Human rights and humanitarian diplomacy

About the Series

Key Studies in Diplomacy is an innovative series of books on the procedures and processes of diplomacy, focusing on the interaction between states through their accredited representatives, that is, diplomats. Thus its volumes focus on factors affecting foreign policy, and the ways in which it is implemented, through the apparatus of diplomacy – the diplomatic system – in both bilateral and multilateral contexts. But they also examine the how diplomats are sometimes able to shape not just the presentation but even the substance of their states' foreign policies. Given that the diplomatic system is worldwide, all the series' volumes, whatever their individual focuses, contribute to an understanding of the nature of diplomacy. They do so authoritatively – in that they are written by scholars specializing in diplomacy and by former diplomats – and comprehensibly. They emphasize the actual practice of diplomacy, and analyze that practice in a clear and accessible manner, hence making them essential primary reading for both beginning practitioners and advanced level university students.

Series Editors

J. Simon Rofe and Giles Scott-Smith
Lorna Lloyd (Editor Emeritus)

Titles in the Series previously published by Bloomsbury Academic

21st Century Diplomacy by Kishan S. Rana
A Cornerstone of Modern Diplomacy by Kai Bruns
David Bruce and Diplomatic Practice by John W. Young
Embassies in Armed Conflict by G.R. Berridge

Titles in the Series published by Manchester University Press

Reasserting America in the 1970s edited by Hallvard Notaker, Giles Scott-Smith, and David J. Snyder

Human rights and humanitarian diplomacy

Kelly-Kate Pease

Manchester University Press

Copyright © Kelly-Kate Pease 2016

The right of Kelly-Kate Pease to be identified as the author of this work has been asserted by her in accordance with the Copyright, Designs and Patents Act 1988.

Published by Manchester University Press
Altrincham Street, Manchester M1 7JA
www.manchesteruniversitypress.co.uk

British Library Cataloguing-in-Publication Data
A catalogue record for this book is available from the British Library

Library of Congress Cataloguing-in-Publication Data applied for

ISBN 978 1 7849 9328 3 hardback
ISBN 978 1 7849 9329 0 paperback

First published 2016

The publisher has no responsibility for the persistence or accuracy of URLs for any external or third-party internet websites referred to in this book, and does not guarantee that any content on such websites is, or will remain, accurate or appropriate.

Typeset by Out of House Publishing
Printed in Great Britain by CPI Group (UK) Ltd, Croydon, CR0 4YY

Contents

List of tables	vi
List of sidebars	vii
Acknowledgements	viii
1 Introduction to human rights and humanitarian diplomacy	1
2 The centrality of the state	19
3 Inside the black box	43
4 The United Nations and multilateral diplomacy	66
5 IGO diplomacy and the international civil service	100
6 NGO diplomacy	134
7 The human rights and humanitarian professional	155
8 Conclusion	173
Glossary	182
Appendix: Statement of ethical commitments of human rights professionals	197
Bibliography	200
Index	211

Tables

2.1	International human rights treaties	38
3.1	Human rights reports issued by the United States	52
4.1	Past UN peacekeeping operations	69
4.2	Current UN peacekeeping operations	73
5.1	Special procedures: thematic and country mandates	115
5.2	Committee Diplomacy: treaty monitoring bodies	122

Sidebars

2.1 Excerpt from Jimmy Carter's commencement address at the
University of Notre Dame, May 22, 1977   32
2.2 Excerpt from Russian President Vladimir Putin's op-ed,
New York Times, September 11, 2013   35
3.1 Address by Minister for Trade and Development, Joe Costello, to
the United Nations Human Rights Council in Geneva, March 3, 2014   53
3.2 Margaret K. McMillion (former ambassador to the Republic of
Rwanda) – human rights diplomacy in Rwanda 2001–04   58
4.1 Special Rapporteur Paulo Sergio Pinheiro, the politicization of the CHR
(Commission on Human Rights) and afterwards   90
5.1 Statement by Navanethem Pillay, United Nations High Commissioner
for Human Rights   105
5.2 Special Rapporteur Paulo Sergio Pinheiro: the independence of
special rapporteurs   119
6.1 Bill Frelick – Human Rights Watch   140
6.2 Open letter to the United Nations   143
6.3 Hosanna Fox – civil society engagement   148
7.1 Ivan Gayton (MSF) – negotiating access   164
7.2 Greg Constantine (photojournalist)   167

Acknowledgements

This book would not have been possible without the hard work and contributions of others. First, I would like to thank Bill Felick, Ivan Gayton, Greg Constantine, Margaret McMillion, and Hosanna Fox for providing original sidebars describing their experiences in human rights and humanitarian diplomacy. Paulo Sergio Pinheiro graciously provided material and permissions related his diplomatic work as a special rapporteur. These first-hand accounts of the conduct diplomacy are invaluable for linking the theory to the practice of diplomacy. Second, I thank Webster University and its Institute for Human Rights and Humanitarian Studies, which provided the institutional support, contacts, and resources necessary to include real-world diplomatic voices. Kevan Morshed, the graduate assistant for Webster University's International Relations Program, is responsible for creating the text's many tables and some of the supplemental teaching materials. He also did an amazing job of editing later versions of the manuscript. Third, I owe an intellectual debt to David P. Forsythe, my mentor, colleague, and friend. His scholarship and advice related to human rights, international relations, and diplomacy helped me conceptualize the book. Fourth, the comments of the anonymous reviewers were extremely useful in revising and tightening the final manuscript. Finally, I must express my appreciation to Allan MacNeill who held my hand during the more trying moments of the drafting process. His counsel, patience, and encouragement were instrumental in helping me finish this important project.

1
Introduction to human rights and humanitarian diplomacy

Human rights and humanitarian diplomacy is the bargaining, negotiating, and advocating process involved with promoting and protecting international human rights and humanitarian principles. This diplomacy is also a secondary mechanism for discovering or defining new rights and principles. For centuries, diplomacy in general was the exclusive preserve of states. States use diplomacy as a foreign policy tool to achieve complicated and often competing goals. Today, human rights and humanitarian diplomacy is conducted on many levels by individuals who represent not only states but also intergovernmental organizations (IGOs) and nongovernmental organizations (NGOs). As such, diplomacy occurs on several tracks, often in interactive and simultaneous ways. **Track 1 diplomacy** refers to the official diplomacy practiced by state and IGO officials using traditional channels and tools. **Track 2 diplomacy** expands diplomatic activity to include the more unofficial interactions that involve civil society actors such as NGOs and prominent individuals. The conduct of human rights and humanitarian diplomacy occurs on multiple levels that can both complement each other, as well as work at cross-purposes.

This introductory chapter explores what international human rights are, why they are controversial, and why diplomacy is necessary for the actualization of human rights. It also explains the narrow distinctions between human rights and humanitarianism; discusses the different kinds of actors involved in multilevel human rights and humanitarian diplomacy; and outlines basic strategies and tools used to promote and protect human rights and humanitarian principles through diplomacy.

The subsequent chapters of the text are devoted to the process and conduct of human rights and humanitarian diplomacy. Chapter 2 examines the continued centrality of the state and how states, as the main duty-bearers, define and implement human rights and humanitarian principles domestically, as well as promote and protect them internationally. Chapter 3 looks inside "the black box" of the state to highlight the roles of secretaries, ministers, ambassadors, bureaucrats, and ombudsmen. It also looks at how human rights reports are created and help frame the diplomatic process. Chapter 4 shifts focus to IGOs. States create IGOs to help them achieve common goals or manage international problems. One of the central purposes of IGOs, such as the United Nations (UN) and the European Union (EU), is to promote and protect human rights and this chapter provides an overview of their respective multilateral architecture. This chapter explains the operation of international human rights commissions and councils, and how international criminal courts have become an important tool of human rights and humanitarian diplomacy. Chapter 5 delves into the international civil service to show how IGO officials such as secretaries-general and high commissioners (and independent experts such as special rapporteurs) bargain and negotiate for human rights and humanitarian principles. It also explains the diplomatic functions of treaty monitoring bodies and courts in advancing respect for international human rights and humanitarian principles.

Chapter 6 details how NGOs engage in human rights and humanitarian diplomacy. Human Rights Watch and Amnesty International are just two of the many NGOs which monitor, report, advocate, and educate on human rights. Médecins Sans Frontières (MSF; Doctors Without Borders) and the International Committee of the Red Cross (ICRC) routinely and, oftentimes, quietly deliver humanitarian assistance. Chapter 7 explores how the human rights and humanitarian professionals employed by NGOs and IGOs conduct day-to-day diplomacy in the field. This includes providing immediate protection, conducting interviews, negotiating humanitarian access, monitoring detention facilities, and creating humanitarian space.

Selected chapters present *sidebars* written by individuals engaged in human rights and humanitarian diplomacy to illustrate its actual practice. These sidebars represent voices from across the spectrum of diplomacy: heads of state, foreign ministers, ambassadors, high commissioners, special rapporteurs, humanitarian affairs officers, and human rights professionals. The voices of civil society are also included to illustrate how human rights and humanitarian diplomacy is conducted at all levels. Chapter 8 concludes the text with a discussion of key challenges facing future human rights and humanitarian diplomatic efforts: globalization, failed states, and illiberal challenges to existing norms, laws, and values.

What are international human rights?

Philosophically, human rights are rights possessed by individuals by virtue of their humanity. Human rights are also a means for achieving minimal human dignity and social justice. From an international relations perspective, international human rights are generally recognized as the rights contained in what is called the **International Bill of Rights**. This includes the rights articulated in the **Universal Declaration of Human Rights (UDHR)** (1948) and the **International Covenant on Civil and Political Rights (ICCPR)** (1966) (and its two optional protocols), and the **International Covenant on Economic, Social and Cultural Rights (ICESCR)** (1966).[1] The UDHR is a nonbinding UN General Assembly resolution that represents the existing international consensus regarding the definition and importance of human rights in the post-World War II order. This is not to say that other human rights do not exist, only that those rights have not achieved the wider international recognition necessary to be codified in international law.

In order to actualize the rights contained in the UDHR, states followed up by pursuing the more binding international law represented by the covenants and protocols. One way to understand human rights is to organize them around generations. **First generation human rights** refer to civil and political rights. This generation grew out of the Western, liberal tradition of political thought that holds that individuals need to be maximally free (including being free from oppression) in order to achieve human dignity. To effectively participate in public life, individuals need to have security of person and equal legal status. Through civil and political rights, individuals would be free to maximize their potential and chart their own course in life. Rights included in the ICCPR include to the right to: the freedom from torture or slavery; recognition and equality under the law; the freedom of thought and religion; the freedom of expression and opinion; and the freedom of assembly and association, among others.

Second generation human rights center on economic, social, and cultural rights. These rights include the right to: work and for a fair wage; an education; an adequate standard of living (including food and housing); and to health (interpreted as the right to health care). This generation of rights is largely a product of socialist values, which is one of the reasons why the right to "social security" was a centerpiece of the ICESCR.

Third generation human rights refer to collective human rights such as the rights of peoples to self-determination, or development, or the rights of specific groups (minorities, children, women, refugees, stateless persons, and indigenous peoples). Collective human rights are possessed by groups and are designed to improve the dignity and lives of group members. Certain groups face unique challenges in actualizing their human rights and thus have their own specialized treaties.

The ICCPR and the ICESCR represent the binding international law that codified many of the human rights contained in the UDHR. These two treaties now are joined by other core international human rights treaties:[2]

- International Convention on the Elimination of All Forms of Racial Discrimination (1965);
- Convention on the Elimination of All Forms of Discrimination against Women (1979);
- Convention against Torture and Other Cruel, Inhuman or Degrading Treatment or Punishment (1984);
- Convention on the Rights of the Child (1989);
- International Convention on the Protection of the Rights of All Migrant Workers and Members of their Families (1990);
- International Convention for the Protection of All Persons from Enforced Disappearances (1996);
- Convention on the Rights of Persons with Disabilities (2006).

In addition to these core instruments, numerous other domestic, regional, and international laws have been inspired by the UDHR. Most call for human dignity within their preambles, suggesting this overarching theme within the international human rights discourse.

Why are human rights controversial?

Legally speaking, states make international law but individuals are the claimants (or the possessors) of human rights. States are the "duty-bearers," which means they have the primary obligation to respect, protect and fulfill those rights.[3] While there is general agreement on the idea of internationally recognized human rights, not all states accept all rights and some states are party to some human rights treaties but not others. States often become party to treaties but issue reservations to parts they do not agree with. Moreover, considerable disagreement exists on the definition and implementation of human rights. In addition, there is no consensus on what is permissible while promoting and protecting human rights. Human rights can also conflict with other important international norms and values. Most states jealously guard their **sovereignty**. Sovereignty is a centuries-old legal principle that holds that the state, or representatives of the state (the government), has the final say within its territorial jurisdiction. For many states, this includes the right to define and implement human rights. A companion legal principle to sovereignty is the principle of **nonintervention**. This means that states have the duty not to intervene in the internal affairs of other states. This certainly applies to coercive military intervention but many states also see sanctions, the withholding of aid, and even the mere discussion of a state's domestic human rights situation as forms of intervention.[4]

Prior to World War II, human rights issues were largely considered to fall within the domestic jurisdiction of states, therefore, not subject to serious outside scrutiny. However with the creation of the UN in 1945, a legal revolution occurred whereby states exercised their sovereign prerogatives and agreed to international human rights laws that clearly regulate what a state can and cannot do to the people within its territory. States, when they join the UN, take on the legal obligation to promote and protect human rights. The UDHR passed without a dissenting vote, although important states such as South Africa, the Soviet Union, and Saudi Arabia abstained. The UN Charter and the UDHR were revolutionary at the time because they challenged the absolute sovereignty of the state and placed human rights squarely on the international agenda. Article 55 of the UN Charter states:

> With a view to the creation of conditions of stability and well-being which are necessary for peaceful and friendly relations among nations based on respect for the principle of equal rights and self-determination of peoples, the United Nations shall promote:

a. higher standards of living, full employment, and conditions of economic and social progress and development;
b. solutions of international economic, social, health, and related problems; and international cultural and educational cooperation; and
c. universal respect for, and observance of, human rights and fundamental freedoms for all without distinction as to race, sex, language, or religion.

Article 56 contains the pledge to take joint and individual action to achieve the purposes contained in Article 55. At the same time, Article 2(1) of the UN Charter also privileges the sovereign equality of states and Article 2(7) prohibits the UN from intervening in the internal affairs of states. With the onset of the Cold War international human rights became politicized as both sides in the East–West conflict of the Cold War used human rights to try to delegitimize the other. The United States condemned the Soviet Union and Eastern Bloc states for suppressing civil and political rights and, conversely, the United States was criticized for its unemployment, racial segregation, and poverty. Moreover, the often violent decolonization process greatly expanded the number of states that constituted "the international community." These newly independent states were not keen to curb their hard-fought sovereignty or necessarily subscribe to existing values or definitions of human rights. The economic and political disparities between North and South led to a divide where developing states began to challenge the rules and values they perceived to privilege the wealthy.

Competing and contradictory international norms, values, and principles, as well as disagreements regarding the definition and implementation of human rights, has led to several ongoing debates. The first debate centers on whether human rights are universal or culturally relative.[5] During the preparatory session for the UDHR, and after it was passed, the American Anthropology Association expressed grave concern regarding the origins and consequences of the "universality" of human rights. Universal human rights centers on the idea that rights are applicable to all humans, whereas the cultural relativist approach holds that rights are relative and to be understood in the context of the culture in which they are being actualized. The rights articulated by the West could be interpreted as a form of colonialism in that they prescribe certain kinds of domestic laws and even government type. In order to have cultural diversity, rights must be defined and implemented by societies differently. At the same time, many cultural and religious practices can be harmful to human dignity and be discriminatory on the basis of sex, sexual orientation, or minority status. After six decades of debate, the literature and development of international and domestic human rights law suggest that human rights are "relatively universal."[6] Certain rights do appear to be universal, such as the right to freedom from torture, while others, like the right to marry, health care, or to participate in public life, are still relative. The tension between cultural relativism and universalism is something that needs to be managed by states and the international community and informs the ways human rights are pursued and promoted through diplomacy.[7]

A related debate centers on the extent to which some rights are "basic" or fundamental versus rights that are aspirational or desirable.[8] The latter risks "rights inflation," such as recent efforts to declare access to the Internet as a human right.[9] On the one hand, the idea of core defensible rights that are necessary for the enjoyment of life, such as the physical security of the person, makes sense in light of cultural diversity concerns and the difficulties of reaching relative consensus among the international community's 193 states. On the other hand, the minimalist approach may unnecessarily limit rights to the lowest possible common denominator and neglect the rights of certain groups that have considerable difficulty in obtaining basic rights.[10]

Another human rights controversy focuses on the relationships between "generations" of rights and between positive and negative rights. These disagreements are rooted in different worldviews and ideologies (discussed in detail in Chapter 2) about how international relations operate. For example, the United States promotes civil and political rights as being more important to human dignity, whereas China stresses economic rights and the right to development. The United States also tends to view human rights protection as restricting state interference with individual freedom as opposed to having the state take strong action to provide for rights, especially if it means heavily regulating business or markets. The United States sees the freedom of conscience as a human right but rejects the idea that health care must be provided by the state for all. Many socialist states are more comfortable with government regulation on behalf of economic and social rights, but may still reject the idea they have to provide jobs paying a living wage for all within their territory, regardless of citizenship. Some totalitarian states feel restricting civil and political rights are necessary for stability, harmonious relations, and economic growth. States tend to prioritize certain kinds of values and human rights based on their dominant ideology or political culture. Other actors, such as IGOs and NGOs, seek to stress the indivisibility and interdependence of human rights.

These disagreements make human rights controversial, in turn making the promotion and protection of human rights through diplomacy complicated, problematic, and necessary. Diplomacy is necessary because the pursuit of human rights and humanitarian principles are part of the global political process. This process also involves the pursuit of other values, such as free markets, sovereignty, government type, and economic development, all of which arguably can promote and preserve human dignity (or threaten it). The process involves prioritizing and pursuing policies, values, and interests that may actually conflict with each other. The world can also be a very dangerous place, with war, terrorism, and other forms of violent conflict occupying the attention of states. War, terrorism, and other forms of violent conflict are certainly not conducive to human dignity and the wrong policies can exacerbate a violent situation and prolong human suffering. Hence, human rights diplomacy is necessary for defining and implementing rights and for keeping human rights as a priority on the global agenda. This invariably involves pursuing some human rights at the expense of others. It also means human rights must be weighed against the other interests of states, many of which have a profound impact on the quality of human life.

Human rights and humanitarianism

Human rights are entitlements that are designed to promote human dignity. Human rights restrict what a state can and cannot do and place a duty on states to protect human rights by preventing abuses and taking action so human rights can be enjoyed. However, action is often taken by states and other actors, not because foreigners have a legal right, but because it is the humane thing to do. This is often referred to as **humanitarianism**. For example, many states will provide emergency food and medical assistance to those experiencing natural disasters and civil disturbances, not because states believe persons have a legal right to that aid or because states feel they have the legal obligation to provide the aid, but because they believe that it is the right thing to do. Since the definition and implementation of international human rights is contested on many levels for a variety of reasons, humanitarianism allows states and others to sidestep the often thorny issue of rights, duties, and obligations and take action.

Complementing, and yet complicating, international human rights law and humanitarianism is **international humanitarian law (IHL)**. Similarly focused on promoting human dignity, IHL governs the conduct of armed conflict. Strictly speaking, international human rights law refers to the relationship between the state and the persons within its territorial jurisdiction. It results from a separate legal history and it allows states to deviate or derogate from the law in certain situations. For example, Article 4(1) of the ICCPR allows states to restrict the enjoyment of many rights during a public emergency. Similarly, Article 9 allows liberty to be curtailed with due process of law, which allows states to deny certain rights to those convicted of a crime.

IHL emanates from a different legislative history, which includes the **Geneva Conventions**, and is designed to preserve the dignity of those who are not engaged in hostilities during armed conflict. These persons are often referred to as the "victims of war" and they include the civilian population, the wounded, and those who have laid down their arms (prisoners of war). One way to think about IHL is that, among other things, it protects human rights and dignity during war by regulating the conduct of war and creating legal obligations for belligerents. It also reinforces the inviolability of certain rights where no derogation is permitted, such as the prohibition of torture, arbitrary detention, and summary execution. Given the overlapping and complementary nature of international human rights, humanitarianism, and IHL, human rights and humanitarian diplomacy are often treated together.

The actors

A variety of actors participate in human rights and humanitarian diplomacy. The first and the most important actor, is the **state**. Since the **Peace of Westphalia** in 1648, international relations has been organized around the territorially-based state that exercises authority over the population within its recognized borders. Representatives of the state (the government) create laws domestically and internationally that define and prescribe its relationships with its people and with other states. Under the Westphalian order, states are the subjects of international law. They have the legal personality to make international law and to assume duties and obligations under that law. States make decisions as to when and how to develop international human rights and humanitarian law. They also decide how to implement human rights at home and whether (and how) to take action abroad for humane reasons. The state remains the greatest protector of, and the greatest threat to, internationally recognized human rights. As such, states remain central to defining and implementing human rights and humanitarian principles.

The pursuit of human rights also involves **intergovernmental organizations (IGOs)**. These organizations are created by states to help them take collective action. When states use IGOs to help them take collective action relating to a specific issue, this is often referred to as **multilateral diplomacy**. Within the UN system, states may use the UN Security Council or the Human Rights Council (HRC) to take action to promote and protect human rights and humanitarian principles. The political will of states is necessary for IGOs to be effective; however, at the same time, once created, IGOs can become independent actors in their own right, challenging states to improve their human rights and humanitarian records. Many IGOs have the protection and promotion of human rights as one of their central purposes and some even have specialized agencies devoted to promoting and protecting human rights. For example, the UN has the Office of the High Commissioner for Human Rights (OHCHR) and the United Nations High Commissioner for Refugees to educate, advocate, and implement human rights and provide humanitarian aid. Similarly, regional organizations, such as the European Union and the Organization of American States, have human rights commissions and even courts to assist individuals in exercising their rights and help states to adhere to international human rights standards. When IGO officials independently advocate or negotiate on behalf of human rights and humanitarian principles, this is known as **IGO diplomacy**.

Nongovernmental organizations (NGOs) are part and parcel of the human rights and humanitarian diplomatic process. NGOs are private, not-for-profit, voluntary organizations that have policy goals. Human rights NGOs monitor human rights and humanitarian situations and pressure states through lobbying and by organizing grassroots campaigns. Many also function as "subcontractors" delivering bilateral and multilateral humanitarian aid provided by states in conflict zones and during the aftermath of natural disasters. Increasingly traditional human rights organizations such as Amnesty International and Human Rights Watch are also involved with promoting IHL, especially as it relates to the treatment of detainees and the questionable legality of renditions and drone strikes during irregular war. The building blocks of international/global civil society are NGOs and **NGO diplomacy** is central for the creation and enforcement of international human rights and humanitarian norms.

The increasing importance of non-state actors in human rights and humanitarian diplomacy, especially as it relates to creating, defining, and implementing human rights and humanitarian principles, means that international relations is no longer the sole domain of states. International relations is more global and more cosmopolitan where civil society actors, such as NGOs, individuals, and business, all play roles in creating international laws and promoting international norms.[11] Much attention has been paid to how business practices can promote (and threaten) human rights. **Corporate Social Responsibility (CSR)** has become a special vehicle for businesses to become part of the human rights network. Originally an initiative of former UN Secretary-General Kofi Annan called the Global Compact, the idea behind CSR is to educate businesses and corporations about internationally recognized human rights and to recruit them as partners in the protection of human rights. While the duty to promote and protect human rights (from harmful business practices if necessary) resides primarily with states, the business sector increasingly has a role in actualizing human rights. The initiative of CSR is voluntary and not without criticism.[12] Nevertheless, it recognizes the dynamic relationship between business practices and human rights and dignity.

No discussion of the actors who participate in human rights and humanitarian diplomacy is complete without attention to the importance of individuals both in influencing how states, IGOs, and NGOs approach human rights and humanitarianism, and in their success of negotiating strategies. States, IGOs, and NGOs are collections of individuals who can affect the development of international human rights and humanitarian norms. The praises of Henry Dunant, Hansa Mehta, Charles Malik, and Eleanor Roosevelt are widely sung for their watershed work in furthering human rights and humanitarian principles. Heads of state, such as US President Jimmy Carter, South African President Nelson Mandela, and Irish President Mary Robinson, have shaped the human rights priorities of their governments. Celebrities such as Angelina Jolie, Bono, and George Clooney call attention to humanitarian disasters around the world and help to raise money to alleviate suffering. The often-unsung heroes of human rights and humanitarian diplomacy are the "human rights professionals" who work every day in offices, or in the field, for states, IGOs, and NGOs to further human rights and humanitarian principles.

One of the central purposes of this book is to help educate those who are, or want to be, engaged in human rights and humanitarian work about the process and complications associated with human rights and humanitarian diplomacy, with all the attendant controversies surrounding the definition and implementation of human rights and humanitarian principles. This book does not purport to say what the right strategy is, but rather, to show that the competition between different perspectives will ultimately determine what human rights and humanitarian values are and how they will evolve in the future.

Types of diplomacy

Diplomacy can take place between different actors and in a variety of venues. While states have been and remain the principal diplomatic actors, diplomacy is also conducted by IGOs, NGOS, and even private individuals. Diplomacy related to human rights and humanitarianism may be public in that the issue is placed squarely on a foreign policy agenda, or in the media, and is subject to public scrutiny and comment. This type of **public diplomacy** also can take the form of propaganda. It is designed to provide information in order to mobilize mass public opinion and/or put pressure on public officials to adopt a course of action. This information comes in the form of reports, speeches, press releases, and media outreach/appearances. States, IGOs, NGOs, and individuals increasingly have taken to social media such as Twitter, Tumblr, Snapchat, and Facebook to communicate with people all around the world. Often referred to as **diplomacy 2.0**, social media can be an effective way for government officials to reach out to domestic and foreign audiences. Social media can level the playing field by allowing a variety of actors to document and publicize violations of human rights and humanitarian principles. Diplomacy 2.0 also enables small groups and individuals to mobilize public opinion and challenge the official narrative articulated by governments.

Private diplomacy, on the other hand, involves the behind-the-scenes, quiet approach to protecting and promoting human rights and humanitarian principles. Also known as "quiet" diplomacy, private diplomacy is usually preferred because it allows the involved parties the opportunity to avoid losing honor or prestige while at the same time improving human rights conditions. Unfortunately, the nature of private diplomacy makes it difficult to analyze, although it clearly takes place, as is evidenced when a political prisoner is released or a UN resolution is publicly announced. The Wikileaks disclosure of private, diplomatic cables between US embassies and consulates and their counterparts around the world show that human rights and humanitarian principles are a significant, if inconsistent, part of the overall diplomacy of states. At the same time, the disclosure also put human rights activists at risks in troubled area such as Afghanistan and Iraq. Public and private diplomacy influence how human rights and humanitarian diplomacy is conducted through multiple channels.

Channels of diplomacy

The bargaining, negotiating, and advocating process associated with human rights and humanitarian diplomacy, whether private or public, occurs through many channels (or modes) of diplomacy. One channel of diplomacy is **summit diplomacy**. Summit diplomacy involves the heads of state or leaders of governments. Summits have the advantage of helping leaders develop personal relationships which could assist them in tackling difficult problems. However, summits often have many agenda items, with human rights sometimes being downplayed or conspicuously absent from the agenda. For example, the 2013 bilateral summit between US President Barack Obama and China President Xi Jinping addressed the ongoing crisis with North Korea, climate change, and cyber-attacks, but not human rights in any significant way. During the Cold War, human rights figured prominently in bilateral summits during the thaw of relations that began in the 1970s.

Multilateral summit diplomacy often occurs in the context of G8 and G20 diplomacy (groups of the eight and twenty largest economies). These summits originally began to promote economic cooperation but, in recent years, the agenda has become more complex, including security, social, and human rights issues. Moreover, such summit meetings involving important states (thus commanding international media attention) can serve as the impetus for "**counter-summits**" or protests by NGOs and other civil society actors who use the gathering to raise human rights issues. The 2013 G20 Summit in St. Petersburg, Russia, was notable because while its main agenda item was the scourge of corporate tax havens, international media attention was focused instead on the counter-summit, which highlighted Russia's human rights record in relation to Lesbian, Gay, Bisexual, Transgender and Queer (LGBTQ) rights and US surveillance tactics worldwide. This kind of diplomacy keeps human rights at the forefront of international relations by bringing international attention towards human rights violations.

Human rights diplomacy is often channeled through IGOs and conducted by independent officials representing IGOs such as secretaries-general or commissioners. This IGO diplomacy happens when officials use their "good offices" (meaning their prestige) to promote and protect human rights. They head relatively autonomous international bureaucracies that support their mandates. While IGO diplomacy centering on human rights usually engages states, IGO officials also engage with other non-state actors in human rights and humanitarian diplomacy. This kind of diplomacy is also known as **network diplomacy** because successful diplomatic strategies today need to mobilize networks of actors.[13]

Conference diplomacy can occur in tandem with summit diplomacy or independently of summits. Conference diplomacy is a form of multilateral diplomacy and is often conducted under the auspices of an IGO, usually the UN or a regional organization. Conferences are sometimes attended by heads of states, but more often conference diplomacy involves high ranking government and IGO officials. Occasionally, conferences can be devoted solely to human rights or humanitarian issues. For example, in 1993 the World Conference on Human Rights was held in Vienna under the auspices of the UN and led to the creation of the office of the UN High Commissioner for Human Rights. In 1995 the Fourth World Conference on Women was held in Beijing to improve the status of women's human rights. NGOs often participate in global conferences or they hold civil society **parallel conferences**. In the realm of humanitarian affairs, **pledging conferences** are organized by the UN and other organizations to raise money for the victims of armed conflict or natural disasters. Recent examples of pledging conferences include UN efforts to raise money for internally displaced persons (IDPs) in Syria and for Syrians who have fled to neighboring states.[14] Another conference involved generating resources for the victims of typhoon Haiyan which devastated entire provinces in the Philippines in 2013. This allows the UN to raise money for humanitarian relief from private actors, as well as states.

Conference diplomacy is also a prelude to the formal codification of international human rights and humanitarian law. International human rights and humanitarian treaties (and organizations) are the result of conferences of interested state parties coming together to hammer out framework agreements to generate international consensus regarding principles, norms, and aims. The conferences often aim to produce the text of international law and often include voices from civil society.

Another channel of human rights diplomacy is **commission diplomacy**. Commission diplomacy has two variations. The first involves "high level panels" and commissions that can have a formative impact on the public good because they issue reports that then shape state and IGO policy.[15] Arguably, all modern panels and commissions impact human rights and humanitarian affairs because they provide a road map for ending a particular armed conflict or addressing a situation that impacts human rights and dignity, broadly defined. Examples include the Independent Commission on International Humanitarian Issues, the Independent International Commission on Kosovo, the International Commission on Intervention and State Sovereignty (ICISS), and the Commission on Human Security.

Another variation of commission diplomacy centers on the work of human rights commissions within IGOs. For the most part, this variation of commission diplomacy is a form of multilateral diplomacy consisting of the representatives of member states who have the responsibility of promoting human rights and sometimes even protecting human rights by hearing individual petitions. The now defunct UN Commission on Human Rights (since replaced by the HRC) was the center of human rights activity at the UN during much of the Cold War, but did not allow individuals to submit petitions. The European Commission on Human Rights (1954–98), similarly defunct, allowed private petitions and investigated complaints. The European Commission was abolished in 1998 when the European Court of Human Rights was expanded and reformed to allow private individuals to bring human rights cases. The League of Arab States, the African Union (AU), Organization of American States (OAS), and the Association of South East Asian Nations (ASEAN) have respective human rights commissions that are engaged more on promotional activities such as standard setting, rather than direct protection. As will be discussed in subsequent chapters, human rights commissions are often criticized by human rights NGOs for focusing their diplomacy more on protecting states and not human rights. The effectiveness of human rights commissions is debatable; however, they do represent international efforts to implement human rights according to agreed-upon international standards.[16]

Committee diplomacy centers on the committees created to monitor the implementation of specific human rights treaties.[17] Most of these treaty monitoring bodies track compliance and issue reports regarding the status of the respective rights covered by their constitutive treaty. Unlike human rights commissions which are comprised of state representatives, human rights monitoring committees are made up of independent experts who are nominated and elected by state parties. Depending on the treaty, some committees are also authorized to conduct country inquiries when there is compelling evidence that a state is systematically violating treaty provisions. Some committees also receive and investigate communications from private individuals. Since investigating complaints and conducting inquiries usually require state consent and cooperation, the committees have to routinely negotiate, bargain, and advocate with state officials to further human rights and humanitarian principles. Committees also issue "general comments" which constitute their interpretations of the meanings of treaty provisions, which is useful since states and NGOs may have competing understandings and interpretations.

The term **humanitarian diplomacy** is used by the International Federation of the Red Cross and other humanitarian aid organizations to refer to the process whereby NGOs are involved with "persuading decision makers and opinion leaders to act at all times in the interests of vulnerable people and with full respect for fundamental humanitarian principles."[18] This is an important aspect of NGO diplomacy. As humanitarianism seeks to minimize the harm during violent conflict, and alleviate suffering during times of crisis, fundamental humanitarian principles involve not only the conduct of armed conflict but also the delivery of humanitarian aid. These fundamental principles of IHL include the distinction between civilians and combatants; proportionality; the humane treatment of prisoners of war (POWs); and refraining from torture.[19] The principles surrounding the delivery of humanitarian assistance include neutrality, impartiality, humanity, and independence.[20] Chapter 6 details the evolution of NGO diplomacy in their efforts to promote respect for humanitarian principles. Chapter 7 focuses on how human rights and humanitarian professionals conduct **field diplomacy** in order to gain access to vulnerable populations.

Tools and strategies

Successful diplomacy, regardless of the actors, involves several elements. First, parties must attempt to empathize with each other and see the issue from the other's perspective. This involves recognizing that human beings understand and perceive the world differently. **Worldviews** are sets of widely held beliefs that provide a mental map as to how the world works. This involves focusing on certain kinds of actors and the motivations for their behavior. In Chapter 2, several approximate worldviews are discussed to show how the promotion and protection of human rights can be seen simultaneously as part of a larger geopolitical power struggle, an effort to destabilize a government, or a form of imperialism that subjugates the poor. Understanding how others view human rights and humanitarian principles and recognizing that there are different conceptions and priorities of human rights and humanitarian principles is the first step in being able to successfully promote them. Second, actors need to recognize that oftentimes they will need to compromise or at least be comfortable with vague language that allows for multiple interpretations and glosses over differences of substance. Sometimes the language of international human rights and humanitarian law must be avoided altogether in order to further human dignity. Third, diplomacy requires trust and, when trust is absent, confidence-building measures must be pursued to bridge the trust deficit. This can affect the venue and the processes of diplomacy. Beyond these three elements, there is no set formula for successful human rights and humanitarian diplomacy because diplomacy is an art form, a picture painted for a specific situation in a specific time. Some people may never be artists, no matter how hard they try, and some artists are qualitatively better than others.

When actors choose to pursue human rights and humanitarian principles, they must decide on the type of diplomacy and the channel(s), given their varying capabilities. States have more resources and access to diplomatic channels than non-state actors. Also, they have the formal architecture of diplomacy. States, therefore, tend to have the most direct effect, both positive and negative, on human rights. On the other hand, NGOs and certain agencies within IGOs have the benefit of being singularly focused on human rights and humanitarian affairs, which gives them more "moral authority" when it comes to human rights and humanitarian protection. They have no ulterior motives, per se. NGOs and IGOs are also well aware that they often have to rely on states for funding, protection, and the necessary visas to operate around the world. An expelled or poorly funded organization finds it very difficult to participate in human rights and humanitarian diplomacy.

Much of diplomacy involves getting an actor to do what they otherwise would not do. Actors must craft a strategy that combines types of diplomacy within the appropriate channels. Actors must also choose which instruments or tools to use. States have a variety of instruments and leverage at their disposal which can be used as carrots and sticks. The carrots serve as positive inducements and can include trade concessions, membership to organizations, economic assistance, military assistance, development aid, and humanitarian aid. The instruments can also be used as sticks when they are withheld. Sanctions and military force are also options. Definitions of diplomacy often distinguish it from war; however, diplomacy often leads up to the use of military force and is used to negotiate a cessation to hostilities. All of these instruments give state actors leverage in diplomatic bargaining or negotiating situations. They can be used to encourage certain kinds of behavior, like respecting and implementing human rights, and also to deter a course of action that threatens human rights and humanitarian principles. These instruments can be used to induce others to change their behavior. Officials must choose the right mixture of encouragement, and deterrence, and decide whether to do it privately or publicly.

State officials must also decide whether to pursue human rights and humanitarian diplomacy through track 1 (official) or track 2 (unofficial) diplomacy, and through multilateral fora (and deciding which one), and whether to use mediation, arbitration, or judicial remedies. **Mediation** is often nonbinding and usually involves finding a solution to a dispute that works for the parties rather than trying to assess who is legally right and wrong. **Arbitration** is similar in that the "legal right or wrong" of the parties are not as important in reaching a settlement. The difference is that the parties agree ahead of time to be bound by the decision of the arbiter. Many states have agreed to create courts and other legal and quasi-legal bodies (such as treaty monitoring bodies) to adjudicate disputes involving violations of human rights or humanitarian law.

Non-state actors are in a very different negotiating and bargaining position than states. Officials from IGOs and NGOs recognize that they have limited resources and options for engaging in human rights and humanitarian diplomacy. It does human rights and humanitarianism (as well as the organizations themselves) no good to alienate states. They have few tools to compel or deter outside of a strategy of "name and shame." If they go against the wishes of states they can be expelled, ignored, or find their funding cut. The name and shame strategy can backfire and officials are wise to use it sparingly. Rather, IGOs and NGOs contribute to the promotion and protection of human rights and humanitarian principles by providing reliable information and engaging in advocacy. Fact-finding and monitoring are crucial for promoting human rights and humanitarian principles. NGOs are also particularly good at organizing at the grassroots level and for setting standards. This kind of track 2 diplomacy can also help states promote and protect human rights and keep human rights as a priority. More recently, NGOs have been engaging in track 1 diplomacy by participating in human rights and humanitarian negotiations, as they were in the conceptualization and implementation of the International Criminal Court (ICC) and the Ottawa Convention which banned antipersonnel landmines.

NGOs, often working in tandem with IGOs, deliver humanitarian assistance in conflict zones which means they can run afoul of governments. Hence another dimension of humanitarian diplomacy means negotiating ceasefires, access, visas, and creating a "humanitarian space" between belligerents. Unlike traditional diplomacy, which occurs within an institutionalized framework, humanitarian diplomacy is more ad hoc and not subject to formal rules.[21] NGOs can also function like pressure groups, lobbying governments for favorable policies and for a rights-based approach to state foreign policy. They can employ direct techniques such as contacting government officials or by testifying before governmental bodies. NGOs can also use indirect techniques like mobilizing public opinion through letter-writing campaigns, paid advertising, letters to the editor, and op-eds. They can make extensive use of social media to publicize issues or cases. They can issue independent reports, file *amicus curiae* briefs with national and international courts, and provide legal services to individuals denied their rights. The distinction between advocacy and diplomacy thus become blurred. The strategies and tools used by NGOs vary but what remains unchanged is that NGOs are central to the landscape of human rights and humanitarian diplomacy.

Conclusion

Human rights and humanitarian diplomacy is conducted by multiple actors, through a variety of channels, using a wide range of tools and instruments. Human rights and humanitarian principles are widely accepted, although considerable disagreement exists regarding prioritizing, defining, and implementing those rights and principles. The remainder of the text is devoted to fleshing out how human rights and humanitarian diplomacy is practiced at a variety of levels. All the chapters illustrate the central themes that:

1. The conduct of human rights and humanitarian diplomacy is often clumsy and cumbersome but is fundamental to the definition, discovery, implementation, and evolution of human rights and humanitarian principles.
2. Nothing is inevitable or inexorable about the progress of human rights and the development of humanitarian principles. It depends on world politics and the skills of diplomats. The art of diplomacy can be effective or it can be inept and problematic.
3. The actors who practice human right and humanitarian diplomacy are flawed, but different interpretations of rights and principles are more likely the result of worldview, rather than ill-will.
4. A multifaceted and concerted effort is necessary to preserve and advance human dignity in world politics.

Key terms

Human rights and humanitarian diplomacy, track 1 diplomacy, track 2 diplomacy, International Bill of Rights, Universal Declaration of Rights, International Covenant on Civil and Political Rights, International Covenant on Economic, Social and Cultural Rights, first generation human rights, second generation human rights, third generation human rights, sovereignty, nonintervention, humanitarianism, international humanitarian law, Geneva Conventions, state, Peace of Westphalia, intergovernmental organizations (IGOs), multilateral diplomacy, IGO diplomacy, non-governmental organizations (NGOs), NGO diplomacy, Corporate Social Responsibility (CSR), public diplomacy, diplomacy 2.0, private diplomacy, summit diplomacy, counter-summits, network diplomacy, conference diplomacy, parallel conferences, pledging conferences, commission diplomacy, committee diplomacy, humanitarian diplomacy, field diplomacy, worldviews, mediation, arbitration.

Discussion questions

1. What is human rights and humanitarian diplomacy? Discuss the differences between human rights and humanitarianism and why they are often analyzed together.
2. What are human rights and why are human rights controversial?
3. Discuss the actors that participate in human rights and humanitarian diplomacy. How do the interests and worldviews of actors affect diplomacy?
4. Discuss and explain the different types and channels of diplomacy.

Notes

1 See the Office of the High Commissioner for Human Rights, "Fact Sheet No.2 (Rev. 1.) The International Bill of Rights," accessed June 25, 2013. www.ohchr.org/Documents/Publications/FactSheet2Rev.1en.pdf.
2 See the Office of the High Commissioner for Human Rights, "The Core International Human Rights Instruments and their Monitoring Bodies," accessed October 15, 2014. www.ohchr.org/EN/ProfessionalInterest/Pages/CoreInstruments.aspx.
3 See Manisuli Ssenyonjo, "Economic, Social and Cultural Rights," in *International Human Rights Law: Six Decades after the UDHR and Beyond*, ed. Mashood A. Baderin and Manisuli Ssenyonjo (Surrey: Ashgate, 2013), 49–88, 86.
4 See United Nations General Assembly Resolution A/RES/20/2131, "Declaration on the Inadmissibility of Intervention in the Domestic Affairs of States and the Protection of their Independence and Sovereignty" (December 21, 1965), accessed September 1, 2013. www.un-documents.net/a20r2131.htm.
5 R.J. Vincent, *Human Rights and International Relations* (Cambridge: Cambridge University Press, 1988); Rhonda L. Callaway and Julie Harrelson-Stephens, *Exploring International Human Rights: Essential Readings* (Boulder: Lynne Rienner, 2007).
6 Jack Donnelly, "International Human Rights: Universal, Relative or Relatively Universal," in *International Human Rights Law: Six Decades after the UDHR and Beyond*, ed. Mashood A. Baderin and Manisuli Ssenyonjo (Surrey: Ashgate, 2013), 39–48.
7 Michael K. Addo, "The Practice of United Nations Treaty Bodies in the Reconciliation of Cultural Diversity with Universal Respect for Human Rights," *Human Rights Quarterly*, 32:2 (2010), 601–664.
8 Michael Ignatieff and Amy Gutman, *Human Rights as Politics and Idolatry* (Princeton: Princeton University Press, 2001), 90.
9 Vinton G. Cerf, "Internet Access is Not a Human Right," *New York Times*, January 5, 2012, accessed October 15, 2014. www.nytimes.com/2012/01/05/opinion/internet-access-is-not-a-human-right.html?_r=0.
10 Greg Dinsmore, "Debate: When Less is Really Less – What's Wrong with Minimalist Approaches to Human Rights," *The Journal of Political Philosophy*, 15:4 (2007), 473–483.
11 Steven Roach (ed.), *Governance, Order, and the International Criminal Court* (Oxford: Oxford University Press, 2009).
12 Olufemi Amao, *Corporate Social Responsibility, Human Rights and the Law: Multinational Corporations in Developing Countries* (New York: Routledge, 2011).
13 See Andrew F. Cooper, Jorge Heine, and Ramesh Thakur, "Introduction: The Challenges of 21st Century Diplomacy," in *The Oxford Handbook of Modern Diplomacy*, ed. Andrew F. Cooper, Jorge Heine, and Ramesh Thakur (Oxford: Oxford University Press, 2013), 22.
14 See the United Nations Office for the Coordination of Humanitarian Affairs, "Second International Pledging Conference for Syria" [last modified January 15, 2014], accessed April 18, 2014. https://docs.unocha.org/sites/dms/Documents/SyriaPledging_MediaInfo_EN.pdf.
15 For an overview of this kind of commission diplomacy see Gareth Evans, "Commission Diplomacy," in *The Oxford Handbook on Modern Diplomacy*, ed. Andrew F. Cooper, Jorge Heine, and Ramesh Thakur (Oxford: Oxford University Press, 2013), 278–302.

16 See the arguments of Emilie Hafner-Burton, *Making Human Rights a Reality* (Princeton: Princeton University Press, 2013).
17 For an overview of the committees see Office of the High Commissioner for Human Rights, "Monitoring the Core the Human Rights Treaties," accessed July 15, 2014. www.ohchr.org/EN/HRBodies/Pages/WhatTBDo.aspx.
18 See the International Federation of the Red Cross and Red Crescent Societies, "Humanitarian Diplomacy," accessed December 26, 2013. www.ifrc.org/en/what-we-do/humanitarian-diplomacy/humanitarian-diplomacy-policy/.
19 Ray Murphy and Mohamed M. El Zeidy, "Prisoners of War: A Comparative Study of the Principles of International Humanitarian Law and the Islamic Law of War," *International Criminal Law Review*, 9:4 (2009), 623–649; and Ben Clark, "Contemporary Legal Doctrine on Proportionality in Armed Conflicts: A Select Review," *Journal of International Humanitarian Legal Studies*, 3:2 (2012), 391–414.
20 See the UN Office for the Coordination of Humanitarian Affairs, "OCHA on Message: Humanitarian Principles," June 2012, accessed October 15, 2014. https://ochanet.unocha.org/p/Documents/OOM-humanitarianprinciples_eng_June12.pdf.
21 See Larry Minear, "The Craft of Humanitarian Diplomacy," in *Humanitarian Diplomacy: The Practitioners and their Craft*, ed. Larry Minear and Hazel Smith (Tokyo: United Nations University Press, 2006), 9.

2
The centrality of the state

States have been, and continue to be, the main actors engaged in human rights and humanitarian diplomacy. One of the central attributes of being a state is the ability to recognize other states and enter into formal diplomatic relations with each other. This involves exchanging ambassadors, opening embassies and consulates, and creating **international law** (the formal rules and principles that govern the relations and the behavior of states). States are the main **subjects** of international law in that they possess **international legal personality**. This means that states create the law and have rights and duties under the law. As such, states are the creators of international human rights and humanitarian law. They are also responsible for applying that law through their domestic and foreign policies. States conduct their international relations and foreign policy using many tools, including diplomacy. State diplomacy can be thought of as one of the ways states negotiate and persuade other states to achieve objectives and promote norms and values without resorting to violence.

States are essentially political actors who pursue a variety of interests and values in an international system where they are competing with other states who have different interests and values. Non-state actors, with their own agendas, are also part of this landscape. All of these actors have preferences and their differences in preferred outcomes can lead to international conflict. In a domestic context, the government often decides which interests and values will prevail. In the international context, no such authoritative body exists to make these kinds of determinations and, thus, disputes are resolved through diplomacy or violence. International relations remains, in large part, the relationship between states. This relationship is complicated and often boils down to either war or diplomacy. Most states are well prepared for both. And even in war and violent conflict, the behavior of states and other kinds of belligerents is still subject to international rules and principles – IHL and human rights norms.

This chapter is organized around three sections. The first section briefly reviews international relations theory and its relationship to widely held worldviews about the nature of international relations. Diplomacy is part of (but not synonymous) with a state's foreign policy in world affairs, therefore, how states and their key decision-makers understand world politics helps explain the place and the role of human rights and humanitarian principles in the overall diplomacy of states. The second section examines the role of heads of state in promoting and protecting and human rights and humanitarianism abroad, while recognizing that these interests are often secondary to other interests, especially when immediate security interests are engaged. The third section examines how states create international human rights and humanitarian law. These laws are necessary for setting international standards and advancing human rights and humanitarian principles.

Theory, worldviews, and human rights

International relations theory describes, explains, analyzes, and predicts world affairs. Theory provides a framework for examining and simplifying the complicated nature of international relations by positing assumptions and propositions that guide analysis. International relations theory, while more formal and academic, approximates widely held worldviews about which actors are important in international relations and what processes determine, influence, or drive their behavior. While it is tempting to try to assess whether one theory is right or wrong, perhaps a better way to understand the value of a theory is how well it explains a particular event or development. Different theoretical frameworks can examine the same situation and generate different explanations, causalities, and interpretations of events. Theory and worldview are very useful in understanding how and why states (and other actors) understand and prioritize human rights and humanitarian principles the way they do.

One of the oldest theories in international relations (and a widely held worldview) is **realism**. Realism has many variations and nuances, in part because its intellectual precursors date back millennia; however, it does lend itself to certain generalizations. Realism centers on the exercise of power by states against other states in the international system. Many realists have a very pessimistic view of human nature, believing that humans, at their essence, are violent, selfish, aggressive, base, and vain.[1] Unless human impulses are controlled or checked by society and government, the human existence will be very unpleasant. This, in part, explains the emergence of the state as the central political unit. Other realists ignore human nature altogether and focus on the international system itself. For them, international relations is characterized as **anarchy**, defined as the absence of a higher authority in international relations. The territorially-based state, of which there are currently 193, represent the highest form of political organization in world affairs. No authority exists above them to protect their territorial integrity, ensure their vital interests, or decide which values and preferences will prevail. While states have created IGOs, they have not seen fit to empower these organizations with sufficient authority to decide many issues relating to their internal and international affairs. As such, states (regardless of the intent of leaders or government type) engage in self-help to ensure their survival, territorial integrity, interests, and values in the international system.

The first step in protecting oneself in an anarchic and dangerous world is to take up arms or risk being attacked or vulnerable to the whims of the powerful. For realists, the substance and the conduct of international relations involve the acquisition and the exercise of power. Power can take many forms. It can be hard, with its emphasis on tangible military and economic resources, such as weapons, technology, armies, and gross domestic product (a measure of the monetary value of all the goods and services a state produces). Hard power allows states to employ both carrots and sticks to guarantee their security and pursue their interests and values. Traditional realists put great stock in military capability because, ultimately, the threat or the use of military force is the final arbiter of disputes. Carl von Clausewitz, a famous Prussian strategist, once said that war "is the continuation of politics by other means."[2] If diplomacy breaks down, violence is always an option. Under conditions of anarchy there is nothing to stop states from resorting to violence except perhaps a balance of power where another state has enough military and economic capability to deter an attack. International laws and norms will not deter states from exercising a military option. For many realists, international relations is characterized by war and violent conflict with periodic outbursts of peace. States who value their survival, their way of life, and their interests had better be prepared to fight for them in an anarchical world.

Economic power can be used to both reward and punish others. Financial aid and trade concessions are often used by states to achieve their goals, either as incentives or disincentives. This form of hard power is particularly effective as a foreign policy tool and is usually the preferred means of achieving goals in a nonviolent way. For realists, the use of economic capabilities to help others is more likely for self-interested reasons, even if it appears to be for moral and humane reasons.

Another dimension of power employed by realists is often referred to as soft power.[3] Soft power is less tangible as it involves sources of influence such as culture and values. The effects of culture and values are difficult to measure and quantify but they frame the global debate. Soft power enables states to achieve their aims by co-opting others rather than threatening and using force. Soft power complements hard power in that it is easier to get another to do what you want them to do because they think they want to do it and it is in their immediate material interests to do so. The threat and the use of violence is always held in reserve and can be used later if circumstances warrant.

A special conceptualization of power used by realists is hegemonic power. **Hegemonic power** is where a state possesses a preponderance of military and economic capabilities, enough so that it is able to create and control the central institutions of the international system. A hegemon usually emerges after a world or global war where the major military powers fight to determine the nature of world order. The last hegemonic war is widely considered to be World War II where the major powers of the day fought to determine which of their ideologies (liberalism, fascism, and communism) would prevail. The United States, with its liberal ideology, emerged as the hegemon and it set about institutionalizing its values and principles through international organizations and law. The structures of the international system are not created out of benevolence, but rather to further the hegemon's interests and to maintain its dominant, privileged position. Soft power is an important part of a hegemon's structural power; however, it is behaving just like any other state trying to acquire power and exercise influence over others.

Realists tend to see the international system as conflictual because state interests are often opposed. More importantly, shifts in the balance of power will always occur as some states rise and others decline. Economic growth and technological innovations invariably means that some states will rise at the expense of others or some states will benefit more than other states. As such states must be vigilant to evolving threats and changes in power capabilities. As the hegemon declines, so does the world order the hegemon created. As other states rise, their interests and values will have to be accommodated by the existing order, or the order will be replaced.

The role of international (universal) human rights and humanitarian principles in the world of the realist is a marginal one for several reasons. First, states are preoccupied with security, internationally and internally. As such, human rights and humanitarian concerns are not a priority and are cast aside when the security of the state is threatened. Human rights can be used, however, as a tool to delegitimize adversaries and political opponents. Second, attention to human rights can be seen a threat to state security or government stability. This is one of the reasons why international human rights law allows states to restrict the enjoyment of certain human rights during a public emergency. During war, human rights are secondary to military necessity. IHL (laws of war) has always been informed by whether it is more humane to take cruel steps to end the war quickly, or follow principles that may actually prolong the conflict, leading to even more human suffering.[4] For realists, a state's military, geostrategic, and economic interests will always trump human rights and humanitarian principles.

Third, even if states decide to pursue human rights through their foreign policy, human rights often mask other, less "moral" interests, or are used to justify their interventionist policies. The principles of sovereignty and nonintervention are long-lived in world politics for a reason. They help states avoid war and other forms of conflict. Also, even an intervention conducted with the best of intentions can make matters significantly worse. Those unfamiliar with the local factions or customs can find themselves in a quagmire and be faced with the unintended humanitarian consequences of an otherwise noble endeavor. For these reasons, among others, human rights are relegated to the realm of low politics, something to be pursued only when other interests are met and even then, not too seriously, lest they disrupt other, more important kinds of state relations.

Fourth, substantive change, either internationally or domestically, rarely happens nonviolently. The powerful do not give up their status or privileges voluntarily. Most of the states in existence today came into being through violence. Wars of national liberation were fought to remove the yoke of colonialism, rebellions ensued to overthrow governments, and local populations used whatever means available, including violence. Prohibitions against the use of force helps the powerful maintain the status quo, which privileges their interests. Of course, violent conflict is a direct threat to the enjoyment of human rights.

Finally, for realists "might" makes "right" and there is no such thing as a universal good or sense of justice, save for what the powerful say it is. Good does not always triumph over evil and issues such as the status and definition of human rights will ultimately depend on power. Even realists who have a neutral or positive view of human nature understand that the nicest, most well-meaning people can disagree and the final arbiter of the dispute will be the power to deter, prevail, or impose. The state is in the best position to define the meaning of human rights and their implementation within its territorial jurisdiction.

Realism informs the worldview of many states and their decision-makers, particularly continental states and developing states whose histories are defined by invasion, war, and shifting territorial boundaries and national identities. The human rights and humanitarian diplomacy pursued by other states is viewed with suspicion because these states have fought hard for their sovereignty and independence. Their human rights situations are their affairs and they will define, protect, and promote them as they see fit. Criticism of another's human rights record is often interpreted as a strategy to embarrass or undermine the government. States also disagree as to what constitutes intervention. Some states see issuing public reports on the human rights situations of other states as a normal part of world politics, while others see it as an impermissible violation of sovereignty.

In the case of the United States, realists tend to see its attention to international human rights, particularly internationally recognized civil and political rights, as serving its self-interest in undermining adversaries, while conveniently ignoring the human rights violations of friendly governments. While the United States pays great lip service to international human rights, the laundry list of human rights, as well as positive and negative rights, means governments, including that of the United States, are going to pick and choose which values and rights to pursue. States conduct their foreign policy with mixed motives, so decision-makers with a realist worldview tend to dismiss the humane motives of other states and interpret their actions in terms of furthering their national interests.

The existing international human rights architecture (laws and institutions) is, in large part, a creation of US hegemony. After World War II, the United States used its preponderant military and economic power to establish a liberal world order that was largely a reflection of itself. For realists, the United States did this not because it was nice or inherently good, but because it wanted to have a world conducive to its political and commercial interests. Human rights, the general prohibition against the threat and use of force, and the regulation of the use of force (permissible weapons and tactics) if war does occur, favors the privileged positon of the United States in the world it created.

The liberal world order created by the United States may represent a revolutionary improvement in the conduct of international relations or simply a pleasant mask for American realpolitik. Still, **liberalism** constitutes another mainstream theoretical approach and widely held worldview. The intellectual foundation of liberalism was laid in the eighteenth century by the likes of Adam Smith, David Ricardo, Jeremy Bentham, and John Locke, and was largely a reaction to realist thinking. Liberalism also has many variations but it is fundamentally an economic theory that is very suspicious of government, often seeing government as a necessary evil. Liberals argue that if selfish, competitive, yet maximally free individuals are allowed to operate within the context of a market they will generate the goods and services a society wants and needs at a price they are willing to pay.

One of the principal threats to markets and the freedom of individuals is the state. The state has the monopoly on violence domestically and can, through authoritative fiat, pick winners and losers in the economy and politics. Liberals hold that in order to check the potentially unlimited power of the state, individuals and groups need to be able to influence and control government. The power of government should also be limited by law and checked by other institutions. Limited government is necessary for the private sector and civil society to thrive and prosper; and the private sector and civil society have a proper role in influencing the government. Thomas Jefferson allegedly once said the famous line, "government that governs best, governs least." Democratic states committed to liberal values (limited government, majority rule, minority rights, individual rights, individual equality and the rule of law) create wealth, progress, and even peace.[5]

Liberalism as an economic and political theory is often divided into two competing schools of liberal thought. The first school includes **neoclassical liberals**, often associated with conservatives in the United States, who see the role of the state to promote free market values, but with very limited government regulation of the market, unless it is to help the supply (business) side of the economic equation. For these kinds of liberals, markets and private individuals are the mechanisms to properly distribute resources and values for a society. Their ideology holds that the market is self-regulating and that the market and private sector are far better than governments and the public sector in promoting values and distributing goods and services. **Keynesian liberals**,[6] on the other hand, see the state as an important force for leveling the economic and political playing field and for correcting for market excesses and imperfections. The government needs to prevent oligopoly and monopoly to ensure market competition. The government should also regulate the economy to prevent the concentration of wealth and prevent illegal behavior such as fraud and discrimination. Keynesian liberals see the government as important for ensuring that those on the demand side of the equation (workers and consumers) are protected in the market and citizens are able to participate effectively in the democracy. Although significant differences exist between these two kinds of liberals, they share common liberal values related to democracy, markets, and individual rights, including property rights.

Internationally, liberals see international law, international organizations, and global civil society as important vehicles for creating peaceful relations. While imperfect, the more liberal these institutions become, the more likely it is that the diverse people can come together to obtain mutual interests and manage global problems, while retaining their right to self-determination. Both domestically and internationally, the similarities between liberals suggest the economic integration and liberal democratic governance perhaps have transformed international relations to the extent that most international conflict can be resolved through peaceful, nonviolent means. The ill effects of anarchy are tempered by international law and organizations that can help states overcome security threats and collective action problems.

The differences among liberals, however, cannot be understated because both neoclassical liberals and Keynesian liberals disagree significantly regarding the efficacy of the state and the role of the state in the lives of individuals. Most internationally recognized human rights are liberal in orientation and are part and parcel of the liberal world order. They restrict what the government can and cannot do, and place a duty on governments to take the necessary steps so that individuals can actualize and enjoy their human rights. Part of the debate regarding the definition and implementation of human rights stems from an intra-liberal debate. Neoclassical liberalism is premised on the idea that the power of government needs to be checked. The state should refrain from interfering in the private sector (markets, homes, family, and religion). The government, even with the best of intentions, has a difficult time providing quality goods and services. Many of the civil and political rights enshrined in liberal democracies are designed to empower individuals to chart their own course in the world and to actualize and enjoy their rights as they see fit. Neoclassical liberalism emphasis on laissez-faire economics often translates into an emphasis on negative human rights, which puts a duty on the state to not do something as opposed to taking action.

Keynesians, on the other hand, see the government as responsible for ensuring that people have food, health care, housing, jobs, and fair wages. The government has the responsibility for leveling the playing field, decreasing inequality and correcting for market failures and volatility. Therefore, government needs to be much more active and involved in the private sphere and in protecting and promoting human rights. It is the government's responsibility to protect individuals from private sector groups (such as businesses) that can threaten individual human rights. Hence the promotion and protection of certain human rights also means promoting a certain *kind* of government. This, in turn, makes the actualization of human rights controversial and inherently political.

Nevertheless, liberals hold that expanding markets, economic interdependence, democratic government, and the development of shared norms and values, although evolving and contested, pave the path to peace. This path begins with the respect for fundamental human rights and dignity. Peace and respect for human rights are highly correlated.[7] States that respect human rights are generally more stable and prosperous than those that do not.

Even when civilized relations break down and societies engage in war, it does not mean it is open hunting season on human beings. States have agreed to, albeit imperfect, rules and laws regarding the methods and means of war. Many states are willing to hold individuals accountable for violating those laws. Human beings even at their worst can still strive for humane behavior.

The liberal worldview is criticized by realists as being naive and idealistic. They note that interdependence and nonviolence makes it very difficult to counter aggression or change the exploitative, oppressive policies of states. For those who hold a **Marxian** worldview, the liberal embrace of **capitalism** is problematic. The Marxian approach is also known as **structuralism** because it characterizes and defines the central structural feature of the international system as capitalism. Capitalism is an economic system and mode of production that is based on markets, private property, wage labor, and private ownership of the means of production. Capitalism is inherently exploitative because a small group of people (the owners/capitalists) benefit at the expense of everyone else (the workers). Whereas the liberal sees private individuals exchanging goods and services in a market as the best way to generate what a society wants at a price they are willing to pay, the Marxian sees the market as a way for the dominant capitalist class to accumulate vast wealth by maximizing profits which comes at the expense of wages. As capitalists accumulate more, wealth becomes concentrated in the hands of the few while impoverishing the masses. Workers are paid so little that they cannot consume the goods and services that they producing, leading to over-production and under-consumption. The state is merely a reflection of the dominant class and is used by that class to control the masses. Democracy is an illusion or a facade because the capitalists are financially more articulate and can buy access to the political decision-making process.[8] Often capitalists can just buy government decisions.

Imperialism (colonialism) occurred when states, controlled by capitalists, scrambled for captive territories to serve as outlets for excess goods and services that could not be consumed at home. The state's role was to secure access to raw materials, markets, and cheap labor overseas and it did so through military force and corruption. When formal colonialism ended in the post-World War II era, it was replaced with neoimperialism/neocolonialism whereby the newly "independent" states had formal sovereignty in that they were now responsible for law and order, schools, health care, and infrastructure. However, their resources, markets, and labor were controlled by foreign multinational corporations which were backed by their powerful home countries. States in the periphery and semi-periphery were controlled by the core states through corruption and economic domination.

In a Marxian context, the greatest threat to human dignity and human rights is capitalism. The plight of industrial workers was chronicled by Karl Marx and the individualistic nature of liberal notions of human rights serve to protect market values, not human dignity.[9] Moreover, the language of human rights was used to justify colonialism under the guise for bringing progress, human dignity and modernity to peripheral countries.[10] States willing to act for the sake of human rights and humanitarian principles abroad are also engaging in a form of neocolonialism.

Many decision-makers from developing countries often have a mixture of a realist and Marxian worldviews because of the historical experience with colonization and their violent struggle for independence. Their experiences with liberalism/capitalism are slavery, exploitation, violence, and poverty. Liberal notions of human rights, especially those civil and political rights espoused by the advanced industrialized countries, as well as negative rights, are viewed with suspicion. These states tend to prioritize economic, social, and cultural rights. Developing countries also highlight collective rights such as rights to self-determination and development.

Realist, liberal, and Marxist worldviews are sets of widely held beliefs about how the world works. They recognize that states are important, but each has a different perspective on what motivates states, and how and why they prioritize different kinds of human rights domestically and internationally. The worldviews appear to be objective in that they describe the world as it is and how certain forces (anarchy, power struggles, markets, or capitalist accumulation) determine the fate of societies. As such, they offer competing narratives of international relations and the role of human rights and humanitarian affairs within those relations. Another approach, albeit not necessarily a worldview, is **constructivism**. Constructivism is used by academics and analysts to explain how the central theories, concepts, norms, and values in international relations are socially constructed and change over time.[11] The social and political institutions in world politics are constructed by human beings and human beings give them importance or relegate them to the trash heap of history. The meanings of institutions and principles change over time because politics are not static. That is to say, what may have been permissible in the eighteenth century is no longer permissible now. States at one time had formal colonies, practiced institutionalized slavery, and treated women as property. Most of these practices are no longer permissible today. The world is what human beings make it and nothing, including human rights and humanitarian principles, is preordained or predetermined.

Theory provides a mental map regarding world affairs and it is at the heart of diplomacy. It explains how and why different, well-meaning people can look at the same issue and event and disagree about the causes and what ought to be done. The other is not necessarily evil or immoral. They are just understanding the situation through a different worldview. Also the differences between theories are not minor. Differences center on how the world works and what causes human misery and improves the human condition. Diplomacy is the process through which actors come to international understandings in a complex world. Decision-makers, regardless of worldview, must engage in world politics and diplomacy. The next sections examine the role of heads of state in the diplomatic process and how states decide whether and how to advance human rights and humanitarian principles in their foreign relations.

Heads of state and diplomacy

An active head of a state is usually a chief executive (a prime minister or president) who makes the big decisions regarding state policy, including the diplomatic recognition of states and whether to accept the credentials of representatives of foreign governments.[12] They also are responsible for negotiating and concluding formal and informal agreements with other states. Obviously, subordinates are responsible for the nuts and bolts of diplomacy including the pre-negotiations and the actual conduct of diplomatic talks; however, heads of state have a defining role in **summit diplomacy**, either as a precursor to launch lower level negotiations by subordinates or to provide a dramatic conclusion to ongoing negotiations. Negotiations may be bilateral or multilateral (meaning the preparations and the conduct of diplomacy are under the auspices of an IGO).

Summit diplomacy is high profile and is used by heads of state to guide policy in a particular direction while recognizing they must also satisfy domestic constituencies. Summits are rare and involve multiple issues that are sources of conflict. Human rights and humanitarian issues were generally not part of summitry until the 1970s, but several summits are noteworthy for their impact on human rights. The **Helsinki Summit** was the capstone to the signing of the **Helsinki Accords** in 1975. The accords were a series of high level agreements that led to a thaw in the Cold War and put human rights on the international agenda. The attention to human rights and the formal monitoring of political oppression in the Soviet Union may have even contributed to the end of Cold War in 1989.[13] Negotiations were formally opened by the Conference on Security and Cooperation in Europe and its final act identified ten principles:[14]

1. Sovereign equality, respect for the rights inherent in sovereignty
2. Refraining from the threat or use of force
3. Inviolability of frontiers
4. Territorial integrity of states
5. Peaceful settlement of disputes
6. Non-intervention in internal affairs
7. Respect for human rights and fundamental freedoms (including the freedom of thought, conscience, religion or belief)
8. Equal rights and self-determination of peoples
9. Cooperation among states
10. Fulfillment in good faith of obligations under international law.

The negotiations dealt with far ranging global issues including arms control and the resolution of territorial disputes. The final agreement was signed with great fanfare by thirty-five heads of state including US President Gerald Ford and the Soviet Premier Leonid Brezhnev. After reaffirming the age-old principles of sovereignty, territorial integrity, and nonintervention, the Cold War antagonists agreed to respect internationally recognized human rights. Specifically, the language of principle 7 states:

> The participating States will respect human rights and fundamental freedoms, including the freedom of thought, conscience, religion or belief, for all without distinction as to race, sex, language or religion.
> They will promote and encourage the effective exercise of civil, political, economic, social, cultural and other rights and freedoms all of which derive from the inherent dignity of the human person and are essential for his free and full development.
> Within this framework the participating States will recognize and respect the freedom of the individual to profess and practice, alone or in community with others, religion or belief acting in accordance with the dictates of his own conscience.
> The participating States on whose territory national minorities exist will respect the right of persons belonging to such minorities to equality before the law, will afford them the full opportunity for the actual enjoyment of human rights and fundamental freedoms and will, in this manner, protect their legitimate interests in this sphere.
> The participating States recognize the universal significance of human rights and fundamental freedoms, respect for which is an essential factor for the peace, justice and well-being necessary to ensure the development of friendly relations and co-operation among themselves as among all States.

> They will constantly respect these rights and freedoms in their mutual relations and will endeavour jointly and separately, including in co-operation with the United Nations, to promote universal and effective respect for them.
> They confirm the right of the individual to know and act upon his rights and duties in this field.
> In the field of human rights and fundamental freedoms, the participating States will act in conformity with the purposes and principles of the Charter of the United Nations and with the Universal Declaration of Human Rights. They will also fulfil their obligations as set forth in the international declarations and agreements in this field, including inter alia the International Covenants on Human Rights, by which they may be bound.[15]

The language is typical of human rights diplomacy. In order for diverse peoples, with different worldviews, and different conceptions of human rights, to agree, diplomatic language must be vague enough to be subject to multiple interpretations and leave room for heads to state to appease multiple domestic constituencies, all the while incrementally furthering the cause of human dignity. In this particular formulation, several worldviews are accommodated: the realist worldview sees the reaffirmation of the principles of sovereignty and nonintervention; the Marxian/structuralist view sees the importance of economic, social, and cultural rights; and the liberal view sees the civil and political rights with special emphasis on "the freedom of thought, conscience, religion or belief, for all without distinction as to race, sex, language or religion." The Helsinki Accords were groundbreaking because they represent the first major multilateral agreement since the start of the Cold War that attempted to bridge the gap between East and West regarding the placement of human rights on the agenda and to comprehensively deal with the sources of conflict. More importantly, the accords link respect for human rights to security and cooperation in Europe.[16] When the thirty-five heads of state embraced the agreement, they increased the diplomatic salience of human rights norms.[17] The Helsinki Accords also resulted in the creation of an NGO called **Helsinki Watch** to monitor the human rights progress of the signatories, particularly the Soviet Union. Helsinki Watch was the precursor to one of the more important non-state actors involved in human rights diplomacy, **Human Rights Watch** (whose history, function, and evolution are discussed in Chapter 6).

The Helsinki Accords represent the most important Cold War diplomatic statement on human rights. Human rights were also featured in the bilateral Cold War summits between US President Ronald Reagan and Soviet Premier Mikhail Gorbachev during the 1980s. While mostly focused on arms control and other security issues, the media buzz surrounding the **Reagan–Gorbachev summits** was whether human rights were going to be on the agenda and how that might affect the negotiations.[18] The first two summits, in Geneva (1985) and Reykjavik (1986), did not have human rights formally on the agenda, but were broached by Reagan. According to US Secretary of State George Schultz recalling the Geneva Summit in his memoirs:

The second summit day, Wednesday, November 20, was tough from start to finish. The Soviets were hosts. Gorbachev began by inviting President Reagan into a side room in their embassy for a private session. We had predicted this would happen, and the president had decided to use the opportunity to take up human rights issues again. When the two leaders emerged, they were not smiling. The atmosphere had been highly charged. The president told me that after he made his points, Gorbachev attacked human rights practices in the United States, citing discrimination against blacks and women and unemployment figures, which he contrasted with full employment in the Soviet Union. The president had argued back. The exchange had been intense. Again, that sounded good to me. The Soviets were talking with us about the subject. They weren't stonewalling. Maybe we could move forward through this process of mutual criticism.[19]

This passage illustrates the contending notions of human rights stemming from different worldviews and whether the human rights should even be part of the international diplomatic dialogue. Subsequent summits in Washington, DC (1987) and Moscow (1988) showed that human rights continued to be a major source of irritation. According to the *New York Times* when reporting on the Moscow summit:

The discussion today ranged over such issues as freedom of religion and the right to emigrate, and Soviet officials said Mr. Gorbachev was irritated not so much at the specific points raised as by Mr. Reagan's insistence on discussing the issues at all. The Soviet Union rejects unsolicited advice. Gennadi I. Gerasimov, the Soviet Foreign Ministry spokesman, accused Mr. Reagan of not understanding the improvement made in human rights policy here, and of trying to lecture the Soviet people about their failings. "We don't like it when someone from outside is teaching us how to live, and this is only natural," he said at a briefing for reporters. Disputes over human rights have punctuated the three previous meetings between the American and Soviet leaders, and as Mr. Gerasimov indicated, the Soviet Union is sensitive about what it considers intrusions into its internal affairs.[20]

The relative importance of Reagan or Gorbachev to the advancement of international human rights is debatable, but these bilateral superpower summits show that international human rights are political, contested, and a central feature of international relations (whether states like it or not). More importantly, discussion of human rights was no longer an egregious breach of diplomatic protocol. Human rights have been on the agenda of other summits since but were not surrounded with the same dramatic media attention. Rather, criticism often has centered on disappointment that human rights were not pursued more vigorously.

Besides summits, heads of state make foreign policy decisions that affects a state's ability to promote and protect human rights abroad. In the 1990s, human rights diplomacy took a different turn when the administration of US President Bill Clinton decided to delink improvements in human rights in the US trade negotiations with China over the renewal of **Most Favored Nation (MFN)** status. Under trade rules, states are not allowed to discriminate among trading partners in terms of tariffs, duties, and quotas. States are also supposed to treat all trading partners equally, hence if the United States grants China MFN status then China has the same trading terms with the United States as, say, the United Kingdom. A state with MFN status is eligible for a special level of trade concessions. Under US law, China's MFN status was granted provisionally in 1980, but was conditional on improvements in human rights and was to be reviewed annually. After the 1989 massacre of pro-democracy demonstrators in Tiananmen Square, the United States, under the administration of President George H.W. Bush, imposed trade sanctions and threatened to revoke MFN status (although it never did).

As trade negotiations continued under the Clinton Administration, the president's decision to delink human rights from trade was widely criticized by human rights groups because trade concessions can be important positive incentives for encouraging states to promote and protect human rights at home. The move was seen as placing profits and geopolitics ahead of human rights in China. In defending the decision, President Clinton took the classical liberal line regarding the promotion of human rights. "This decision offers us the best opportunity to lay the basis for long-term sustainable progress on human rights and for the advancement of our other interests with China … Let me ask you the same question I have asked myself," he said. "Will we do more to advance the cause of human rights if China is isolated?"[21] Only by engaging states can human rights be promoted.[22] Coercion rarely, if ever, works. The idea that trade liberalization will lead to higher living standards and translate into more political liberalization and improved human rights is a common liberal theme. This theme also provides the rationale for liberal strategies of promoting human rights through trade in foreign policy. The 1997 and 1998 summits between China President Jiang Zemin and President Bill Clinton had human rights on the agenda but also paved the way for permanent MFN status in 2001 when China officially joined the World Trade Organization (WTO).

The WTO is widely criticized by human rights activists because it limits the extent to which trade measures may be used for social and political reasons, such as pressuring states to improve their human rights.[23] It is also criticized because free trade privileges the profit interests of multinational corporations and undermines economic and labor rights such as the rights to work, unionize, and receive just wages.[24] The merits of these criticism will always be debated because they are grounded in different worldviews. But it is safe to say that the choices made by leaders of powerful states shape the way international human rights are defined and implemented. Nearly twenty years later, China has made tremendous progress in terms of development, dramatically improving quality of life of its people in terms of access to food, water, housing, education, and health care. China's record on civil and political human rights, however, remains sketchy at best.

Heads of state also engage in other kinds of "public diplomacy" promoting human rights and humanitarian principles. This involves taking their message directly to a wider public audience and can take the form of speeches and other kinds of media encounters. President Jimmy Carter's 1977 commencement speech at the University of

Notre Dame (Sidebar 2.1) is widely remembered as one of the first public expositions which placed international human rights at the forefront of US foreign policy. This speech was designed to build public support for a series of changes in the direction of US foreign policy.

> **Sidebar 2.1 Excerpt from Jimmy Carter's commencement address at the University of Notre Dame, May 22, 1977**[25]
>
> But I want to speak to you today about the strands that connect our actions overseas with our essential character as a nation. I believe we can have a foreign policy that is democratic, that is based on fundamental values, and that uses power and influence, which we have, for humane purposes. We can also have a foreign policy that the American people both support and, for a change, know about and understand.
>
> I have a quiet confidence in our own political system. Because we know that democracy works, we can reject the arguments of those rulers who deny human rights to their people.
>
> We are confident that democracy's example will be compelling, and so we seek to bring that example closer to those from whom in the past few years we have been separated and who are not yet convinced about the advantages of our kind of life.
>
> We are confident that the democratic methods are the most effective, and so we are not tempted to employ improper tactics here at home or abroad.
>
> We are confident of our own strength, so we can seek substantial mutual reductions in the nuclear arms race.
>
> And we are confident of the good sense of American people, and so we let them share in the process of making foreign policy decisions. We can thus speak with the voices of 215 million, and not just of an isolated handful.
>
> Democracy's great recent successes–in India, Portugal, Spain, Greece–show that our confidence in this system is not misplaced. Being confident of our own future, we are now free of that inordinate fear of communism which once led us to embrace any dictator who joined us in that fear. I'm glad that that's being changed.
>
> For too many years, we've been willing to adopt the flawed and erroneous principles and tactics of our adversaries, sometimes abandoning our own values for theirs. We've fought fire with fire, never thinking that fire is better quenched with water. This approach failed, with Vietnam the best example of its intellectual and moral poverty. But through failure we have now found our way back to our own principles and values, and we have regained our lost confidence.
>
> By the measure of history, our Nation's 200 years are very brief, and our rise to world eminence is briefer still. It dates from 1945, when Europe and the old international order lay in ruins. Before then, America was largely on the

periphery of world affairs. But since then, we have inescapably been at the center of world affairs.

Our policy during this period was guided by two principles: a belief that Soviet expansion was almost inevitable but that it must be contained, and the corresponding belief in the importance of an almost exclusive alliance among non-Communist nations on both sides of the Atlantic. That system could not last forever unchanged. Historical trends have weakened its foundation. The unifying threat of conflict with the Soviet Union has become less intensive, even though the competition has become more extensive.

The Vietnamese war produced a profound moral crisis, sapping worldwide faith in our own policy and our system of life, a crisis of confidence made even more grave by the covert pessimism of some of our leaders.

In less than a generation, we've seen the world change dramatically. The daily lives and aspirations of most human beings have been transformed. Colonialism is nearly gone. A new sense of national identity now exists in almost 100 new countries that have been formed in the last generation. Knowledge has become more widespread. Aspirations are higher. As more people have been freed from traditional constraints, more have been determined to achieve, for the first time in their lives, social justice.

The world is still divided by ideological disputes, dominated by regional conflicts, and threatened by danger that we will not resolve the differences of race and wealth without violence or without drawing into combat the major military powers. We can no longer separate the traditional issues of war and peace from the new global questions of justice, equity, and human rights.

It is a new world, but America should not fear it. It is a new world, and we should help to shape it. It is a new world that calls for a new American foreign policy – a policy based on constant decency in its values and on optimism in our historical vision.

We can no longer have a policy solely for the industrial nations as the foundation of global stability, but we must respond to the new reality of a politically awakening world.

We can no longer expect that the other 150 nations will follow the dictates of the powerful, but we must continue – confidently – our efforts to inspire, to persuade, and to lead.

Our policy must reflect our belief that the world can hope for more than simple survival and our belief that dignity and freedom are fundamental spiritual requirements. Our policy must shape an international system that will last longer than secret deals.

We cannot make this kind of policy by manipulation. Our policy must be open; it must be candid; it must be one of constructive global involvement, resting on five cardinal principles.

I've tried to make these premises clear to the American people since last January. Let me review what we have been doing and discuss what we intend to do.

> First, we have reaffirmed America's commitment to human rights as a fundamental tenet of our foreign policy. In ancestry, religion, color, place of origin, and cultural background, we Americans are as diverse a nation as the world has even seen. No common mystique of blood or soil unites us. What draws us together, perhaps more than anything else, is a belief in human freedom. We want the world to know that our Nation stands for more than financial prosperity.
>
> This does not mean that we can conduct our foreign policy by rigid moral maxims. We live in a world that is imperfect and which will always be imperfect – a world that is complex and confused and which will always be complex and confused.
>
> I understand fully the limits of moral suasion. We have no illusion that changes will come easily or soon. But I also believe that it is a mistake to undervalue the power of words and of the ideas that words embody. In our own history, that power has ranged from Thomas Paine's "Common Sense" to Martin Luther King, Jr.'s "I Have a Dream."
>
> In the life of the human spirit, words are action, much more so than many of us may realize who live in countries where freedom of expression is taken for granted. The leaders of totalitarian nations understand this very well. The proof is that words are precisely the action for which dissidents in those countries are being persecuted.
>
> Nonetheless, we can already see dramatic, worldwide advances in the protection of the individual from the arbitrary power of the state. For us to ignore this trend would be to lose influence and moral authority in the world. To lead it will be to regain the moral stature that we once had.
>
> The great democracies are not free because we are strong and prosperous. I believe we are strong and influential and prosperous because we are free.
>
> Throughout the world today, in free nations and in totalitarian countries as well, there is a preoccupation with the subject of human freedom, human rights. And I believe it is incumbent on us in this country to keep that discussion, that debate, that contention alive. No other country is as well-qualified as we to set an example. We have our own shortcomings and faults, and we should strive constantly and with courage to make sure that we are legitimately proud of what we have.

The impact of Carter on furthering human rights has been widely analyzed.[26] Carter's policy shift is credited with the creation of the "Country Reports on Human Rights Practices" written by the US Department of State (discussed more thoroughly in Chapter 3) and for linking US military, economic, and development aid to progress on human rights. Carter was not always successful in keeping human rights a foreign policy priority, but his administration did put international human rights squarely into US relations with other states. Other heads of state also are noted for their eloquent advocacy of human rights and humanitarian principles in their public diplomacy. South African President Nelson Mandela, Irish President Mary Robinson, and Czech Republic President Vaclav Havel are icons in the human rights movement because they took concrete action to match their inspirational words.

Heads of state must juggle competing interests. Domestic and international security is always a concern. War and other forms of violent conflict pose some of the gravest threats to human rights and dignity. Failing and failed states also create seemingly intractable diplomatic problems for states (as extensively detailed in Chapter 4). The principles of sovereignty and nonintervention have been around for a long time, in part, because they contribute to state stability, which is arguably necessary for the actualization of human rights. In Sidebar 2.2, Russian President Vladimir Putin urges the United States and its allies not to launch a military strike on Syria (in response to the use of chemical weapons in that country) in a 2013 editorial to the *New York Times*. This op-ed is an example of public diplomacy designed to shape mass and elite international opinion regarding the priority of human rights and humanitarian values vis-à-vis other international values.

Sidebar 2.2 Exerpt from Russian President Vladimir Putin's op-ed, *New York Times*, September 11, 2013[27]

The United Nations' founders understood that decisions affecting war and peace should happen only by consensus, and with America's consent the veto by Security Council permanent members was enshrined in the United Nations Charter. The profound wisdom of this has underpinned the stability of international relations for decades.

No one wants the United Nations to suffer the fate of the League of Nations, which collapsed because it lacked real leverage. This is possible if influential countries bypass the United Nations and take military action without Security Council authorization.

The potential strike by the United States against Syria, despite strong opposition from many countries and major political and religious leaders, including the pope, will result in more innocent victims and escalation, potentially spreading the conflict far beyond Syria's borders. A strike would increase violence and unleash a new wave of terrorism. It could undermine multilateral efforts to resolve the Iranian nuclear problem and the Israeli-Palestinian conflict and further destabilize the Middle East and North Africa. It could throw the entire system of international law and order out of balance.

Syria is not witnessing a battle for democracy, but an armed conflict between government and opposition in a multireligious country. There are few champions of democracy in Syria. But there are more than enough Qaeda fighters and extremists of all stripes battling the government. The United States State Department has designated Al Nusra Front and the Islamic State of Iraq and the Levant, fighting with the opposition, as terrorist organizations. This internal conflict, fueled by foreign weapons supplied to the opposition, is one of the bloodiest in the world.

Mercenaries from Arab countries fighting there, and hundreds of militants from Western countries and even Russia, are an issue of our deep concern. Might they not return to our countries with experience acquired in Syria? After all, after fighting in Libya, extremists moved on to Mali. This threatens us all.

From the outset, Russia has advocated peaceful dialogue enabling Syrians to develop a compromise plan for their own future. We are not protecting the Syrian government, but international law. We need to use the United Nations Security Council and believe that preserving law and order in today's complex and turbulent world is one of the few ways to keep international relations from sliding into chaos. The law is still the law, and we must follow it whether we like it or not. Under current international law, force is permitted only in self-defense or by the decision of the Security Council. Anything else is unacceptable under the United Nations Charter and would constitute an act of aggression.

No one doubts that poison gas was used in Syria. But there is every reason to believe it was used not by the Syrian Army, but by opposition forces, to provoke intervention by their powerful foreign patrons, who would be siding with the fundamentalists. Reports that militants are preparing another attack – this time against Israel – cannot be ignored.

This editorial was widely panned in the West as a cynical Russian attempt to protect its brutal ally Syrian President Bashar al-Assad. At the same time, it also resonated in other parts of the world, especially those that have experienced Western military intervention. To them, Putin was trying to get the leaders of liberal democracies to see that their proposed course of action was beyond what was currently acceptable in terms of the norms and law of international relations. Good intentions and military air strikes had the very real potential to make the human rights and humanitarian situation in Syria and the region significantly worse. Whether Putin's public diplomacy was cynical or sage is subject to worldviews that generate competing narratives about who is at fault and what factors precipitated the Syrian humanitarian crisis. Its effect was to help forestall an armed intervention and eventually led to the removal of chemical weapons from Syria. At the same time, the Syrian conflict rages on with more than 200,000 killed. The extremist elements that Putin opined would be advantaged by a US military strike have proven that they indeed pose a very real threat to regional stability, not to mention international human rights and the rights of ethnic and religious minorities.

States and the development of international human rights and humanitarian law

Intervention is but one dimension of human rights and humanitarian protection. The progressive development of international law is another, more expansive effort. States are the creators and principal enforcers of international law. They have used their sovereignty to create more than one hundred human rights agreements, each designed to preserve human dignity and prescribe certain kinds of state behavior. While many of these treaties are far from being universal, they do represent the incremental evolution of human rights and humanitarian protection through state diplomacy. After the states of UN General Assembly adopted the UDHR in 1948, they also adopted the **Convention on the Prevention and the Punishment of Genocide** (1948). It entered into force in 1951 when the requisite number of states (forty-one at the time) had become formal signatories.

States then moved outside of the UN to redress the atrocities that were committed during World War II, thereby greatly expanding the scope of IHL. In 1949, states codified international expectations regarding the treatment of civilians in international conflict and in occupied territories in four Geneva Conventions. **Common Article 3** extended the protection of civilians to include internal, as well as international, conflicts. The dimensions of this protection includes access to besieged populations and, by extension, the security of persons delivering humanitarian aid. The ICRC was given the right to visit detainees and POWs to monitor their treatment. In 1977, two protocols were added. Protocol I provides additional rules for international armed conflict and the protection of those not participating in hostilities. Protocol II extends those protections to victims in non-international armed conflict, which have made up more than 80 percent of all armed conflicts since 1945.[28] Additional Protocol III (2005) protects the neutral emblems of humanitarian aid groups.

States also created international law to address the continuing human rights problems associated with refugees and migrants after World War II and the onset of the Cold War. The **1951 Convention Relating to the Status of Refugees (and the 1967 Protocol)**, the **1954 Convention Relating to the Status of Stateless Persons**, and the **1961 Convention on the Reduction of Statelessness** provide the legal framework for the protection of refugees and stateless persons. These laws also define a refugee and stateless person and codify how states are to protect these vulnerable persons.

The Cold War generated at lag between the soft law of the UDHR and the more binding international law necessary for UDHR aspirations to take effect. Table 2.1 lists the major human rights treaties that were created by states under the auspices of an IGO and monitored by the UN. The table also includes regional human rights law. Even though important states, such as the United States and Russia, are not formal parties to many human rights and humanitarian treaties (including optional protocols), the principles enshrined in the law (whether ratified or not) contribute to the development of customary international law.[29] Just because a state has not signed or ratified the treaty on torture or the disabled, it is expected to abide by the law nevertheless.

The proliferation of international law has also meant the creation of international agencies, commissions, and committees to help states implement the law and to fulfill their duties and responsibility. Many of the treaties listed in Table 2.1 have complementary committees that are responsible for monitoring state compliance.

Table 2.1 International human rights treaties

Name of treaty	Date opened for signatures	Date entered into force	Number of parties
International Convention on the Elimination of All Forms of Racial Discrimination (ICERD)	1965	1969	177
International Covenant on Civil and Political Rights (ICCPR)	1966	1976	168
International Covenant on Economic, Social and Cultural Rights (ICESCR)	1966	1976	162
Convention on the Elimination of All Forms of Discrimination against Women (CEDAW)	1979	1981	188
Convention against Torture and Other Cruel, Inhuman or Degrading Treatment or Punishment (CAT)	1984	1987	155
Convention on the Rights of the Child (CRC)	1989	1989	194
International Convention on the Protection of the Rights of All Migrant Workers and Members of Their Families (ICMW)	1990	2003	47
International Convention for the Protection of All Persons from Enforced Disappearance (CPED)	2006	2010	43
Convention on the Rights of Persons with Disabilities (CRPD)	2006	2008	148
Optional Protocol to the Convention on Economic, Social and Cultural Rights (ICESCR-OP)	2008	2013	15
Optional Protocol to the International Covenant on Civil and Political Rights (ICCPR-OP1)	1966	1976	115
Second Optional Protocol to the International Covenant on Civil and Political Rights, aiming at the abolition of the death penalty (ICCPR-OP2)	1989	1991	81
Optional Protocol to the Convention on the Elimination of Discrimination against Women (OP-CEDAW)	1999	2000	188
Optional Protocol to the Convention on the Rights of the Child on the Involvement of Children in Armed Conflict (OP-CRC-AC)	2000	2002	156
Optional Protocol to the Convention on the Rights of the Child on the Sale of Children, Child Prostitution and Child Pornography (OP-CRC-SC)	2000	2002	167
Optional Protocol to the Convention against Torture and Other Cruel, Inhuman or Degrading Treatment or Punishment (OP-CAT)	2002	2006	73
Optional Protocol to the Convention on the Rights of Persons with Disabilities (OP-CRPD)	2006	2008	148

Source: Compiled from www.ohchr.org.

Chapter 5 explores the work of these committees; however, they warrant recognition here because states have agreed to have their diplomacy supplemented by committees, and in some cases human rights courts. This growing body of international law represents empirical evidence of the human rights and humanitarian diplomacy of states. Human rights and humanitarian principles are important to states, although their relative importance vis-à-vis other state interests is the subject of considerable debate.

Conclusion

The diplomatic history of human rights and humanitarian rights necessarily revolves around states as they bear the main duties and responsibilities. Their different experiences, geopolitical situation, history, culture, and identity mean states understand the world and the processes/dynamics of world politics very differently. As a result, they have different conceptions about the definition of human rights and about the importance and the role of human rights and humanitarian principles domestically and internationally. States formulate their policies based largely on their worldview, material interests, and capabilities. These factors inform their understanding of international law in international relations. Post-World War II human rights and humanitarian diplomacy by states evolved from efforts to ensure that the horrors of World War II never occurred again with the UDHR, the Genocide Convention, and the Geneva Conventions to the treaties relating to the status of refugees and stateless persons. Then a Cold War stalemate set in. Still, efforts to codify human rights continued and, in the 1970s, a thaw in the Cold War relations led to a breakthrough in human rights protections. This breakthrough is evidenced by the diplomacy surrounding the Helsinki Accords, which led to an important human rights dialogue between the world's superpowers which continued in the 1980s. Moreover, the binding covenants on civil and political rights, and economic, social, and cultural rights (which opened for signatures in 1966), became legally binding in 1977 when the requisite number of states ratified the treaties.

The aftermath of the Cold War saw failed states and ethnic conflict as additional causes of gross violations of human rights, war crimes, genocide, and crimes against humanity. The next chapter explores the mechanics of the conduct of state diplomacy and Chapter 4 explores how states have responded multilaterally to contemporary challenges by strengthening human rights and humanitarian protection in internal conflict and expanding the boundaries of human rights protection during peace. This, and subsequent chapters, show why states remain the most important actors in protecting and promoting human rights and humanitarian principles and are also the ones who can most undermine them.

Key terms

International law, subjects, international legal personality, international relations theory, realism, anarchy, hegemonic power, liberalism, neo-classical liberals, Keynesian liberals, Marxian, capitalism, structuralism, imperialism, constructivism, summit diplomacy, Helsinki Summit, Helsinki Accords, Helsinki Watch, Human Rights Watch, Reagan-Gorbachev summits, Most Favored Nation (MFN), Convention on the Prevention and the Punishment of Genocide, Common Article 3, 1951 Convention Relating to the Status of Refugees (and the 1967 Protocol), 1954 Convention Relating to the Status of Stateless Persons, 1961 Convention on the Reduction of Statelessness.

Discussion questions

1. What is worldview and how does worldview affect the definition and implementation of human rights and humanitarian principles?
2. Discuss how heads of state can engage human rights and humanitarian diplomacy. Your answer should include the role of summitry in general to the process, and the Helsinki Accords/Summit in particular.
3. Discuss the role of states in diplomacy and the creation of international law. Your answer should include how the human rights and humanitarian principles have evolved through state actions.

Notes

1 See Hans Morgenthau, *Politics Among Nature: The Struggle for Power and Peace*, 5th edition (New York: Knopf, 1978), 4–15; E.H. Carr and Michael Cox, *The Twenty Years Crisis, 1919–1939: An Introduction to International Relations* (New York: Palgrave Macmillan, 2001).
2 Carl von Clausewitz, *On War*, ed. and trans. Michael Howard and Peter Paret (Princeton: Princeton University Press, 1976).
3 Joesph Nye, *Soft Power: The Means to Success in World Politics* (New York: Public Affairs, 2004).
4 This is one of the central themes of John Fabian Witt, *Lincoln's Code: The Law of War in American History* (New York: Free Press, 2012).
5 See Bruce Russett, *Grasping the Democratic Peace: Principles of a Post-Cold War World* (Princeton: Princeton University Press, 1994), 1–7.

6 These liberals are influenced by the writings of the British economist John Maynard Keynes (1883–1946) who is widely considered the father of the modern capitalist welfare state.
7 David P. Forsythe, *Human Rights and Peace: International and National Dimensions* (Lincoln: University of Nebraska Press, 1993); and Steven C. Poe and C. Neal Tate, "Repression of Human Rights to Personal Integrity in the 1980s: A Global Analysis," *American Political Science Review*, 88:4 (1994), 853–872.
8 Daniel C. Hellinger and Dennis R. Judd, *The Democratic Façade*, 2nd edition (New York: Wadsworth, 1994).
9 Eric Engle, "Human Rights According to Marxism," *Guild Practitioner*, 65:4 (Winter 2008), 249–256, 249.
10 See Bonny Ibhawoh, *Imperialism and Human Rights: Colonial Discourses of Rights and Liberties in African History* (Albany: State of New York University Press, 2007); and Alice L. Conklin, "Colonialism and Human Rights, A Contradiction in Terms? The Case of France in West Africa, 1895–1914," *The American Historical Review*, 103:2 (April 1998), 419–442.
11 Alexander Wendt, "Anarchy is what States Make of It: The Social Construction of Power Politics," *International Organizations*, 46 (Spring 1992), 291–324.
12 Some states have a split executive where executive powers are divided between a symbolic/figurehead representative (often a monarch) and a chief executive who is charge of the government. Others have a dual executive (usually a prime minister and president) who share executive powers with one usually responsible for the conduct of foreign affairs.
13 See Daniel C. Thomas, *The Helsinki Effect: International Norms, Human Rights, and the Demise of the Cold of Communism* (Princeton: Princeton University Press, 2001).
14 The Final Act of the Conference on Security and Cooperation in Europe, August 1, 1975, 14 I.L.M. 1292 (Helsinki Declaration).
15 *The Conference of Security and Co-Operation in Europe Final Act* (Helsinki, 1975), 6–7. www.osce.org/mc/39501?download=true.
16 William Korey, "The Helskinki Accords: Good Intentions," *New Republic*, August 2, 1975, 6–7.
17 Daniel C. Thomas, "Boomerangs and Superpowers: International Norms, Transnational Networks, and US Foreign Policy," *Cambridge Review of International Affairs*, 15 (2002), 25–44, 25.
18 See Bernard Weintraub, "Reagan to Resist One Issue Summit," *New York Times*, August 22, 1986; and Anthony Lewis, "Abroad at Home; Human Rights Dilemma," *New York Times*, February 13, 1986, accessed October 15, 2014. www.nytimes.com/1986/02/13/opinion/abroad-at-home-human-rights-dilemma.html.
19 George Schulz, *Turmoil and Triumph: My Years as Secretary of State* (New York: Charles Scribner's Sons), 602–603.
20 Steven V. Roberts, "The Moscow Summit: The Serious Side; Reagan and Gorbachev Begin Summit Parley in the Kremlin; Strike Sparks Rights Issue," *New York Times*, May 30, 1988, accessed October 15, 2014. www.nytimes.com/1988/05/30/world/moscow-summit-serious-side-reagan-gorbachev-begin-summit-parley-kremlin-strike.html.
21 Ann Devroy, "Clinton Grants China MFN, Reversing Campaign Pledge," *The Tech Online Edition*, 114:27 (May 27, 1994), accessed October 15, 2014. http://tech.mit.edu/V114/N27/china.27w.html.

22 Yitan Li and A. Cooper Drury, "Threatening Sanctions When Engagement Would Be More Effective: Attaining Better Human Rights in China," *International Studies Perspectives*, 5:4 (November 2004), 378–394.
23 Sarah Joseph, *Blame it On the WTO? A Human Rights Critique* (Oxford: Oxford University Press, 2011); and Thomas Pogge, "Recognized and Violated by International Law," *Leiden Journal of International Law*, 18:4 (2005), 717–745.
24 Razeen Sappideen, "Property Rights, Human Rights, and the New International Trade Regime," *International Journal of Human Rights*, 15:7 (October 2011), 1013–1030.
25 Available at the *American Presidency Project*, accessed September 21, 2014. www.presidency.ucsb.edu/ws/?pid=7552.
26 K. Clymer, "Jimmy Carter, Human Rights and Cambodia," *Diplomatic History*, 27:2 (April 2003), 561–593; and David F. Schmitz and Vanessa Walker, "Jimmy Carter and the Foreign Policy of Human Rights: The Development of a Post-Cold War Foreign Policy," *Diplomatic History*, 28:1 (January 2004), 113–143; and Steven C. Poe, "Human Rights and Economic Allocation Under Ronald Reagan and Jimmy Carter," *American Journal of Political Science*, 36:1 (February 1992), 147–167.
27 Vladimir V. Putin, "A Plea for Caution from Russia: What Putin has to say to Americans about Syria," *New York Times*, September 23, 2013. Accessed October 5, 2015. www.nytimes.com/2013/09/12/opinion/putin-plea-for-caution-from-russia-on-syria.html?pagewanted=all&_r=0.
28 The International Committee for the Red Cross, Treaties States Parties to Such Treaties, accessed September 14, 2014. www.icrc.org/applic/ihl/ihl.nsf/Treaty.xsp?documentId=AA0C5BCBAB5C4A85C12563CD002D6D09&action=openDocumenthttps://www.icrc.org/applic/ihl/ihl.nsf/Treaty.xsp?documentId=AA0C5BCBAB5C4A85C12563CD002D6D09&action=openDocument.
29 See Jeffery L. Roberg, "The Importance of International Treaties: Is Ratification Necessary," *World Affairs*, 169:4 (Spring 2007), 181–186.

3

Inside the black box

States are central to modern diplomacy. Analytically, it is common to view the state as a unitary actor with specific preferences, interests, capabilities, and worldviews. However, the entity that represents the state, the government, is a really complex collection of bureaucratic agencies and individuals bound by domestic laws and culture. They are also conditioned by the international, legal diplomatic framework that has been under construction for centuries. This chapter reviews the international laws and norms of traditional diplomacy. It sketches out the general diplomatic architecture of states to show how bureaucratic agencies ensure the continuity of diplomatic relationships with other governments and IGOs in spite of changes in personnel or leadership. These external and internal factors shape how, and if, human rights and humanitarianism are systematically pursued by the diplomatic arms of states. Inside the black box of the state are government agencies that interact with each other and their foreign counterparts. These agencies must balance their human rights and humanitarian interests and values with other interests and values pursued by governments in international affairs.

This chapter pays special attention to the United States because it has one of the more developed and elaborate diplomatic structures and has made a point of promoting human rights as part of its diplomacy, albeit its own preferred notion of international human rights. Its unwillingness to formally embrace many international standards, laws, and monitoring mechanisms leaves it open to legitimate criticism and affects its ability to lead on human rights. At the same time, the United States is not alone in its hypocrisy and feelings of exceptionalism. Human rights and humanitarian diplomacy by states is about advancing certain rights, priorities, and principles which will often conflict with the priorities and preferences of other actors. Diplomacy is about that negotiating, bargaining, and advocating process essential to defining and implementing human rights and humanitarian principles.

International diplomatic law

The legal framework of modern diplomacy shapes the way states conduct their foreign and diplomatic relations. The keystone treaty, the **1961 Vienna Convention on Diplomatic Relations**, codifies centuries of custom related to how states are to treat each other and their emissaries.[1] The Vienna Convention recognizes and reaffirms the age old principles of the independence and sovereignty of states and codifies others as well.[2] One principle is **diplomatic recognition** where states formally acknowledge each other by establishing embassies and consulates in each other's territory and accepting the credentials of their representatives. Article 22 of the convention articulates the inviolability of the embassy. Officials from the host state cannot enter the premises or enforce local laws without consent of the embassy's government. This is why dissidents and asylum-seekers (many of whom are human rights activists) often seek refuge at another state's embassy or consulate.

Relatedly, the principle of **diplomatic immunity** affords diplomats special protection while conducting relations abroad. Host states cannot incarcerate or harm the official representatives of another state. Diplomatic immunity is necessary for state representatives to conduct often tense negotiations or deliver unwelcome messages. Diplomatic immunity sometimes means that diplomats cannot be criminally prosecuted for breaking the host countries' laws. Diplomats are obligated to respect and obey the national laws of their host countries. When there is a diplomatic or "international" incident, governments usually work behind the scenes to quietly resolve the dispute. Sometimes the situation is dropped and other times the diplomat is "voluntarily" recalled by their government.

A state can also declare a diplomat *persona non grata* **(PNG)** and require that individual to leave the country for any reason. This happens when a diplomat seriously offends the host government and the situation is not resolved informally. Diplomats are encouraged not to offend host governments and states usually try to avoid declaring someone PNG, but it frequently happens. This makes human rights and humanitarian diplomacy a little tricky because states are sensitive to foreign governments (or IGO officials) meddling in what they see as their domestic affairs. For example, in July of 2014, senior US diplomat Tom Malinowski was PNG'd (in diplomatic jargon) by the government of Bahrain and asked to leave the country because he had "intervened flagrantly in Bahrain's internal affairs" by meeting with a political party (the Shiites) "to the detriment of other interlocutors."[3] Malinowski, the Assistant Secretary of State for the Bureau of Democracy, Human Rights and Labor, had been in Bahrain for a three-day series of meetings. Prior to this diplomatic post, he headed Human Rights Watch and was an outspoken critic of Bahrain's suppression of the Shiite minority. Sometimes being "diplomatic" means turning a blind eye or downplaying a human rights situation because a PNG'd official will find it hard to engage in human rights and humanitarian diplomacy on the flight back home. Even if an official is not formally PNG'd, states can ignore the diplomat or make it clear to their government that the individual is unable to fulfill their responsibilities effectively.

Complications can also arise when human rights violations are allegedly committed by diplomats.[4] The diplomatic row between the United States and India regarding Indian deputy consul general Devyani Khobragade in 2014 is illustrative. Khobragade was arrested in New York City on visa fraud and underpayment of her housekeeper.[5] While in custody, she was processed in the same way as anyone else who is accused of a crime in New York City. She was fingerprinted, strip-searched, and placed with the general prison population. Prior to Khobragade's arrest, the housekeeper had fled the residence and alleged mistreatment and underpayment (the visa application stated that the housekeeper would be paid $4,500 per month and records show she was paid less than $600 a month). Moreover, the housekeeper claimed her family in India had been threatened and that a warrant for her arrest had been issued in India. After the diplomat's arrest in the United States, mass protests erupted in India because of the perceived disrespect of India by the United States. The Indian government responded by removing the security barriers around the US embassy in New Delhi and began strictly enforcing diplomatic rules to the letter. Jason Burke of the *Guardian* succinctly describes the issues:

> The arrest of Khobragade touches a range of sensitivities in India. Almost all middle-class households in India employ at least one, and often several, members of staff who will undertake tasks from cleaning and cooking to childcare and driving.
>
> With few Indian diplomats paid wages that would allow them to legally employ local staff to perform such functions in postings in the West, the practice has long been for Indian workers to be flown out and paid rates that, if illegal in US and elsewhere, would be generous at home.
>
> Preet Bharara, the prosecutor in Khobragade's case, said last month: "In fact the Indian government itself has been aware of this legal issue, and that its diplomats and consular officers were at risk of violating the law." The question then may be asked: is it for US prosecutors to look the other way, ignore the law and the civil rights of victims ... or is it the responsibility of the diplomats and consular officers and their government to make sure the law is observed?[6]

The initial indictment against Khobragade was brought because she had a more limited form of immunity as a consular official. The day before she was indicted, she was appointed by India to be a diplomat to its UN mission, giving her full diplomatic immunity. The charges were then dismissed by a federal judge and Khobragade left the United States before she was PNG'd. Once she left the United States, she no longer had immunity and the United States refiled charges against her and placed her on the US visa watch list. The US government informed the Indian government that Khobragade was not to return to the United States, except to answer the charges.

The Khobragade case illustrates several issues surrounding international law, diplomacy and human rights. First, worldview matters when understanding motives and facts. Both India and the United States understandably perceived ill-treatment by the other. Both were arguably promoting and protecting the human rights of the housekeeper (with India facilitating a job opportunity with higher wages than could be found in the local Indian economy and the United States by ensuring that she was treated in accordance with US law). Second, protecting human rights often involves bumping up against traditional ways of conducting relations. The plight of domestic workers on "special visas," i.e. those working for foreign diplomats, was brought to light by Human Rights Watch, forcing officials to confront their own personal records on human rights.[7] At the same time, successful diplomacy sometimes involves "looking the other way" for the sake of stable relationships. While state officials are sometimes forced to do so because of other interests, NGOs are invaluable for keeping human rights and humanitarian principles front and center. Third, formal international diplomatic law is one thing, but the practice of diplomacy is quite another. The behind-the-scenes negotiations and the public stances of officials are often very different.

Since embassies and the diplomatic corps are some of the main conduits through which states conduct their foreign policy, Article 27 of the Vienna Convention guarantees the free communication between the diplomatic mission and their home government. This means that the diplomatic pouch or bag carrying such communication may not be inspected or confiscated or its carrier arrested. Not surprisingly, the legal framework creates opportunity for states to bend the rules and they often do. States are known to use their embassies and diplomatic staff to spy on host states and even to conduct covert activities. Host states routinely bug or conduct surveillance activities on embassies and consulates, as well as their staff. This is an open secret in international diplomacy regardless of the feigned shock of public officials when there are public revelations of eavesdropping and other spying activities. It is also why when embassy officials associate with domestic human rights activists and dissidents, host governments grow suspicious.

States are sensitive to public criticism and interference in domestic matters, which is one of the reasons the legal language of international human rights and humanitarian principles may not be formally invoked. Human rights and humanitarian diplomacy is peppered with vague phrases. For example, "complex humanitarian emergency" is used instead of armed conflict, or war, or natural disaster in the context of war. The phrase "persons detained by reason of events" is used instead of using the term political prisoners or detainees in armed conflict. "Areas of civil unrest" is used to mean conflict zone. By using fuzzy language rather than asserting legal categories, progress can be made in improving a human rights and humanitarian situation while allowing parties to maintain friendly relations.

Diplomatic custom encourages states to maintain diplomatic dialogue even when relationships are difficult and strained. States usually continue to keep their diplomatic relations even while engaging in war. When there is a breach of diplomatic relations, states often will continue to communicate through a third state willing to serve as an intermediary. For example, the United States and Iran have not had diplomatic relations with each other since 1979 (when the US embassy was taken over by radicals and embassy staff held hostage for 444 days). Yet, both states communicate with each other through the diplomats of other states. The Swiss embassy represents US interests in Tehran and the Pakistani embassy represents Iran's interest in Washington, DC. This arrangement allows relations to continue between determined adversaries.

The conduct of diplomacy involves following established protocols and rules. Existing international diplomatic law reflects long-standing norms and principles – the sovereignty and independence of states, nonintervention, diplomatic recognition, and diplomatic immunity. This law frames the way states conduct their diplomatic relations including their human rights and humanitarian diplomacy. Most states establish embassies and consulates to represent their interests abroad and while at home they have complicated bureaucracies to assist in creating and executing foreign policy. The **Ministry of Foreign Affairs (MFA)** performs many roles including staffing and supporting missions abroad, dealing with foreign diplomats at home, and public diplomacy.[8] States call their MFAs by different names, such as Department of State (the United States), Ministry of External Affairs (India), or the Foreign and Commonwealth Office (the United Kingdom), but they all are generally responsible for maintaining diplomatic relations with other states and IGOs.

The internal structure of the MFA varies from state to state but it generally has offices or "desks" that deal with specific countries and regions on a variety of issues including security, terrorism, trade, energy, human rights, and humanitarian affairs. Not all MFAs prioritize human rights and humanitarian affairs as part of their overall diplomacy, and many do not even mention international human rights as foreign policy or diplomatic objectives on their webpages. As a general rule, human rights figure prominently within the MFA mission of the Western liberal democracies, while the MFAs of non-Western or developing states downplay human rights or have them as a lower diplomatic priority. Powerful non-Western states, such as Brazil, Russia, India and China (the BRICs) privilege sovereignty and nonintervention over human rights and do not systematically advocate for international human rights and humanitarian principles. That said, the MFAs of Russia and China have taken to issuing their own human rights reports on the United States and EU in response to the critical reports issued by their Western counterparts. The MFAs of Russia and China are often placed in a position of having to respond to criticism of their country's domestic human rights records. Still, they do not systematically pursue international human rights or humanitarian principles abroad.

For many developing states in the Global South, bilateral diplomacy is expensive to maintain. Scarce resources are directed toward select missions, and all other diplomatic functions are generally conducted multilaterally through IGOs. Thus, they also tend to be strong advocates of the UN system and upholders of international law.[9] They must invariably navigate between the competing politics of the great powers, especially when it comes to human rights and humanitarian principles, as well as advancing their own interests and preferences.

The foreign minister or secretary

Chapter 2 explained how heads of state can shape the conduct of human rights and humanitarian diplomacy. The nuts and bolts of diplomacy are channeled through the MFA, and on the top this bureaucratic pyramid is the **foreign minister or secretary**. The foreign minister reports to the head of state and is the public face of a state's day-to-day diplomacy. The foreign minister must balance multiple interests. The extent to which human rights and humanitarian affairs are priorities depends on the person and their boss. Lloyd Axworthy, the former Foreign Minister of Canada, is widely recognized for situating human rights at the center of Canadian diplomacy. He played a central role in putting the clout of Canadian government behind the

ICISS, which laid the intellectual foundation for the doctrine of the Responsibility to Protect (R2P; discussed in Chapter 4). He also was instrumental in facilitating the diplomacy that ultimately led to the **Convention on the Prohibition of the Use, Stockpiling, Production and Transfer of Anti-Personnel Mines and on their Destruction**, also known as the Ottawa Treaty or the Anti-Personnel Mine Ban Convention; and developing and promoting the concept of human security. His work with the Ottawa Treaty earned him a Nobel Peace Prize nomination. He also was a strident, necessary voice in the diplomatic negotiations that resulted in the creation of the ICC.

Also noteworthy is former US Secretary of State Madeleine Albright, whose "assertive multilateralism" pushed the United States and its allies to militarily confront the human rights and humanitarian crisis in Kosovo in 1997. As Ivo Daalder, the US permanent representative to the North Atlantic Treaty Organization (NATO), states: "There's a reason that *Time* magazine called Kosovo 'Madeleine's war.' Because it was! When the lawyers told her Kosovo couldn't be done without a UN mandate, she said 'get me another lawyer.' They did, and the rest is history. Kosovo freed hundreds of thousands of Albanians."[10] The diplomatic tensions created by this unprecedented intervention continues to be felt in international relations today, especially as it relates to calls for humanitarian intervention in Libya, Syria, Iraq, Georgia, and Ukraine. It also puts secessionism and self-determination front and center as sources of violent conflict because it pits the government against large segments of its population.

More recently, in 2015, Sweden Foreign Minister Margot Wallstrom was barred from addressing the Arab League by Saudi Arabia because the topic and content of her speech was women's rights.[11] The resulting diplomatic row led Saudi Arabia to recall its ambassador and Sweden to cancel an arms deal with Saudi Arabia. Saudi Arabia deemed her remarks an impermissible interference in Saudi internal affairs, even though her published remarks did not mention Saudi Arabia specifically. Sweden's choice to take a strong stand is notable because it is rare for Western states to make human rights a priority in their relations with the oil-rich kingdom. Assertive public diplomacy on behalf of human rights and humanitarian principles by foreign ministers is often the exception rather than the norm.

The Ministry of Foreign Affairs and human rights and humanitarian diplomacy

The foreign minister or secretary is the leader of the diplomatic bureaucracy. The MFA at home and its missions abroad are quite different. The MFA at home has a great deal of responsibility for contributing to, formulating, and executing government foreign policy. This includes interacting with the domestic actors such as legislatures, courts, and the military. For example, US State Department officials routinely testify before the US Congress on human rights and humanitarian issues. Below is a list of selected testimony from January 2013 to April 2014:[12]

- 02/14/13 The Crisis in Mali: US Interests and the International Response; Assistant Secretary Johnnie Carson, Bureau of African Affairs; Before the House Committee on Foreign Affairs (As Prepared); Washington, DC.
- 02/28/13 Human Rights in Burma; Assistant Secretary Michael H. Posner, Bureau of Democracy, Human Rights, and Labor; Tom Lantos Human Rights Commission; Washington, DC.
- 02/28/13 Human Rights in Burma; Special Representative and Policy Coordinator for Burma W. Patrick Murphy; Tom Lantos Human Rights Commission; Washington, DC.
- 03/21/13 Democracy and Human Rights In the Context of the Asia Rebalance; Acting Assistant Secretary Joseph Yun, Bureau of East Asian and Pacific Affairs; Before the Senate Committee on Foreign Relations Subcommittee on East Asian and Pacific Affairs; Washington, DC.
- 03/21/13 Democracy and Human Rights in the Context of the Asia Rebalance; Deputy Assistant Secretary Daniel Baer, Bureau of Democracy, Human Rights, and Labor; Senate Committee on Foreign Relations, Subcommittee on East Asian and Pacific Affairs; Washington, DC.
- 03/20/13 Crisis in Syria: The US Response; Ambassador Robert S. Ford, Syria; House Foreign Affairs Committee; Washington, DC.
- 03/20/13 Crisis in Syria: The US Response; Assistant Secretary Anne C. Richard, Bureau of Population, Refugees, and Migration; Before the Committee on Foreign Affairs, US House of Representatives; Washington, DC.
- 03/19/13 The Syrian Humanitarian Crisis; Assistant Secretary Anne C. Richard, Bureau of Population, Refugees, and Migration; Committee on Foreign Relations Subcommittee on Near Eastern and South and Central Asian Affairs, United States Senate; Washington, DC.
- 03/07/13 US Policy Toward North Korea; Special Representative for North Korea Policy Glyn Davies; Testimony Before the Senate Committee on Foreign Relations; Washington, DC.
- 05/21/13 The Growing Crisis in Africa's Sahel Region; Acting Assistant Secretary Donald Y. Yamamoto, Bureau of African Affairs; Opening Statement; Washington, DC.
- 06/18/13 Examining Prospects for Democratic Reform and Economic Recovery in Zimbabwe; Acting Assistant Secretary Donald Y. Yamamoto, Bureau of African Affairs; Testimony Before the US Senate Committee on Foreign Relations Subcommittee on African Affairs; Washington, DC.
- 06/06/13 Labor Issues in Bangladesh; Assistant Secretary Robert O. Blake, Jr., Bureau of South and Central Asian Affairs; As-prepared statement to Senate Foreign Relations Committee; Washington, DC.
- 06/25/13 Religious Minorities in Syria: Caught in the Middle; Deputy Assistant Secretary Thomas O. Melia, Bureau of Democracy, Human Rights, and Labor; House Foreign Affairs Subcommittees on Africa, Global Health, Global Human Rights, and International Organizations and on Middle East and North Africa; Washington, DC.

- 07/11/13 The State Department 2013 Trafficking in Persons Report; Ambassador-at-Large Luis CdeBaca, Office to Monitor and Combat Trafficking in Persons; Subcommittee on Africa, Global Health, Global Human Rights, and International Organizations of the House Foreign Affairs Committee; Washington, DC.
- 09/10/13 Proposed Authorization to Use Military Force in Syria; Secretary of State John Kerry; Opening Remarks Before the House Armed Services Committee; Washington, DC.
- 09/12/13 Troubling Path Ahead for U.S.-Zimbabwe Relations; Before the U.S. House Foreign Affairs Subcommittee on Africa, Global Health, Global Human Rights, and International Organizations; Washington, DC.
- 09/19/13 Examining the Syrian Refugee Crisis; Assistant Secretary Anne C. Richard, Bureau of Population, Refugees, and Migration; As Delivered Opening Remarks Before the House Foreign Affairs Subcommittee on the Middle East and North Africa; Washington, DC.
- 10/08/13 Security and Governance in Somalia: Consolidating Gains, Confronting Challenges, and Charting the Path Forward; Assistant Secretary Linda Thomas-Greenfield, Bureau of African Affairs; Before the Senate Foreign Relations Committee Subcommittee on African Affairs; Washington, DC.
- 10/31/13 Efforts of the United Nations and the Organisation for the Prohibition of Chemical Weapons to Accomplish the Elimination of Syrian Chemical Weapons; Assistant Secretary Thomas M. Countryman, Bureau of International Security and Nonproliferation; Senate Foreign Relations Committee; Washington, DC.
- 11/19/13 U.S. Government's Response to Super Typhoon Haiyan; Principal Deputy Assistant Secretary Scot Marciel, Bureau of East Asian and Pacific Affairs; Statement Before the Senate Committee on Foreign Relations; Washington, DC.
- 11/19/13 Crisis in the Central African Republic; Principal Deputy Assistant Secretary Robert P. Jackson, Bureau of African Affairs; House Foreign Affairs Committee Subcommittee on African Affairs, Global Health, Human Rights and International Organizations; Washington, DC.
- 11/20/13 The Global Gender-Based Violence Threat; Ambassador-at-Large for Global Women's Issues Catherine M. Russell; Tom Lantos Human Rights Commission; Washington, DC.
- 11/21/13 Convention on the Rights of Persons with Disabilities; Secretary of State John Kerry; Opening Statement Before the Senate Foreign Relations Committee; Washington, DC.
- 12/17/13 Responding to the Humanitarian, Security, and Governance Crisis in the Central African Republic; Assistant Secretary Linda Thomas-Greenfield, Bureau of African Affairs; Senate Foreign Relations Committee, Subcommittee on African Affairs; Washington, DC.
- 01/07/14 The Syrian Refugee Crisis; Assistant Secretary Anne C. Richard, Bureau of Population, Refugees, and Migration; Statement Submitted for the Record to the Senate Committee on the Judiciary, Subcommittee on the Constitution, Civil Rights and Human Rights; Washington, DC.

- 01/09/14 The Situation in South Sudan; Assistant Secretary Linda Thomas-Greenfield, Bureau of African Affairs; US Senate Committee on Foreign Relations; Washington, DC.
- 01/15/14 The Situation in Ukraine; Deputy Assistant Secretary Thomas O. Melia, Bureau of Democracy, Human Rights, and Labor; Statement Submitted for the Record to the Senate Foreign Relations Committee; Washington, DC.
- 01/15/14 South Sudan's Broken Promise?; Assistant Secretary Linda Thomas-Greenfield, Bureau of African Affairs; Washington, DC.
- 01/27/14 Testimony Before the House of Representatives Foreign Affairs Subcommittee on Africa, Global Health, Global Human Rights, and International Organizations; Ambassador-at-Large Luis CdeBaca, Office to Monitor and Combat Trafficking in Persons; As-Delivered Statement; Washington, DC.

The testimony by State Department officials before Congress involves briefing committee and subcommittee members about human rights and humanitarian situations, as well as providing country-specific information as required by US law. This testimony also informs congressional decisions regarding overseas development assistance and trade preferences.

The US Department of State also participates in human rights litigation, either by filing or signing onto *amicus curiae* briefs in domestic and international courts.[13] While not necessarily always on the side of human rights litigants, the State Department has argued that US federal courts can exercise jurisdiction over international human rights claims.[14] At the same time, it is cautious about human rights cases that could potentially interfere with other kinds of foreign relations. It is selective about which cases to support and how to support them. Diplomacy requires the maintenance and nurturing of long-term relationships and State Department officials do not like to disrupt those relations unnecessarily. Relatedly, the department's Office of Global Criminal Justice coordinates the US government's position on ongoing international criminal cases involving genocide, war crimes, and crimes against humanity and also assists governments, IGOs, and courts with domestic commissions of inquiry and fact-finding missions.[15] It also responsible for advising the Secretary of State on the formulation of policy to prevent and respond to mass atrocities.

The US Department of State has a complicated working relationship with the US Department of Defense which assists with State Department humanitarian activities.[16] The military participates in human rights and humanitarian diplomacy through a number of programs. The Denton Program permits the military to transport privately donated humanitarian aid to foreign country on a space available basis and the Humanitarian Assistance and Civic Program authorizes the military to engage in humanitarian and disaster relief operations "as part of training missions." This relationship involves often complex coordination with the Department of State and private NGOs. The military involvement in the delivery of humanitarian aid has many diplomatic benefits, especially in generating goodwill toward the United States by the local population. It does, however, contribute to the blurring of lines between combatants and humanitarian aid workers.

Table 3.1 Human rights reports issued by the United States

Name of the report	In compliance with:
Country Reports on Human Rights Practices (Human Rights Reports)	Foreign Assistance Act of 1961
Trafficking in Persons Report	Victims of Trafficking and Violence Prevention Act of 2000
Advancing Freedom and Democracy	Advance Democratic Values, Address Nondemocratic Countries, and Enhance Democracy Act of 2007
Findings on Bahrain's Compliance with its Labor Commitments	Labor Chapter of the U.S.-Bahrain Free Trade Agreement (FTA)
International Religious Freedom Reports	International Religious Act of 1998
United States Universal Periodic Review	United Nations Human Rights Council's Universal Periodic Review
Findings on the Worst Forms of Child Labor	Trade and Development Act of 2000
US Treaty Reports	States Parties Obligations

Source: Compiled from www.humanrights.gov/reports/.

The MFA at home is also usually responsible for the bulk of a state's public diplomacy, for maintaining missions with IGOs, and supporting the work of international courts and tribunals. The public diplomacy relating to human rights involves creating and maintaining a significant web presence, press releases, media packets, webcasts, and the creation and dissemination of human rights country reports. **Human rights reports** are often a point of contention as many states do not appreciate having their human rights records scrutinized and or criticized. Table 3.1 contains a list of reports prepared by the US State Department, along with the domestic or international law that requires the report.

The European Union issues the **EU Annual Report on Human Rights and Democracy**. The extent to which important non-Western states, such as Russia and China, pursue public human rights diplomacy through the MFA is often limited to responding to critical reports or issuing retaliatory reports. For example, in 2012, Russia published its first human rights report systematically criticizing the EU human rights record.[17] The report claimed that EU record was far from perfect and that "Russia is ready for a constructive dialogue of equals with the European Union on human rights and democratic development, which would to the full extent correspond to the relations of strategic partnership with the EU. This cooperation will gain a lot if our counterparts from the EU abandon their policy of imposing their priorities, stop looking down on the interests of other partners and creating an artificial systematization of international human rights obligations."[18] The sentiments expressed by Russia resonates with many developing states, many of whom are reluctant to publicly criticize or sanction violators of human rights. Rather they wish to pursue human rights diplomacy through ongoing dialogue and standard-setting.[19] The human rights diplomacy of states is a push–pull process involving how to prioritize rights and what kinds of state policies are permissible in the pursuit of those rights.

Social media is now a significant part of the public "diplomacy 2.0" of the MFA and creates opportunities, as well as challenges. One the one hand, the MFA is conservative by nature and slow to change its values and standard operating procedures. This means it has been slower than NGOs in taking advantage of social media and its message often can be drowned out by paid pro-government bloggers.[20] On the other hand, social media provides a way of bypassing government controlled media and communicating directly with the population. Obviously, the use of social media to articulate Western positions on human rights and humanitarian situations has its limits in censorious states such as China, Russia, Iran, Turkey, and Venezuela. And just because these states ban social media at home, it has not deterred them from using Twitter and Facebook diplomacy to reach foreign audiences abroad.

Human rights and humanitarian affairs are part and parcel of the work of MFAs in most the Western liberal democracies. Many small states, however, choose to channel much of their human rights and humanitarian diplomacy through IGOs, such as the UN (see Chapter 4). By pooling their diplomatic clout, small states can amplify their voices regarding human rights. Since the MFA is responsible for maintaining missions with IGOs, they often have permanent representatives/ambassadors to those organization, and high level MFA officials often appear as well. Sidebar 3.1 is a statement of Ireland's Foreign Minister Joe Costello before the UN HRC in 2014. This sidebar shows how a small country like Ireland can advance its human rights and priorities through a multilateral body such as the UN HRC.

Sidebar 3.1 Address by Minister for Trade and Development, Joe Costello, to the United Nations Human Rights Council in Geneva, March 3, 2014[21]

Mr. President, Excellencies, ladies and gentlemen.

The agenda of the Council has always been ambitious, and this session is no exception. In my address today, I would propose to identify a number of the priorities for my delegation at this session and during our term of membership of the Council.

DPRK

The Commission of Inquiry for the Democratic People's Republic of Korea will present its final report to the Council on 17th March. This is the first time that the full accounts of atrocities have been presented to the international community in such detail. The Commission's conclusions and recommendations must be taken very seriously.

The international community has an obligation to the people of the DPRK, who have suffered so grievously. Ireland will strongly support efforts to ensure follow-up to the recommendations, including those on accountability for human rights violations.

Ukraine

We have witnessed in recent weeks some very disturbing violations of basic human rights in Ukraine, including repressive legislation, intimidation, violence, cases of missing persons and torture. I have been particularly appalled at the many deaths and injuries in Kiev just last month. While I am relieved that the violence and bloodshed has been brought to an end, Ireland, together with our EU partners, has called for an urgent, transparent and impartial investigation into all acts of violence and for the perpetrators to be brought to justice. There should be no atmosphere or culture of impunity. We very much hope that the International Advisory Panel set up by the Council of Europe can start its work soon and will receive the cooperation necessary to bring its investigations to a successful conclusion.

The situation in Ukraine remains a very volatile and fragile one and we are deeply concerned about developments over the weekend. It is imperative that the sovereignty and territorial integrity of Ukraine is fully respected in accordance with international law. All parties must work to ensure that, through dialogue, all legitimate concerns are addressed.

We would encourage the new Government in Ukraine to work together with all stakeholders in an inclusive and transparent way to prepare for the elections that have been scheduled for May.

Syria

The people of Syria have endured ceaseless atrocities and crimes in recent years, in the course of a conflict characterised by mass violations of basic human rights.

Ireland has played its part in helping alleviate the suffering of the Syrian people and is one of the more generous contributors to the humanitarian response on a per capita basis. Ireland's overall funding commitment over the period 2011 to 2014 is more than €26 million. We have called for all parties to the conflict to fully respect international humanitarian law and to refrain from the targeting of civilians. We welcome the adoption of UN Security Council Resolution 2139 which calls on all parties to the conflict to facilitate the delivery of life-saving humanitarian assistance. It is now critical that its terms are fully implemented by all sides and especially the Syrian authorities.

Human Rights and Development

Ireland's commitment to the promotion and protection of human rights is at the heart of our development cooperation programme – Irish Aid. Coordinated efforts centred on the Millennium Development Goals framework have helped to deliver significant progress in reducing poverty.

In recent months Ireland, together with Denmark and Norway, has been actively engaged in the UN Open Working Group on Sustainable Development Goals.

We have highlighted the need for the next development framework to stay true to the spirit of the Millennium Declaration and the indivisible nature of human rights. The internationally agreed human rights framework can help identify priorities and set standards for the next generation of goals. Doing so will ensure that the post 2015 global development efforts target those who do not currently enjoy the fruits of economic growth, those who are discriminated against and especially those who are in greatest need. The Post 2015 framework should be aligned with international human rights standards and mechanisms, be attached to meaningful accountability mechanisms and measure both means and outcome.

We believe that Human Rights principles such as equality and non-discrimination, particularly as they relate to gender, participation, transparency and accountability should be mainstreamed across all goals in a post-2015 framework. It will also be important to address the legitimate rights of citizens to participate in decision-making, to seek and receive information, to enjoy personal security and freedom from violence. We believe that the protection of the space for civil society is integral to the realisation of many of these rights.

Irish National Initiatives

Ireland has worked to translate the dual vision of *"freedom from fear and freedom from want"* in our two national initiatives; the first on preventable mortality and morbidity of children under five and the second on the protection of civil society space.

Preventable Under-5 Morbidity and Mortality

Each year, some 6.6 million children under the age of five die mainly from preventable and treatable causes. At the Human Rights Council in September 2013, Ireland, along with Austria, Botswana, Mongolia and Uruguay, presented a resolution on preventable mortality and morbidity of children under five as a human rights concern. The resolution focused on how the Human Rights Council can support the articulation and adoption of a human rights based approach to this issue and support the much needed engagement of the human rights community in strengthening accountability for children's health.

Following on the resolution, the Office of the High Commissioner for Human Rights – in close consultation with the World Health Organisation – will develop technical guidance for national Ministries and other actors to design policies and programmes to reduce and eliminate preventable morbidity and mortality of children under five. Ireland is looking forward to continuing work with partners on this vital issue.

Civil Society Space

Just as a resounding call is being heard for a political and economic order that delivers on the promises of "freedom from fear and want," States must recognise the crucial importance of the active involvement of civil society, particularly in promoting good governance, transparency and accountability, at all levels. This is indispensable for building peaceful, prosperous and democratic societies.

As the UN Secretary General has stated, *"Civil society is crucial for advancing human rights by raising awareness, and ringing the alarm about abuse, inequality, or creeping authoritarianism. Indeed, civil society is central to advancing the work of the United Nations across our agenda, not only for human rights but also for peace and security, as well as development. Civil society has never been more important or needed."*

In recent years, civil society actors have come under increasing pressure in many parts of the world; in some countries the space for civil society engagement is narrow or shrinking. Restrictive legislation and repressive practices have led to stigmatisation, harassment, and even criminalisation of civil society actors.

To address this, Ireland took the lead, together with Chile, Japan, Sierra Leone, and Tunisia, on a new resolution entitled *"Civil society space; creating and maintaining, in law and in practice a safe and enabling environment"* at the September 2013 session of the Human Rights Council. This resolution addresses, for the first time at the Human Rights Council, the issue of civil society space as a human rights concern. It calls on States to create and maintain a safe and enabling environment in which civil society can operate effectively and free from intimidation and harassment. The first formal debate in the Council on civil society space will take place next week.

We hope that the discussion will stimulate debate and identify strategies and steps for all stakeholders in order to develop and protect civil society space and further promote a constructive interactive partnership between States and civil society.

Reprisals

We deplore the fact that some civil society representatives have been subjected to reprisals because of cooperating or seeking to cooperate with the UN. Reprisals, intimidation, threats or harassment against individuals cooperating with the United Nations is unacceptable.

Gender Equality

Gender-based discrimination is the most longstanding and fundamentally discriminatory form of inequality and is pervasive across most societies. It compounds and is reinforced by other inequalities. Achieving gender equality is a key to reducing community poverty and is both a moral and a practical imperative. It is important that gender equality is a central theme in the post-2015 development agenda. Gender equality should be a stand-alone goal and also mainstreamed across the other post-2015 goals.

Rights of LGBTI Individuals

Ireland strives to consistently support the promotion and protection of the human rights of all persons, irrespective of their sexual orientation or gender identity.

In 2011 Ireland was a co-sponsor of the landmark UN Human Rights Council resolution on human rights, sexual orientation and gender identity. We are particularly concerned about the introduction of draconian legislation in some countries affecting the rights of LGBTI individuals. The Council's voice needs to be heard louder than ever, as the most basic rights of LGBT persons continue to be violated on a daily basis.

Our own national experience is an illustrative example of the breadth and pace of change that is possible, where there is political will. In 1993, homosexuality was decriminalised in Ireland. Since that time, we have made steps to help ensure towards achieving equality, through the introduction of legislation prohibiting discrimination on the grounds of sexual orientation in employment, the provision of goods and services and many other areas of life. In 2010, civil partnership for same-sex couples was introduced in Ireland, and a referendum to change the Constitution so as to permit same-sex marriage is due to take place in 2015.

Ireland supports the commitment of the High Commissioner for Human Rights, Navi Pillay, to the principle of non-discrimination and considers that the international community must now move beyond the debate on whether all human beings have equal rights, to securing the climate for full implementation of these rights.

Human Rights Monitoring Body Strengthening Process

Ireland is very pleased that the General Assembly recently agreed on the text of a draft resolution on strengthening the human rights treaty body system. This draft resolution is potentially a positive turning point for the UN. Ireland is proud that many of the reforms contained in the resolution originated in the Dublin Consultations and that we played an active role in bringing the process to a successful conclusion. When adopted by the General Assembly, States, the Office of the High Commissioner for Human Rights and the Treaty Bodies themselves must strive to ensure that the system is renewed and re-energised to ensure that it can meet the ever increasing challenges which it faces.

Conclusion

At this time of enormous challenges it is appropriate to recall Article 1 of the Universal Declaration of Human Rights: "*All human beings are born free and equal in dignity and rights. They are endowed with reason and conscience and should act towards one another in a spirit of brotherhood.*"

As a member of the Human Rights Council, Ireland pledges to consolidate the modest gains we have made and continue our work to promote and protect the innate dignity of the human person in every way we can.

Thank you, Mr. President.

The MFA maintains relationships with the embassy and consulates of foreign governments located at home. Bilaterally, the MFA may pursue human rights or humanitarian principles through **démarches**, which are official government diplomatic positions of protests delivered by one government to another through the MFA. The level of the démarche may vary, but diplomatic custom holds that governments are to respond to démarches when required. Some démarches are quite public (as with the Khobragade incident) but mostly they are private correspondences trying to persuade a government to adopt a certain position or policy. The volume of diplomatic cables pertaining to human rights reflects that the issue is of some importance to states.[22]

The MFA also solicits, processes, and interprets information collected from its resident missions abroad. The MFA abroad (its embassies, consulates, and mission overseas) is the frontline of diplomacy. Ambassadors and members of the diplomatic corps are responsible for troubleshooting human rights situations and for responding to démarches. The embassy is also involved in preparing or providing information for country reports. In Sidebar 3.2, former US Ambassador to Rwanda, Margaret McMillion, highlights how human rights diplomacy was pursued by the United States in post-genocide Rwanda.

Sidebar 3.2 Margaret K. McMillion (former ambassador to the Republic of Rwanda) – human rights diplomacy in Rwanda 2001–04

Human rights diplomacy presents some of the greatest challenges for any ambassador. The need for human rights diplomacy suggests that there are problems. These problems are likely to affect the tenor of the bilateral relationship and in many cases, the ambassador's personal relationships with host country interlocutors. Human rights diplomacy involves three aspects:

- Working with host governments in areas of agreement;
- supporting and coordinating with like-minded countries and organizations, and;
- engaging host governments on specific questions involving human rights norms, in effect, setting boundaries based on international human rights law.

American law clearly indicates a commitment to advancing human rights. For example, in accordance with the Foreign Assistance Act of 1961 and the Trade Act of 1974, each embassy must prepare an annual human rights report on its host nation. The African Growth and Opportunity Act requires, among other things, consideration of a country's record in protecting human and labor rights before granting trade preferences. The Treasury Department must review human rights practices before approval of loans in international financial institutions. The Millennium Challenge Corporation considers indicators for ruling justly in determining eligibility for a compact. These requirements can be both carrot and stick, but for governments eager to receive outside recognition for their work, as Rwanda's development-minded government was, they can be powerful incentives.

In Rwanda, during 2001–2004, human rights were a sensitive issue, particularly in the period preceding the end of the nine-year transition that followed the 1994 genocide. The Rwandan Patriotic Front-led government had a full domestic agenda that included drafting and ratifying a new constitution, presidential and legislative elections, and the inauguration of a new government in 2003. Long term goals included the launch of the community-based gacaca courts, where people accused of genocide would be tried, and reform of the legal code.

Our strategy was to work closely with likeminded governments and international organizations on areas of agreement with the Rwandan government and to seek improvement on issues of concern. One important area of accord was the need for decentralization of the government, a response to the widely accepted conclusion that a high degree of government centralization and top-down direction had contributed to the 1994 genocide. Consequently, in designing projects, USAID kept decentralization in mind. Public health projects, for example, included grassroots decision making committees whose members represented local communities. Another common interest was legal reform. The public diplomacy section helped organize a major conference that included representatives from the U.S. and Africa. A principal topic was how to combine the civil code tradition inherited from the Belgian trusteeship and the Anglo-Saxon common law tradition familiar to members of the RPF returning from Uganda. A third interest was promotion of women's rights. Women had assumed important roles in the aftermath of the genocide. USAID and the public diplomacy section supported programs to teach leadership skills.

The embassy also worked with likeminded partners. Nearly every donor offered some assistance to the 1993 elections. The United Nations Development

Program was particularly well-placed to engage the government, perhaps because it was perceived as more neutral. It was therefore able to ensure equity and accountability in the management of funds that supported government entities and civil society organizations involved in the elections. In another area, the International Committee of the Red Cross and the Netherlands worked to improve conditions in overcrowded prisons where thousands accused of genocide awaited trials.

Engaging the government on specific cases was far more contentious due to the RPF's desire to manage the potentially divisive ethnic issue and to win a convincing victory at the polls. A particular concern was the flight or disappearance of seven prominent leaders, who had served in the transitional government but had associations with the former government. They included a former Minister of Defense, a former Supreme Court judge, and a sitting member of parliament. Candidates for parties competing with the RPF-led coalition and their supporters faced harassment and in some cases, arrest. These events and others raised questions about whether the elections would be free and fair and about the RPF's intentions over the long term.

U.S. actions included formal demarches to the government, both alone and in concert with the United Kingdom, discussions with the Rwandan Human Rights Commission at regularly scheduled meetings with members of the diplomatic corps, and ultimately, a public reminder to the Ministry of Foreign Affairs of the requirements of American law during a meeting with the diplomatic corps. The government did not like these approaches, and despite repeated requests, provided very little information about those people who had fled or disappeared. It did make formal replies by diplomatic note in August 2003 and June 2004. However, perhaps in part because of these repeated discussions, the wave of flights and disappearances abated by May 2003. Harassment continued throughout the election period.

This experience led to two important conclusions for the embassy. First, advancing human rights goals should be a cross-cutting goal in all of our activities. We would continue to work in areas of mutual agreement with the GOR, such as decentralization and the promotion of women's rights, where we saw positive results. Second, reconciliation would remain a second cross-cutting goal in our programs. The end of the political transition did not signal the end of the need for reconciliation between Tutsi and Hutu. Events surrounding the elections clearly indicated that a long term commitment to reconciliation was needed to encourage greater tolerance and in turn permit more openness to debate and competition in future elections.

As this discussion indicates, human rights diplomacy is multi-faceted. It can be difficult, and it requires a long term commitment. Results might not accrue quickly, but continued dialogue and cooperation often prepare the way for rapid and sometimes surprising changes when the time is ripe.

Ambassador McMillion explains how finding common ground with the government of Rwanda was essential to advancing human rights, especially after the international community failed to halt the genocide in 1994. The Tutsi-led government was, and continues to be, sensitive to human rights issues, so states must tread carefully, yet not abandon principle.

The embassy and consulate represent the state abroad and many of their duties revolve around citizen services. Also, more than one ministry usually has staff at the embassy. Ministries of trade, commerce, agriculture, and defense have personnel that work out of the embassy, as do the intelligence services. The embassy or consulate can come under scrutiny by the host state when human rights advocates seek diplomatic asylum on their premises. In 2012, Wikileaks founder Julian Assange sought and was granted asylum at the Ecuador embassy in London after it became clear the UK government would extradite him to Sweden to face sex abuse charges. Assange maintained that the charges were a ruse designed to allow the United States to extradite him back to the United States to face charges for his role in damaging leaks including "cablegate" where Wikileaks posted hundreds of thousands of diplomatic cables that were stolen by a low ranking US army soldier. Also in 2012, just before a visit by Secretary of State Hillary Clinton and Treasury Secretary Timothy Geitner to China, Chinese human rights activist Chen Guangcheng fled house arrest and sought refuge at the US embassy in Beijing. Creative diplomatic solutions to such incidents must be sought. In the case of Assange, a solution has eluded diplomats as he remains at the embassy because the UK is unwilling to allow him passage to Ecuador. Guangcheng was not granted asylum but a backroom deal was struck where China granted him a visa to study in the United States. These cases created awkward situations for the countries involved, and while human rights concerns were factors, they were not decisive. In diplomacy, the norm of offering a "face-saving" way out is often the key to resolving conflict and maintaining quality relations.

National commissions and ombudsman offices

The traditional diplomatic arms of state clearly engage in some form of human rights and humanitarian diplomacy abroad. At the same time, many states set up **national human rights commissions** and **ombudsman** offices to help them promote and protect human rights at home.[23] These bodies are designed to play both an investigative and mediation role between individuals and government officials (including the police). They hear complaints, assess them, and attempt to informally resolve human rights disputes. National commissions are also often used as a tool to evaluate a state's domestic progress on implementing international human rights standards or to investigate human rights abuses. Prominent examples include the national Human Rights Commissions of Cameroon, India, and Ghana. For states with troubled human rights records, these bodies can signal a turning point in their diplomatic relations, or, conversely be a cynical attempt to create a puppet to legitimize the government and deflect international scrutiny of their oppressive policies.[24]

More than seventy states have some kind of national human rights commission or ombudsman office.

Special human rights commissions at the national level also may be established on an ad hoc basis to investigate human rights violations that occurred under previous regimes. Also known as **truth commissions**, these bodies can help societies come to terms with their troubled past and provide a mechanism for holding gross violators of human rights and humanitarian law accountable for their actions. They do not have the same procedures as legal bodies but they do allow individuals to air grievances and give officials an opportunity to atone for their actions, without necessarily triggering legal penalties. The idea is that the "less legal" process allows for more effective mediation and more swift determination of the facts. Truth commissions have been around for nearly forty years, however, the most famous is the Truth and Reconciliation Commission in South Africa, which was created in 1995 to address apartheid-era crimes. To date, more than sixty-seven states have used truth commissions; however, their effectiveness in helping states internalize international human rights norms is uncertain.[25]

The creation of national human rights commissions, ombudsman offices, or truth commissions often requires extensive bilateral, multilateral, IGO, and NGO diplomacy. States may provide incentives to (or pressure) other states by linking development and military aid to national human rights protection. Canada has chosen to encourage national human rights commissions abroad by offering training programs, formal and informal consultations, expert exchanges, and networking opportunities.[26] Ad hoc truth commissions are often a part of a larger multilateral diplomatic effort to resolve complex emergencies. IGOs encourage compliance with international human rights and humanitarian standards for all of these bodies and even provide training. Domestic and international NGOs advocate for the creation of national human rights bodies and a formalized monitoring role for themselves. The diplomatic activities of these many actors are designed to advance human rights and humanitarian principles, albeit from the actor's perspective, interest, and worldview relating to human rights and humanitarian principles.

Conclusion

Human rights and humanitarian diplomacy occurs in the context of institutionalized diplomatic protocols and norms that can complicate the promotion of human rights and humanitarian principles internationally. The MFA traditionally has been responsible for the conduct of a state's bilateral and multilateral diplomacy, including its human rights and humanitarian diplomacy. This kind of diplomacy tends to center the promotion and protection of internationally recognized human rights as a state defines and prioritizes them. It also involves challenging the definitions and priorities of other actors. Active human rights and humanitarian diplomacy involves engaging foreign counterparts abroad without alienating them. Many states have also created human rights commissions, ombudsman offices, and truth commissions to help them fulfill their international human rights obligations. These commissions and ombudsman offices can provide administrative oversight of police functions and mediate disputes between private individuals and agencies of the state. They also reflect a state's commitment to international human rights and humanitarian principles.

Key terms

1961 Vienna Convention on Diplomatic Relations, diplomatic recognition, diplomatic immunity, *persona non grata* (PNG), Ministry of Foreign Affairs (MFA), foreign minister or secretary, Convention on the Prohibition of the Use, Stockpiling, Production and Transfer or Anti-Personnel Mines and on their Destruction, human rights reports, EU Annual Report on Human Rights and Democracy, démarches, national human rights commissions, ombudsman, truth commissions.

Discussion questions

1. Discuss how the traditional diplomatic architecture affects a state's human rights and humanitarian diplomacy.
2. What are the diplomatic divides among states relating to human rights and humanitarian principles? How does diplomacy bridge and reinforce those divides?
3. What role does the MFA play in human rights and humanitarian diplomacy?
4. What are the advantages of national human rights commissions and ombudsman offices?

Notes

1 See for example the 1961 Vienna Convention on Diplomatic Relations. This treaty formally codified many of the customary behaviors related to the conduct of diplomacy.
2 The following principles can be found at the United Nations, "Vienna Convention on Diplomatic Relations," *The Audio Visual Library of International Law*, accessed January 23, 2014. http://legal.un.org/avl/ha/vcdr/vcdr.html.
3 Ernesto Londono, "Bahrain Orders Senior U.S. Diplomat to Leave," *Washington Post*, July 7, 2014, accessed July 8, 2014. www.washingtonpost.com/world/national-security/bahrain-orders-senior-us-diplomat-to-leave/2014/07/07/982655 4c-0609-11e4-8a6a-19355c7e870a_story.html.
4 See for example Steven Greenhouse, "Report Outlines the Abuse of Foreign Domestic Workers," *New York Times*, June 14, 2001, A16, accessed October 15, 2014. www.nytimes.com/2001/06/14/us/report-outlines-the-abuse-of-foreign-domestic-workers.html.

5 BBC, "Devyani Khobragade Row: India Targets US Nationals," December 28, 2013, accessed April 11, 2014. www.bbc.com/news/world-asia-india-25534144.
6 Jason Burke, "India Cracks Down on US Embassy Club in Diplomatic Row," *Guardian*, January 8, 2014, accessed April 12, 2014. www.theguardian.com/world/2014/jan/08/india-us-american-embassy-club-row.
7 Steven Greenhouse, "Report Outlines the Abuse of Foreign Domestic Workers," *New York Times*, June 14, 2001, A16, accessed October 15, 2014. www.nytimes.com/2001/06/14/us/report-outlines-the-abuse-of-foreign-domestic-workers.html.
8 G.R. Berridge, *Diplomacy: Theory and Practice* (New York: Palgrave, 2002), 5.
9 Kishan S. Rana, *21st Century Diplomacy: A Practitioner's Guide* (New York: Bloomsbury Academic, 2011), 65.
10 Ivo Daalder, "Leadership, Lisbon and Libya: Remarks to the Aspen Group," June 10, 2011, accessed August 21, 2014. http://nato.usmission.gov/ambassador-speeches/aspenstrategy20110610.html.
11 Ishaan Tharoor, "At Last, A Western Country Stands Up to Saudi Arabia on Human Rights," *Washington Post*, March 12, 2014, accessed March 15, 2015. www.washingtonpost.com/blogs/worldviews/wp/2015/03/12/at-last-a-western-country-stands-up-to-saudi-arabia-on-human-rights/?tid=HP_more?tid=HP_more.
12 Compiled from the US State Department, accessed October 5, 2015. www.state.gov/s/h/tst/2013/index.html.
13 For a discussion of state participation through *amicus* briefs see William A. Schabas, *The International Criminal Tribunals: The Former Yugoslavia, Rwanda and Sierra Leone* (Cambridge: Cambridge University Press, 2006), 619.
14 Beth Stephens, Judith Chomsky, Jennifer Green, Paul Hoffman, and Michael Ratner, *International Human Rights Litigation in U.S. Courts*, 2nd edition (Leiden: Martinus Nijhoff, 2008), 434.
15 "Office of Global Justice," accessed October 1, 2014. www.state.gov/j/gcj/index.htm.
16 See "Humanitarian Operations," accessed April 25, 2014. www.state.gov/t/pm/iso/c21542.htm.
17 See The Ministry of Foreign Affairs of the Federation of Russia, "The Report on the Human Rights Situation in the European Union," December 6, 2012, accessed August 1, 2014. www.mid.ru/brp_4.nsf/0/F6501F42C40A25EE44257ACC004971FC. For analysis of the report see BBC, "Russia Attacks EU Human Rights Record after Criticism," December 7, 2012, accessed August 2, 2014. www.bbc.com/news/world-europe-20644214.
18 The Ministry of Foreign Affairs of the Federation of Russia, "The Report on the Human Rights Situation in the European Union."
19 David Petrasek, "New Powers, New Approaches? Human Rights Diplomacy in the 21st Century," *International Journal on Human Rights*, 10:19 (2013), 6–15.
20 Michele Kelemen, "Twitter Diplomacy: State Department 2.0," *All Things Considered*, National Public Radio, February 21, 2012, accessed October 15, 2014. www.npr.org/blogs/alltechconsidered/2012/02/21/147207004/twitter-diplomacy-state-department-2-0.
21 *Statement by Minister Costello at UN Human Rights Council*, March 3, 2014, accessed March 5, 2015. www.dfa.ie/news-and-media/speeches/speeches-archive/2014/march/minister-costello-un-human-rights-council/.

22 For a sampling of such cables see the *Public Library of US Diplomacy*, accessed April 28, 2014. www.wikileaks.org/plusd/cables/02ROME3647_a.html.
23 Kamal Hussain, Leonard F.M. Besselink, Haile Selassie, Gebre Selassie, and Edmond Volker (eds.), *Human Rights Commissions and Ombudsman Offices: National Experiences Throughout the World* (The Hague: Kluwer Law International, 2000).
24 Niki Esse de Lang, "The Establishment and Development of the Myanmar National Human Rights Commission and its Conformity with International Standards," *Asia Pacific Journal on Human Rights and Law*, 13:1 (2012), 2–3.
25 Matiangai V.S. Sirleaf, "The Truth about Truth Commissions: Why they Do Not Function Optimally in Post-Conflict Societies," *Cardozo Law Review*, 35:6 (2014), 2263–2347.
26 Sonia Cardenas, "Transgovernmental Activism: Canada's Role in Promoting National Human Rights Commissions," *Human Rights Quarterly*, 25:3 (2003), 775–790, 775.

4
The United Nations and multilateral diplomacy

States have used their sovereignty to not only create international law but also IGOs to help them address collective action problems, resolve conflict, and achieve common goals. This chapter reviews the relationship between states and IGOs, as well as the human rights architecture of selected IGOs to show how states use IGOs to shape and conduct human rights and humanitarian diplomacy. The distinction between organs controlled by states and agencies headed and staffed by officials independent of states is made here. When states use and control IGO fora to conduct their diplomacy, it is known as **multilateral diplomacy**. How states conduct human rights and humanitarian diplomacy multilaterally is the focus of this chapter. The next chapter centers on **IGO diplomacy** where independent IGO officials engage in diplomatic activities to galvanize international attention, carry out their mandates, and liaise with states, NGOs, and other IGOs.[1] These forms of diplomacy are analyzed separately but as a practical matter, their diplomacy is interactive, with each shaping and influencing the other.

Multilateral Human Rights and Humanitarian Diplomacy at the United Nations

The UN is a universal global IGO and the center for global multilateral diplomacy. According to Article 1 of the UN Charter the purposes of the UN are:

1. To maintain international peace and security, and to that end: to take effective collective measures for the prevention and removal of threats to the peace, and for the suppression of acts of aggression or other breaches of the peace, and to bring about by peaceful means, and in conformity with the principles of justice and international law, adjustment or settlement of international disputes or situations which might lead to a breach of the peace;
2. To develop friendly relations among nations based on respect for the principle of equal rights and self-determination of peoples, and to take other appropriate measures to strengthen universal peace;

3. To achieve international co-operation in solving international problems of an economic, social, cultural, or humanitarian character, and in promoting and encouraging respect for human rights and for fundamental freedoms for all without distinction as to race, sex, language, or religion; and
4. To be a centre for harmonizing the actions of nations in the attainment of these common ends.

To understand the interactive role of the UN and states in human rights and humanitarian diplomacy, it is helpful to think about the UN as three interactive entities.[2] The **first UN** is an organization comprised of sovereign states who bring their different capabilities, values, interests, and rivalries to the table. When state representatives populate and make the decisions in UN bodies, such as the Security Council or the HRC, the same tensions and conflicts that are manifest in world politics are present at this first UN as well. The first UN is where multilateral diplomacy takes place. The **second UN** is the system of decision- and policy-making by UN officials (the UN bureaucracy) who are independent and not instructed by states. This second UN can be an important actor in its own right. While it cannot function well if its actions and choices stray too far from the preferences of powerful member states, it does play monitoring, mediating, and educating roles. This kind IGO diplomacy involves pushing, prodding, pressuring, and cajoling states, as well as helping them define and fulfill their international human rights and humanitarian obligations. The **third UN** can be thought of as the network of NGOs, independent experts, and other civil society actors that attempt to influence states and IGOs to adopt certain values and develop certain policies.

During much of the Cold War, the first UN was largely marginalized. Superpower competition led to paralysis at the UN in international security matters and human rights were a political tool to bludgeon the other side. The groundbreaking UDHR was adopted by the UN General Assembly in 1948 but it was nonbinding. The drafters intended to follow up the UDHR with the more binding international law; however, the Covenant on Civil and Political Rights and the Covenant on Economic, Social, and Cultural Rights were not ready for signatures until 1966 and did not get the requisite signatories to enter into force until 1976.[3] So while some progress was made, human rights diplomacy geared toward creating binding international law formalizing state obligations was very slow in developing. Still, the UN has and continues to engage in multilateral human rights and humanitarian diplomacy in multidimensional ways.

The United Nations Security Council

States were initially slow to pursue multilateral human rights and humanitarian diplomacy through the UN Security Council. The Security Council is a fifteen-member body that is responsible for maintaining international peace and security. The Security Council includes five permanent members (Russia, China, the United Kingdom, the United States, and France), **the P-5**, each which has veto power over council decisions.

The remaining ten members are nonpermanent and those seats are allotted to specific regions and elected by the General Assembly. Nonpermanent members are elected in two-year staggered terms so that five new members join the council each year. The Security Council's Cold War record was rather spotty because of difficulties in reaching consensus among the veto-wielding P-5. Yet, it did reach "decisions" under Chapter VII (which makes the decision binding on all UN member states) and linked human rights and humanitarian situations occurring materially within states to international peace and security. States acted multilaterally when the council voted mandatory sanctions against the racist regimes in Rhodesia (1966 and 1968) and South Africa (1977). While not explicitly mentioning human rights conditions, concerns about apartheid and self-determination motivated council actions.[4] These actions stand out because they represent a rare Cold War consensus among the P-5.

Even though the Security Council was largely paralyzed during the Cold War, it did innovate **peacekeeping**.[5] While not provided for in the UN Charter, peacekeeping was created as a kind of halfway point between Chapter VI which provides for the peaceful settlement of disputes through diplomacy and Chapter VII, which allows for more forceful measures. Originally, the first peacekeeping missions were security oriented with the only humanitarian purpose of ensuring that violent conflict did not flare up again. Often termed **first generation peacekeeping**, missions included lightly armed personnel and observers who were deployed with the consent of the host government and other belligerents after a ceasefire had been negotiated. To ensure that these missions were as neutral as possible, they were placed under the control of the UN Secretary-General.[6] No "aggressor" is identified and singled out for blame, giving belligerents time to cool off and disengage without humiliation.

Second generation peacekeeping (often referred to as **peace enforcement**) represents an evolution of mission in response to the changing nature of post-Cold War conflicts in the 1990s (discussed below). Increasingly, the deteriorating human rights and humanitarian situations means UN peacekeepers are often called upon to create safe areas and use more "robust" measures to deliver humanitarian aid. If there is a peace to keep, it is a fragile one, with violations occurring from all sides. Second generation peacekeeping often involves preventative diplomacy and enforcing Security Council decisions.[7] The human rights and humanitarian tragedies in Rwanda and the former Yugoslavia forced a rethinking of the idea of neutrality when gross violations of human rights are being perpetrated. The rules of engagement of peacekeepers have been modified to include mandates not only for using force in self-defense but also to protect the civilian population.

Third generation peacekeeping, also known as **peacebuilding**, centers on the reconstruction of post-conflict societies. When there is no government, or it is effectively inoperative, UN peacekeeping missions functionally become the government. Activities involve capacity-building in addition to performing government roles such as policing and administering educational, health, and social services. Peacebuilding is necessary for long-term stability in conflict-ridden societies. At the 2005 World Summit, world leaders agreed to create and fund the **Peacebuilding Commission** that currently has activities in Sierra Leone, Burundi, Central African Republic, Guinea, Cote d'Ivoire, Haiti, Liberia, and Kenya. The diplomacy involved

Table 4.1 Past UN peacekeeping operations

Name	Dates of operation	Size of operation
United Nations Angola Verification Mission I (UNAVEM I)	Jan. 1989 to May 1991	70 military observers
United Nations Angola Verification Mission II (UNAVEM II)	May 1991 to Feb. 1995	171 military observers; 122 civilian police; 11 military medical staff
United Nations Angola Verification Mission III (UNAVEM III)	Feb. 1995 to June 30, 1997	4,220 military personnel, composed of: 283 military observers; 3,649 troops; 288 civilian police
United Nations Aouzou Strip Observer Group (UNASOG)	May to June 1994	9 military observers, supported by 6 international civilian staff
United Nations Assistance Mission for Rwanda (UNAMIR)	Oct. 1993 to March 1996	5,500 military personnel composed of: 5,200 troops; 320 military observers; 90 civilian police (max. deployment)
United Nations Mission in Ethiopia and Eritrea (UNMEE)	July 31, 2000 to July 31, 2008	4,154 uniformed personnel including: 3,940 troops and 214 police supported by 229 international civilian personnel and 244 local civilian staff (max. deployment)
United Nations Mission in Sierra Leone (UNAMSIL)	Oct. 22 1999 to Dec. 31 2005	17,368 military personnel; UN Police: 87; international civilians: 322; local civilians: 552 (max deployment)
United Nations Mission in the Central African Republic (MINURCA)	Apr. 1998 to Feb. 2000	1,350 military personnel and 24 civilian police; 114 international civilian staff; 111 local staff; 13 UN volunteers (max. authorized)
United Nations Mission in the Central African Republic and Chad (MINURCAT)	Sept. 25, 2007 to Dec. 31, 2010	3,814 uniform personnel supported by: 422 international civilian personnel; 524 local civilian staff; 143 UN volunteers
United Nations Observer Mission in Angola (MONUA)	June 1997 to Feb. 1999	3,026 troops and military personnel; 253 military observers; 289 civilian police observers (max. deployment)
United Nations Observer Mission in Liberia (UNOMIL)	Sept. 1993 to Sept. 1997	303 military observers; 20 military medical personnel; 45 military engineers; 90 international and 136 local civilian staff; 58 UN volunteers
United Nations Observer Mission in Sierra Leone (UNOMSIL)	July 13 1998 to Oct. 22 1999	192 military observers; 15 other military personnel and a 2-person medical team (max. deployment)
United Nations Observer Mission Uganda-Rwanda (UNOMUR)	June 1993 to Sept. 1994	81 military observers

Table 4.1 (*cont*)

Name	Dates of operation	Size of operation
United Nations Operation in Burundi (ONUB)	June 1, 2004 to Dec. 31, 2006	5,665 uniform personnel including: 5,400 troops; 168 military observers; 97 police; supported by 316 international civilian personnel; 383 local civilian staff; 156 UN volunteers
United Nations Operations in Cote d'Ivoire (MINUCI)	May 2003 to Apr. 2004	75 military observers supported by 54 international civilian personnel and 55 local staff
United Nations Operation in Mozambique (ONUMOZ)	Dec. 1992 to Dec. 1994	6,576 all ranks
United Nations Operation in Somalia I (UNOSOM I)	Apr. 1992 to Mar. 1993	54 military observers; 893 troops and military support personnel (max. deployment)
United Nations Operation in Somalia II (UNOSOM II)	Mar. 1993 to Mar. 1995	28,000 military and civilian police personnel; provision for 2,800 international and local civilian staff (max. authorized)
UN Mission in the Sudan (UN MIS)	Mar. 24, 2005 to July 9, 2011	10,519 total uniform personnel (max. deployment)
United Nations Operation in the Congo (ONUC)	July 1960 to June 1964	19,828 all ranks (max. deployment)
United Nations Organization Mission in the Democratic Republic of the Congo (MONUC)	Nov. 30 to June 2010	22,016 total uniform personnel (max. authorized)
United Nations Transition Assistance Group (UNTAG)	Apr. 1989 to Mar. 1990	4,493 all ranks (max. deployment)
Mission of the Representative of the Secretary-General in the Dominican Republic (DOMREP)	Mar. 1965 to Oct. 1966	2 military observers
United Nations Civilian Police Mission in Haiti (MIPONUH)	Dec. 1997 to Mar 2000	300 civilian police personnel
United Nations Mission in Haiti (UNMIH)	Sept. 1993 to Jun. 1996	6,065 troops and military support personnel; 847 civilian police (max. deployment)
United Nations Observer Group in Central America (ONUCA)	Nov. 1989 to Jan. 1992	1,098 military observers and troops

Mission	Dates	Personnel
United Nations Observer Mission in El Salvador (ONUSAL)	Jul. 1991 to Apr. 1995	368 military observers and 315 civilian policy (max. deployment)
United Nations Support Mission in Haiti (UNSMIH)	Jul. 1996 to Jul. 1997	1,297 military and 291 civilian police personnel (max. deployment)
United Nations Transition Mission in Haiti (UNTMIH)	Aug. to Nov. 1997	250 civilian police personnel and 50 military personnel (max. authorized)
United Nations Verification Mission in Guatemala (MINUGUA)	Jan. to May 1997	132 military observers and 13 medical personnel
United Nations Advance Mission in Cambodia (UNAMIC)	Oct. 1991 to Mar. 1992	1,090 military personnel
United Nations Good Offices Mission in Afghanistan and Pakistan (UNGOMAP)	May 1988 to Mar. 1990	50 military observers (max. deployment)
United Nations India-Pakistan Observation Mission (UNIPOM)	Sept. 1965 to Mar. 1966	96 military observers (max. deployment)
United Nations mission of Observers in Tajikistan (UNMOT)	Dec. 1994 to May 2000	81 military observers (max. deployment)
United Nations Mission of Support in East Timor (UNMISET)	May 20, 2002 to May 20, 2005	4,776 military personnel; 771 UN Police; 465 international civilian personnel; 856 local civilians
United Nations Security Force in West Guinea (UNSF)	Oct. 3, 1962 to Apr. 30, 1963	1,500 infantry personnel and 76 aircraft personnel
United Nations Transitional Administration in East Timor (UNTAET)	Oct. 25 to May 20, 2002	9,150 military personnel; 1,640 civilian police (max. authorized)
United Nations Transitional Authority in Cambodia (UNTAC)	Feb. 1992 to Sept. 1993	15,991 military personnel; 3,359 civilian police component (max. deployment)
United Nations Integrated Mission in Timor-Leste (UNMIT)	Aug. 25, 2006 to Dec. 31, 2012	1,608 police personnel; 34 military liaison and staff officers (max. authorized)
United Nations Civilian Police Support Group (UNPSG)	Jan. 16 to Oct. 15, 1998	114 police (max. deployment)
United Nations Confidence Restoration Operation in Croatia (UNCRO)	Mar. 1995 to Jan. 1996	6,581 troops; 194 military observers; 296 civilian police

Table 4.1 (cont)

Name	Dates of operation	Size of operation
United Nations Mission in Bosnia and Herzegovina (UNMIBH)	Dec. 1995 to Dec. 2002	2,047 civilian police (max. deployment)
United Nations Mission of Observers in Prevlaka (UNMOP)	Feb. 1996 to Dec. 2002	28 military observers; 3 international civilian personnel; 6 local civilian staff
United Nations Observer Mission in Georgia (UNOMIG)	Aug. 1993 to June 2009	129 military observers; 16 police officers; 105 international staff; 208 local staff; 1 UN volunteer
United Nations Preventive Deployment Force (UNPREDEP)	Mar. 31, 1995 to Feb. 28, 1999	1,049 troops; 35 military observers; 26 civilian police
United Nations Protection Force (UNPROFOR)	Feb. 1992 to Mar. 1995	38,500 military personnel, including: 684 UN military observers; 803 civilian police; 2,017 other international civilian staff; 2,615 local staff
United Nations Transitional Authority in Eastern Slavonia, Baranja and Western Sirmium (UNTAES)	Jan. 1996 to Jan. 1998	2,346 troops: 97 military observers; 404 civilian police
First United Nations Emergency Force (UNEF I)	Nov. 1956 to Jun. 1967	6,073 military personnel (max. deployment)
United Nations Emergency Force II (UNEF II)	Oct. 1973 to Jul. 1979	6,973 military personnel (max. deployment)
United Nations Iran-Iraq Military Observer Group (UNIMOG)	Aug. 1988 to Feb. 1991	400 military personnel (max. deployment)
United Nations Iraq-Kuwait Observation Mission (UNIKOM)	Apr. 1991 to Oct. 2003	1,187 all ranks, including 300 military observers
United Nations Observation Group in Lebanon (UNOGIL)	June to Dec. 1958	591 military personnel (max. deployment)
United Nations Yemen Observation Mission (UNYOM)	Jul. 1963 to Sept. 1964	189 military personnel
UN Supervision Mission in Syria (UNSMIS)	Apr. 21 to Aug. 2012	300 unarmed military observers (max. authorized)

Source: Compiled from www.un.org/en/peacekeeping/operations.

Table 4.2 Current UN peacekeeping operations

Name	Start of operation	Size of operation
United Nations Mission for the Referendum in Western Sahara (MINURSO)	April 1991	237 military personnel; 6 police officers (max. authorized)
United Nations Multidimensional Integrated Stabilization Mission in the Central African Republic (MINUSCA)	April 2014	11,820 total uniformed personnel (max. authorized)
United Nations Multidimensional Integrated Stabilization Mission in Mali (MINUSMA)	April 2013	12,640 total uniformed personnel (max. authorized)
United Nations Stabilization Mission in Haiti (MINUSTAH)	June 2004	6,700 military personnel (max. authorized)
United Nations Organization Stabilization Mission in the Democratic Republic of the Congo (MONUSCO)	July 2010	22,016 total uniformed personnel (max. authorized)
United Nations Assistance Mission in Afghanistan (UNAMA)	March 2014	1,789 civilian staff (as of Jan. 31, 2014)
African Union/United Nations Hybrid operation in Darfur (UNAMID)	July 2007	16,200 military personnel; 4,690 police (max. authorized)
United Nations Disengagement Observer Force (UNDOF)	May 1974	1,223 troops; 49 international staff; 108 local civilian staff
United Nations Peacekeeping Force in Cyprus (UNFICYP)	March 1964	920 total uniformed personnel; 38 international civilian personnel; 111 local civilian staff (as of July 31, 2014)
United Nations Interim Force in Lebanon (UNIFIL)	March 1978	15,000 troops (max. authorized)
United Nations Interim Security Force for Abyei (UNISFA)	June 2011	5,326 military personnel; 50 police (max. authorized)
United Nations Interim Administration Mission in Kosovo (UNMIK)	June 1999	4,718 police personnel; 38 military liaison officers (max. authorized)

Table 4.2 (*cont*)

Name	Start of operation	Size of operation
United Nations Mission in Liberia (UNMIL)	September 2003	6,020 total uniformed personnel; 398 international civilian personnel; 860 local staff; 288 UN volunteers (as of July 31, 2014)
United Nations Mission in the Republic of South Sudan (UNMISS)	July 2011	12,500 military personnel; 1,323 civilian police personnel (max. authorized)
United Nations Military Observer Group in India and Pakistan (UNMOGIP)	January 1949	44 military observers; 23 international civilian personnel; 46 local civilian staff (as of July 31, 2014)
United Nations Operation in Cote d'Ivoire (UNOCI)	April 2004	6,945 total uniformed personnel (max. authorized)
United Nations Truce Supervision Organization (UNTSO)	May 1948	157 military observers; 88 international civilian personnel; 134 local civilian staff (as of July 31, 2014)

Source: Compiled from www.un.org/en/peacekeeping/operations.

to make peacekeeping, peace enforcement, and peacebuilding happen occurs at many levels through a variety of networks. The "success" of peacekeeping missions is hard to quantify, because it cannot be known what would have happened if the UN had not become involved. What is important is that direct diplomatic action was taken to promote and protect human rights and improve the humanitarian situation in conflict-ridden countries. UN peacekeeping is the story of evolution and innovation and, along with it, the notions of security and peace. No longer does international security mean only state security, it also means **human security**. Peace is not just understood in a negative sense (the absence of violence), but also in a positive sense, in that humans must be secure, have access to resources to meet their basic human needs, and have their human rights respected. Table 4.1 and Table 4.2 detail the extent of past and ongoing UN peacekeeping missions. All of these missions were authorized by the Security Council and are evidence of the international community efforts to mitigate the human suffering caused by violent conflict. The missions are the result of the extensive multilateral and IGO diplomacy necessary to create, staff, deploy, and fund the operations.

Post-Cold War. The end of the Cold War generated renewed interest in the United Nations and other IGOs for multilateral diplomacy in general, and human rights and humanitarian diplomacy in particular. Perhaps the most dramatic event in the immediate post-Cold War era was the invasion of Kuwait by Iraq in 1991. For the first time since the Korean War, the UN Security Council authorized a collective security operation to expel Iraq from Kuwait. After the cessation of international hostilities, Iraqi leader Saddam Hussein brutally cracked down on rebelling Kurds in northern Iraq and Shiites in southern Iraq. In response, the Security Council passed **Resolution 688** which was the first unambiguous recognition of a human rights and humanitarian situation within a state as a threat to international peace and security. The resolution:[8]

1. Condemns the repression of the Iraqi civilian population in many parts of Iraq, including most recently in Kurdish populated areas, the consequences of which threaten international peace and security in the region;
2. Demands that Iraq, as a contribution to remove the threat to international peace and security in the region, immediately end this repression and express the hope in the same context that an open dialogue will take place to ensure that the human and political rights of all Iraqi citizens are respected;
3. Insists that Iraq allow immediate access by international humanitarian organizations to all those in need of assistance in all parts of Iraq and to make available all necessary facilities for their operations;
4. Requests the Secretary-General to pursue his humanitarian efforts in Iraq and to report forthwith, if appropriate on the basis of a further mission to the region, on the plight of the Iraqi civilian population, and in particular the Kurdish population, suffering from the repression in all its forms inflicted by the Iraqi authorities;
5. Requests further the Secretary-General to use all the resources at his disposal, including those of the relevant United Nations agencies, to address urgently the critical needs of the refugees and displaced Iraqi population;

6. Appeals to all Member States and to all humanitarian organizations to contribute to these humanitarian relief efforts;
7. Demands that Iraq cooperate with the Secretary-General to these ends;
8. Decides to remain seized of the matter.

While not explicitly authorizing the use of force to end the repression or to deliver humanitarian aid, the United States and United Kingdom used Resolution 688 to forcibly establish no-fly zones and protected areas in Iraq, which remained in effect, more or less, until the US-led invasion of Iraq in 2003. Resolution 688 is important in the history of human rights and humanitarian diplomacy, not only because it clearly mentions the human rights situation occurring materially within the domestic jurisdiction of a state as a threat to international peace and security, but also because a majority of the states on the Security Council were willing to override another state's sovereignty for humanitarian reasons. Also noteworthy was that China abstained from the resolution (which it could have vetoed); and Cuba, Yemen, and India voted against it. Many developing states, especially those with a history of colonialism or foreign occupation, were (and continue to be) wary of loopholes that would provide a justification for the powerful to intervene.

Another noteworthy aspect is that the United States and the United Kingdom had the material capabilities and were willing to use them in this situation. The UN has no independent military capability and must rely on states to enforce decisions and provide resources. This means that any state willing to risk its treasure and blood on behalf of the human rights of foreign nationals is also likely to have other motives as well. The United States and the United Kingdom have geostrategic and oil interests in the area. Coupled with the UK's colonial history in Iraq, suspicions were fueled that the United States and United Kingdom were using human rights to retain their influence and control over the region.

The sensitivities of the issues before the Security Council in the immediate post-Cold War era meant member states often conducted their council diplomacy quietly, behind closed doors. Unlike the Cold War where council resolutions were routinely and publicly vetoed, the renewed commitment to multilateralism meant states were less willing to push an issue to embarrass others. The resolutions that resulted reflected the compromise between competing interests and worldviews and, when passed formally by the council, the outcome was already predetermined.

The next post-Cold War humanitarian crises involved the Balkans, Somalia, and Rwanda, with events unfolding both simultaneously and serially. The Cold War balance of power checked many of simmering ethnic conflicts in states around the world and, when it ended, some of those conflicts erupted. The causes of these conflicts are beyond the scope of this book but what is relevant is that states, acting through the UN Security Council, engaged in multilateral diplomacy on behalf of human rights and humanitarianism. First, the disintegration of Yugoslavia in 1991 led the Security Council to deploy peacekeeping forces to try to stabilize the ensuing secessionist conflict between rival nationalities that included Serbs, Croats, Bosniaks, Albanians, Slovenes, Macedonians, and Kosovars. These rivalries were complicated by religious conflicts between Muslims and the area's Christian religions. The locus of violent conflict was in Bosnia-Herzegovina where competing attempts to forcibly carve out territory led to widespread killing, rape, ethnic cleansing, and gross violations of human rights. In addition to authorizing a peacekeeping mission, the Security Council also authorized "all necessary means" (the diplomatic euphemism for military force) to protect the delivery of humanitarian assistance to besieged populations. At first, states were reluctant to "enforce" the resolutions but after attacks on UN peacekeepers and humanitarian aid workers, some member states (under the auspices of NATO) bombed selected Serb targets. Yet, the fighting among the belligerents continued taking a high toll on the civilian population. The Security Council responded by attempting to disarm the belligerents and creating safe haven areas around certain population centers.[9] They also deployed lightly armed peacekeepers to protect the safe areas. Nevertheless, the violence continued and in 1993 the Security Council responded by establishing the first international criminal tribunal since the Nuremberg and Tokyo Tribunals were created after World War II. The **International Criminal Tribunal for the former Yugoslavia (ICTY)** had a slow start and did not hold its first trial until 1996; however, it would eventually indict 161 individuals for genocide, war crimes, and crimes against humanity, including a sitting head of state.

Unfortunately, the creation of a lightly armed peacekeeping force, safe havens, and a criminal tribunal still did not curb killings. The notorious 1995 massacre of 7,000 Muslim men and boys in the safe area of Srebrenica by a Serb militia (as Dutch peacekeepers stood aside) finally prompted more decisive action by states on the Security Council. The council endorsed the Dayton Peace Accords and authorized the deployment of a robust 60,000-strong peacekeeping force (under the auspices of NATO), which included approximately 20,000 US forces. A tenuous peace remained in effect in the former Yugoslavia until the Kosovo War in 1998–99. The lag between Security Council decisions and decisive military action shows the importance of political will and the centrality of states willing to execute multilateral decisions for humanitarian purposes.

Also unfolding at that time was the humanitarian crisis in Somalia after the collapse of its government in 1992. Extensive media attention on the mass starvation of civilians, as well as alarms raised by UN and NGO officials, spurred states on the Security Council to authorize UNSC Resolution 794 to "use all necessary means to establish as soon as possible a secure environment for humanitarian relief operations in Somalia." The resolution also "strongly condemns all violations of international humanitarian law occurring in Somalia, including in particular the deliberate impeding of the delivery of food and medical supplies essential for the survival of the civilian population, and affirms that those who commit or order the commission of such acts will be held individually responsible in respect of such acts." This was another groundbreaking Security Council resolution because it extends criminal responsibility to persons interfering with the delivery of humanitarian aid. It also foreshadowed the creation of the ICTY and other international criminal courts to prosecute those accused with gross violations of international human rights and humanitarian law. The United States, acting with this UN authorization, deployed roughly 37,000 military personnel to provide internal security and assist the UN and NGOs in providing food, water, and medical services to millions of starving people. Eventually, a UN peacekeeping force took over stability operations in 1993; however, the partnership between the United States and UN would be tested as a UN operation under independent US military command (to capture a warlord) led to the deaths of eighteen US servicemen. As dramatized in the US film *Black Hawk Down*, the bodies of these servicemen were mutilated and dragged through the streets of Mogadishu. These events were broadcast around the world on CNN and would color future humanitarian operations in Rwanda.[10]

The 1994 genocide in Rwanda is perhaps the most dramatic failure of contemporary international diplomacy to stop genocide and other gross violations of human rights and humanitarian law. In one hundred days, more than 800,000 Rwandan Tutsis and moderate Hutus were murdered. Events unfolded quickly. The plane carrying the presidents of Uganda and Rwanda was shot down as it was returning to the Rwandan capital of Kigali from a regional peace conference. Almost immediately thereafter, militias from the Hutu majority began attacking the Tutsi minority indiscriminately. In spite of prior warnings from some UN peacekeeping officials about planned attacks on civilians, the "first UN" was slow to react. Even after several Belgian peacekeepers were murdered and it had become clear the killings amounted to genocide, member states of the UN Security Council were reluctant to intervene (in part because of Somalia). Rwanda, which was a nonpermanent member of the Security Council, escaped criticism, in part because diplomatic protocol frowns upon public confrontation. Even more unsettling, the UN withdrew its peacekeeping force, leaving only a token observer mission. Some member states sent military forces, not to stop the mass killings, but to evacuate foreign nationals. The member states of the UN Security Council lacked the political will (perhaps because they had no compelling national interests in Rwanda) to act in any meaningful way to stop the genocide.

The genocide mercifully ended when Tutsi rebels invaded from Uganda and defeated the Hutu army and associated militias. However, fear of reprisals sent over a million Hutus fleeing into neighboring Zaire (now the Democratic Republic of Congo). Fearing a genocide in reverse, coupled with a willingness of France to lead and provide troops for a military intervention force, the Security Council authorized **Operation Turquoise** to stabilize the situation.[11] Again using the diplomatic "all necessary means," the UN sought to prevent another humanitarian catastrophe. The intervention also had an unintentional consequence of allowing those who perpetrated the genocide to escape and to hide behind the UN and NGOs. Operation Turquoise protected the resulting refugee camps in Zaire and the personnel of the second and third UN as they provided food, shelter, and medical care to the Rwandan refugees. Embedded within those refugees were the *genocidaires* and the safe havens soon became militarized. The camps were then used by the extremists to launch cross-border attacks on Tutsis in Rwanda. The problem became so acute that some NGOs withdrew (including MSF) rather than be complicit in use of refugee camps as military sanctuaries.[12] The UN was unable to demilitarize the camps and the cross-border attacks continued. In 1996, Tutsi-led Rwanda invaded Zaire/Congo, triggering a wider conflict that eventually claimed the lives of millions of people.

The atrocities led the Security Council to create the **International Criminal Tribunal for Rwanda (ICTR)**. Security Council Resolution 955 of 1994 states that the ICTR is to "prosecute persons responsible for genocide and other serious violations of international humanitarian law committed in the territory of Rwanda and neighbouring States, between 1 January 1994 and 31 December 1994."[13] It is the first international tribunal in history to indict persons for genocide. It was also the first to define rape as a war crime because it was used as a weapon of war and to commit genocide. Ninety-three people have been indicted by the ICTR.[14]

In 1998, violence in the Balkans erupted again, this time in Kosovo, where the majority ethnic Albanians sought to break away from Serbia (the successor state to Yugoslavia). Kosovo had enjoyed autonomous status within the Federal Republic of Yugoslavia but that status was revoked in 1989. With the federation breaking apart, Kosovo also sought to secede. Serbian President Slobodan Milosevic brutally cracked down on the rebels and began a policy that looked a lot like the same ethnic cleansing that took place in Bosnia a few years prior. Kosovar Albanians were expelled from their homes, summarily executed, raped, and systematically stripped of their identity. Tense diplomatic negotiations ensued, with no success in stopping the violence. This time, Security Council consensus was elusive as China and Russia opposed military intervention. Western allies, led by US Secretary of State Madeline Albright and acting through NATO, bypassed the UN and began a seventy-seven-day bombing campaign against Serbian forces. Serbia responded by engaging in a mass expulsion of ethnic Albanians from Kosovo, forcibly displacing nearly two million people. The worsening humanitarian situation and escalating violence complicated diplomatic efforts to end the hostilities. Russia was furious, condemning the NATO attack as illegal. Russia hastily introduced a Security Council resolution calling for the cessation of the use of force against Serbia, but it was defeated by a wide margin (3–12) with only China, Russia, and Namibia voting in favor.[15] Tensions were exacerbated when US planes bombed the Chinese embassy in Belgrade, killing three people. After that incident, violent, mass anti-American protests erupted in China and the US embassy, consulates, and interests were targeted. China maintained (and continues to do so) that the attack was deliberate and notes that the bombs hit the intelligence unit within the embassy. The United States claims it was an accident.[16]

Considerable quiet diplomacy eventually resulted in a deal whereby Milosevic agreed to a ceasefire and to withdraw Serbian forces from Kosovo. The UN Security Council would then authorize a peacekeeping mission that would include NATO as well as Russian forces. Russia was involved extensively in the backroom negotiations, exerting considerable pressure on Serbia. Russia was under the impression that its forces would police its own sector, largely populated by ethnic Serbs, independent of NATO.[17] When NATO refused, Russian troops took over the Pristina airport, leading to the very real threat of a military confrontation between Russian and NATO forces. Again, intensive quiet diplomacy ensued and an agreement was reached where Russian forces would stand down from the airport, and while technically part of the peacekeeping mission, Russian forces would patrol under independent Russian command. This led to what emerged as an unprecedented peacekeeping mission involving several

IGOs, including NATO, the EU, the Organization for Security and Cooperation in Europe (OSCE), all under UN oversight. Subsequent NATO and the ICTY investigations made the scale of human rights and humanitarian violations public. Milosevic and his close associates were indicted in May 1999 for crimes against humanity committed in Kosovo, and later for crimes committed in Croatia and Bosnia.[18] Milosevic was forced from office in 2000 and was arrested and transferred to the Hague to stand trial before the ICTY in 2001. He died in prison before the ICTY issued a verdict.

The Kosovo situation has stabilized but not yet resolved in part because it encapsulates the clash of worldviews and international values. The government of Sweden, concerned that conflict was not being independently analyzed, decided to initiate and fund the **Independent International Commission on Kosovo**. South African jurist Richard Goldstone was tapped to chair the commission and it was comprised of many human rights proponents. The commission concluded that the NATO intervention was "illegal but legitimate" and while NATO did not have Security Council authorization, the ethnic cleansing and gross violations of human rights made intervention morally legitimate. The Kosovo Commission recommended that the international community, through the United Nations, needed to bridge the gap between existing international law and moral legitimacy.[19] This *commission diplomacy* complements the multilateral diplomacy in generating shared understandings, even though a great many states are still deeply suspicious of international efforts to create a legal right to humanitarian intervention. The Kosovo Commission suggested that the province should have "conditional independence" and after several successive and ultimately unsuccessful efforts to resolve Kosovo's status diplomatically, Kosovo unilaterally declared its independence in 2008. In a narrow advisory opinion, the International Court of Justice found that international law did prohibit the Kosovo declaration. Currently, 110 states, including the United States and major European powers, have recognized Kosovo as an independent state; however, important states including Russia, China, Brazil, Spain, Greece, Argentina, India, and Mexico have not.

The 1990s: assessing outcomes. The Balkans, Somalia, Rwanda were by no means the only humanitarian crises in the immediate post-Cold War era. The multidimensional crises in Sudan, Haiti, East Timor, Sierra Leone, and the Democratic Republic of Congo also generated extensive diplomatic efforts to protect human rights in humanitarian crises. The extent to which human rights and humanitarian diplomacy is effective is difficult, if not impossible, to discern. Outcomes are subject to worldview interpretation. What is viewed as a success (or at least a preferable outcome) for a liberal and constructivist is often seen as a failure (or as prolonging or exacerbating a situation) for a realist or a structuralist. Kosovo is a clear example. The temporal aspects of these crises also complicates analysis. At what point does a crisis end in a state or region and another begin? Post-genocide Rwanda is widely considered a success story whereas the mass human suffering in Somalia and Congo continues to this day. Some areas of the Balkans, like Croatia and Slovenia, are thriving while the loci of conflict and intervention, Bosnia and Kosovo, continue to experience instability and unrest. The crisis in the Balkans also casts a long shadow over ongoing crises in Ukraine and Georgia.

These complex emergencies are very different from one another, but all manifest the tension between the primacy of state sovereignty and nonintervention as values on the one hand, and the growing importance and imperative of human rights and humanitarian values, on the other. Intertwined is the overlapping issue of secession and its relationship to self-determination that is considered by most to be a human right. These crises illustrate the tensions between the first and second/third UN where states have had difficulty mustering the political will and resources necessary to enable IGO and NGO personnel to protect human rights or implement humanitarian policies.

These tensions resulted in the ongoing, coordinated effort to redefine sovereignty as the **Responsibility to Protect (R2P)**. In 2000, UN Secretary-General Kofi Annan eloquently claimed that the principle of sovereignty cannot be used as a shield by those who engage in gross violations of human rights.[20] With the support of the Canadian government and the UN General Assembly, the **International Commission on Intervention and State Sovereignty (ICISS)** was created to explore the issue of humanitarian intervention. The ICISS report, *The Responsibility to Protect*, sought to redefine sovereignty to mean responsibility. Specifically, "where the population is suffering serious harm, as a result of internal war, insurgency, repression or state failure, and the state in question is unwilling or unable to halt or avert it, the principle of non-intervention yields to the international responsibility to protect."[21] The ICISS report bridges the intellectual, legal, and operational gaps between sovereignty and respect for human rights by recognizing the centrality of states in the promotion and protection of internationally recognized human rights but also allows the international community to step in if the state is either committing, or is unable to prevent, genocide, war crimes and crimes against humanity. This includes gross violations of international human rights.

As a result of this commission diplomacy, member states at the **2005 World Summit** at the United Nations embraced the principle of R2P by stating that the UN may "take collective action, in a timely and decisive manner, through the Security Council, in accordance with the Charter, including Chapter VII, on a case-by-case basis and in cooperation with the relevant regional organizations as appropriate, should peaceful means be inadequate and national authorities are manifestly failing to protect their populations from genocide, war crimes, ethnic cleansing and crimes against humanity."[22] This represents an important step in refining what sovereignty means and now shapes international attempts at humanitarian action. It also creates additional space for international human rights and humanitarian diplomacy. At the same time, forceful action still requires P-5 consensus in order to authorize an intervention. While rare, this has always been possible when the UN Security Council links human rights and humanitarian concerns to the maintenance of international peace and security (as it did with Rhodesia, South Africa, Somalia, and Iraq). It is still innovative because for the first time the states that comprise the international community formally recognized that sovereignty can no longer be used to shield states committing gross violation of human rights or unable stop such violations or prevent the international community from acting. Such is the nature of diplomatic-speak. Every side finds language to support their position while at the same time allowing everyone to move forward. Human rights violations are something states can agree are a problem, even if they disagree as to the causes and the strategies for managing the problem.

Responsibility to Protect diplomacy. R2P is an evolving norm, but not a formal legal principle. The launching of the norm was an arduous diplomatic process because it bumps up against centuries of diplomatic practice, much of which has been codified by international law for more than fifty years. The meaning, effect, and evolution of R2P are also subject to diplomacy.[23] The extent to which R2P can become formally institutionalized is debatable because a large number of states, including powerful Russia and China, are deeply suspicious that human rights might be used as a justification for intervention and regime change. Arguably, they are deliberately trying to undermine R2P especially if means resorting to more forceful measures. As the ICISS explains, the international community's responsibility involves preventing, reacting, and/or rebuilding. Using military force is only one of the many means that can be utilized. Many states are comfortable with nonviolent means such as mediation, quiet diplomacy, and reconstruction assistance on behalf of human rights and humanitarian principles; however, most still are uncomfortable with more forceful measures, especially if it results in regime change. At the UN, states are central to the operation of the Security Council and the General Assembly, so any failure of the "international community to act" is due to the states that comprise the first UN. They possess the political will and the material capabilities necessary for decisive action, military and otherwise.

The struggle to embed R2P in international relations involves diplomacy as does the pushback by other states who are uncomfortable with fundamentally altering the norms of international relations. The paradox of R2P diplomacy specifically, and human rights and humanitarian diplomacy in general, is that state sovereignty is the cornerstone of diplomatic relations and states are necessary for the promotion and protection of human rights and humanitarian principles. At the same time, undermining state sovereignty compromises a state's ability to further international human rights and humanitarian principles. Several cases are illustrative and are discussed below. However, it is noteworthy that the states that have put much of their diplomatic muscle behind human rights and humanitarianism, the United States and the United Kingdom, suffered serious diplomatic setbacks because of their decision to invade Iraq in 2003 without Security Council authorization. Although this intervention pre-dates the 2005 Summit which adopted R2P, their willingness to act without international authorization (justifying that intervention in part on humanitarian grounds) damaged their credibility in future multilateral interventions.

Kenya. The 2007 post-election violence in Kenya was the first application of R2P after its adoption at the 2005 UN Summit. After a contested national election, rioting and ethnic violence interrupted, and several hundred people from the ethnic Kikuya were killed while seeking sanctuary at a house of worship.[24] The killings sparked retaliatory violence eventually leading to more than 1,300 people killed and several hundred thousand displaced. Alarmed by the speed with which the violence unfolded, the African Union assisted by the UN, as well as private individuals, engaged in **preventative diplomacy**. Preventative diplomacy involves taking steps to stop a conflict from escalating. Officials reacted both publicly and privately to the violence, and dispatched envoys to mediate the conflict in its early stages. French Foreign Minister Bernard Kouchner brought the matter to the attention of the Security Council and Archbishop Desmond Tutu and the heads of state from neighboring countries attempted to mediate through constructive dialogue. The African Union took the lead, sending former Secretary-General Kofi Annan to negotiate a power-sharing agreement and helped establish independent national commissions to investigate the violence and propose electoral reforms.[25] The ICC would go on to investigate individuals and eventually charge four individuals, including Uhuru Kenyatta, who was elected President of Kenya in 2012. The decision on the part of the ICC to investigate and indict prominent political leaders in Kenya obviously complicated the work of the ICC and the Kenyan government. In 2014, the ICC dropped the charges against Kenyatta because it lacked evidence (which is not surprising given the lack of cooperation from the Kenyan government). The initial preventative diplomacy, however, kept the violence from spiraling out of control and enabled the international community to avoid more coercive measures and the controversies surrounding permissible uses of force.

Myanmar. In 2008, Cyclone Nargis stuck Myanmar, affecting 2.4 million people. Approximately 84,000 people were killed, nearly 54,000 people missing, and the remaining displaced.[26] The isolated and reclusive government of Myanmar initially rejected most offers of international humanitarian assistance and, when pressured to accept help, it does so on a very limited basis. The government imposed strict conditions on the delivery of humanitarian assistance, particularly in areas of unrest or where large minority populations, such as the Muslim Rohingya, reside. Debate in the UN Security Council revolved around whether the Myanmar government response to the crisis justified invoking R2P. French Foreign Minister, Bernard Kouchner, said that Myanmar's reaction amounted to a crime against humanity and he attempted to rally Security Council support for more forceful action to deliver aid without the consent of the government.[27] However, Security Council members (China, Indonesia, and Vietnam) took the position that R2P did not apply to natural disaster and, with China's veto, the French proposal went nowhere.[28] When France proposed invoking R2P publicly, the position of the council's Southeast Asian member states actually hardened.[29] These states, as well as many observers, thought the situation fell short of what was necessary to justify military action.[30] France's diplomacy in this case demonstrates that sometimes the best approach is not to invoke formal principles or assign blame.

Libya. Anti-government street protests in 2011, inspired by the "Arab Spring" which began in Tunisia and then moved to Egypt in 2010, led to a brutal crackdown by then Libyan President Muammar Gaddafi. Opposition forces organized and militarized, and Libya quickly descended into a civil war. When the opposition took control of Benghazi, Gaddafi's forces besieged the city threatening to annihilate those who opposed him. The international response was to condemn the violence and the Security Council, under Chapter VII, instituted an arms embargo, targeted travel bans, and an asset freeze. The situation was also referred to the ICC. The violence continued to escalate, and after considerable quiet diplomacy to obtain the necessary abstentions from Russia and China, the Security Council passed Resolution 1973 which authorized a no-fly zone and "all necessary measures" to protect civilians. The resolution also prohibited a foreign occupation force, a measure necessary to prevent vetoes from Russia and China. Nonpermanent members Germany, Brazil, and India also abstained from the resolution and warned against the unintended consequences of armed intervention.[31] Gaddafi ignored the resolution, escalated the violence, and NATO (US, British, and French forces) launched air attacks against Libyan government forces threatening civilians.

The NATO campaign lasted seven months, much longer than originally anticipated. It also involved much more than the use of military force to create the no-fly zone and protect civilians. NATO provided intelligence to the opposition and attacked Libyan forces in the field. Also, British and American special forces on the ground helped organize and eventually complemented opposition forces. Gaddafi was forced from power and went into hiding. He was eventually captured (and brutally sodomized and murdered) by opposition forces. Russia and China were angered by what they saw as a contortion of Resolution 1973 and publicly expressed concern that R2P was being interpreted an excuse for as regime change. Western states saw Gaddafi's downfall as a logical consequence of his unwillingness to stop attacking civilians.

After the formal end of NATO military operations in Libya, Brazil (a nonpermanent member of the Security Council) proposed modifying R2P to mean responsibility *while* protecting (RWP). Brazil's reformulation called for stricter criteria to justify intervention and more council oversight of military operations. It is unclear whether RWP is gaining much diplomatic traction as its merits are still being debated at the UN. What is clear is that the Libyan application of R2P continues to cloud diplomatic efforts to respond to humanitarian crises in other parts of the world.

The postscript for Libya is still being written. The current government is unstable and Islamic militants dominate the political and military landscape. The ICC investigations have floundered and the US consulate in Benghazi was attacked by militants, killing the US ambassador who had taken refuge there. Violence and terrorist attacks remain a part of everyday life and, in 2014, Americans were advised to leave Libya. An editorial in the *Guardian* captures disparity between R2P theory and practice:

> The UN-authorised air campaign in 2011 is often lauded as a shining example of successful foreign intervention. Sure, the initial mandate – which was simply to protect civilians – was exceeded by nations who had only recently been selling arms to Muammar Gaddafi, and the bombing evolved into regime-change despite Russia's protests. But with a murderous thug ejected from power, who could object?
>
> Today's Libya is overrun by militias and faces a deteriorating human rights situation, mounting chaos that is infecting other countries, growing internal splits, and even the threat of civil war. Only occasionally does this growing crisis creep into the headlines: like when an oil tanker is seized by rebellious militia; or when a British oil worker is shot dead while having a picnic; or when the country's prime minister is kidnapped.
>
> According to Amnesty International, the "mounting curbs on freedom of expression are threatening the rights Libyans sought to gain". A repressive Gaddafi-era

law has been amended to criminalise any insults to officials or the general national congress (the interim parliament). One journalist, Amara al-Khattabi, was put on trial for alleging corruption among judges. Satellite television stations deemed critical of the authorities have been banned, one station has been attacked with rocket-propelled grenades, and journalists have been assassinated.

Some human rights abuses began in the tumultuous days that followed Gaddafi's removal, and were ignored by the west. Ever since the fall of his dictatorship, there have been stories of black Libyans being treated en masse as Gaddafi loyalists and attacked. In a savage act of collective punishment, 35,000 people were driven out of Tawergha in retaliation for the brutal siege of the anti-Gaddafi stronghold of Misrata. The town was trashed and its inhabitants have been left in what human rights organisations are calling "deplorable conditions" in a Tripoli refugee camp. Such forced removals continue elsewhere. Thousands have been arbitrarily detained without any pretence of due process; and judges, prosecutors, lawyers and witnesses have been attacked or even killed. Libya's first post-Gaddafi prosecutor general, Abdulaziz Al-Hassadi, was assassinated in the town of Derna last month.[32]

For R2P to become institutionalized, intervention must improve human rights and humanitarian situations in sustainable ways, not just confront an immediate threat. Libya validates the concerns of R2P critics and those who abstained from Resolution 1973 because of the unintended consequences associated with armed intervention for humanitarian purposes.

Syria. In March 2011, Syria also experienced an Arab Spring crisis. Events in Libya and Egypt influenced and continue to shape human rights and humanitarian diplomacy in Syria. The Syrian government, under Bashar al-Assad, responded to mass demonstrations by arresting hundreds and brutalizing the protesters. Hardly known for its stellar human rights record, Syria's response was predictable. Assad still enjoyed considerable domestic support, but unlike Libya, Syria's diversity made it more difficult for the opposition to speak with one voice. Matters were made worse because opposition and militia groups also engaged in violence against civilians. The Security Council was paralyzed and efforts to halt the violence or formally support regional plans were vetoed by Russia and China.

The violence continued and Syria slid into a full-fledged civil war that continues today with more than 250,000 killed and at least two million internally displaced. Millions more have fled to other countries. In August 2013, chemical weapons were used in the conflict, prompting renewed calls for intervention, with or without Security Council authorization. Drafts of Security Council resolutions authorizing military intervention were rejected by Russia and China. Russian President Vladimir Putin resorted to unusual public diplomacy by publishing a *New York Times* editorial to caution the United States and its allies from using military force when it appeared that course of action was likely (see Chapter 2). The United States ultimately decided against military action. At the Security Council, China and Russia crafted a plan to remove chemicals weapons from Syria under the international oversight of the

Organization for the Prohibition of Chemical Weapons (OPCW) and the UN. While the violence continues almost unabated, the UN confirmed in June 2014 that chemical weapons had been removed from Syria.[33]

The norm of R2P is off to a rough start especially in terms of influencing multilateral human rights and humanitarian diplomacy in the Security Council. However, the council has always had difficulty in acting in a collective manner, especially when it comes to authorizing military force under any circumstances. This is why innovations in preventative diplomacy such as peacekeeping have come about. R2P will remain part of the diplomatic conversation; however, the focus will likely be on preventing or rebuilding, and less on responding.

The Security Council and courts. Another way the Security Council has responded to gross violations of international human rights and humanitarian law in the post-Cold War era has been to authorize the creation of **ad hoc international criminal tribunals** and **hybrid courts**. These courts were created for a specific situation and for a limited time. The Security Council sought to use legal remedies to complement other measures in complex conflict situations. Similar to the evolution of peacekeeping, the nature, mandate, and operation of criminal courts have been adapted to try to compensate for perceived weaknesses of predecessors. The ICTY and the ICTR were the first legal ventures authorized by the Security Council, and while they made many advancements in international criminal law, they also have been criticized for being biased, expensive, and cumbersome.

The limited mandates of the ad hoc tribunals led many states and civil society actors to establish a permanent criminal court with broad jurisdiction. The ICC is independent of the UN, but loosely associated with it. Beginning in 2004 with efforts to manage the humanitarian crisis in the Darfur region of Sudan, the Security Council has referred situations to the ICC to pressure states to change their policies. Even states that reject the court's jurisdiction voted for the referral. The ICC eventually indicted Sudanese President Omar el-Bashir for crimes against humanity and genocide. It also indicted Kenya's President Uhuru Kenyatta for crimes against humanity. States on the council are not only seeking justice but they are also using the courts as a potential "stick" to deter others from engaging in similar crimes.

A central weakness of international criminal courts and tribunals is that justice is imposed from outside, usually by the strong against the weak. It challenges state sovereignty and can lack legitimacy, especially when domestic and international law are in conflict. To address this, the Security Council has also authorized the creation of hybrid courts, which blend both international and domestic law. Hybrid courts are staffed by local judges and lawyers, as well as international jurists and legal experts. Hybrid courts have the advantages of holding trials close to where crimes were committed and helping local communities develop a culture of legalism. The courts have more legitimacy and assist with post-conflict reconciliation. The Security Council has authorized hybrid courts for Sierra Leone, Lebanon, and Cambodia. Decisions to create international and hybrid courts, or to refer situations to the ICC, are the result of extensive quiet diplomacy among council member states, who know that, once created, these courts need to be funded and politically supported. States need to help with fact-finding, formal investigations, executing warrants, arresting those indicted, and protecting witnesses. Courts also need state and IGO cooperation with incarcerating those convicted of crimes.

The Security Council's diplomatic record on behalf of human rights and humanitarian principles is, at best, mixed, but it has acted and continues to find politically acceptable ways of promoting and protecting human rights and humanitarian principles. Though its multilateral efforts have met with varying degrees of success and criticism, the Security Council has innovated peacekeeping, linked international peace and security to the protection of human rights and humanitarian principles, authorized forceful interventions, invoked R2P, created international and hybrid criminal courts, and referred situations to the ICC.

The United Nations General Assembly

The plenary body of the UN is the General Assembly and it is currently comprised of 193 member states. Since member states have their representatives attend the assembly, the human rights and humanitarian diplomacy of the assembly is multilateral in nature. The Security Council often speaks for the "international community," but the General Assembly is much more representative of the international community of states. The UN Charter spells many roles including oversight of the UN bureaucracy and deliberating and passing resolutions (nonbinding) on issues arising under the charter, including human rights and humanitarian situations. Decisions are taken through majority rule, so states from the Global South can exercise their numerical muscle and be active diplomatically in the General Assembly to promote human rights and humanitarian principles.

The Cold War decolonization process allowed states from the Global South to exercise their new-found majority in the assembly to promote collective human rights such as the freedom from colonialism and self-determination. In 1962, the General Assembly condemned apartheid in South Africa, called for a voluntary boycott, and established the UN Special Committee on Apartheid.[34] It would go on to condemn the brutal white racist rule until apartheid formally ended in 1994. The General Assembly also repeatedly condemned the human rights situation in Israeli-occupied territories. The Cold War record of human rights and humanitarian diplomacy of the assembly mostly centered on the policies of Israel and South Africa; however, member states also pursued a more equitable distribution of wealth and the right to economic development. This diplomatic push culminated in the call for a New International Economic Order in 1974 and the recognition of development as a human right in 1986.[35] These initiatives did not result in significant reforms but indicated that the Global South saw poverty and inequality as a threat to human rights and sought to define human rights more broadly.

Since the end of the Cold War, the General Assembly routinely passes resolutions calling attention to, or condemning, human rights violations occurring within states. Approximately one-third of its resolutions annually pertain to human rights.[36] This is further evidence of a shift in norms. Diplomatic discussion of human rights is now a routine part of international relations. The General Assembly also allows the "international community" of states to express its sentiment, which is important because division among the P-5 often means the Security Council is unable to act or speak with a unified voice. For example, while the Security Council is at an impasse on Syria, the General Assembly has overwhelmingly condemned the violence and called for al-Assad to step down.

The General Assembly is also responsible for initiating studies and making recommendations promoting the progressive development of international law. As such, the General Assembly oversees and assists with the formulation of international law. It often passes "declarations" which are a form of soft law that can lead to the hard law codified in treaties. The General Assembly "approves" human rights treaties, although their approval does not mean the treaties become formal international law. Rather, it means that the drafts have UN approval and the treaties are open for state signatures. Once a treaty has the requisite number of signatories, it enters into force, becoming law. Many human rights treaties have committees of independent experts known as monitoring bodies that also report to the General Assembly.

Another important role for the General Assembly is to provide a forum for smaller states to voice their preferences and concerns relating to human rights and humanitarian principles. The call for a New International Economic Order is a Cold War example. More recently, R2P has been the focus of assembly consideration and informal debate. Since R2P was adopted at the 2005 UN Summit, states in the assembly gather periodically to discuss the implementation of R2P. While many developing states laud the goals of R2P, they are wary of its selective implementation. In the words of Miguel d'Escoto Brockman, the president of the General Assembly and representative of Nicaragua, during the Opening of the Thematic Dialogue in 2009:

> So why do many of us hesitate to embrace this doctrine and its aspirations? Certainly it is not out of indifference to the plight of many who suffer and who may yet be caused to suffer at the hands of their own governments. Recent and painful memories related to the legacy of colonialism, give developing countries strong reasons to fear that laudable motives can end-up being misused, once more, to justify arbitrary and selective interventions against the weakest states. We must take into account the prevailing lack of trust from most of the developing countries when it comes to the use of force for humanitarian reasons.[37]

The General Assembly is more than a debating society. It is an important forum for multilateral human rights and humanitarian diplomacy where every member state gets one vote and an equal opportunity to promote their perspective. Like powerful states, other states in the General Assembly can exhibit a certain selectivity in the kind of human rights they promote or situation they wish to highlight. The General

Assembly is quick to condemn human rights violations committed by Israel but not gross violations of rights in other Middle Eastern states. It passed a resolution that equated Zionism with racism and even though this resolution was rescinded in 1991, the assembly's continued disproportionate focus on Israel weakens its credibility as an unbiased advocate of human rights and humanitarian principles.[38] Assembly members also are quick to question the motives of states wishing to forcibly implement R2P while conveniently overlooking the gross violations of human rights and humanitarian law occurring within targeted states. This is the nature of multilateral human rights and humanitarian diplomacy.

The United Nations Human Rights Council

The General Assembly is responsible for the creation of the HRC (in 2006) and for electing the council's forty-seven members. Before addressing the multilateral human rights diplomacy through the Human Rights Council, a discussion of its predecessor, the **Commission on Human Rights** (1946–2006) is necessary. Originally, human rights at the UN revolved around the Commission on Human Rights and its legacy encapsulates the politics of multilateral human rights diplomacy at the UN in its first sixty years. The commission was a fifty-three-member body that was elected by the Economic and Social Council (ECOSOC), the UN organ responsible for promoting economic and social cooperation in the interrelated fields of economic development, human rights, and social welfare. The role of the commission, in large part, involved setting human rights standards. It served as the technical drafting body for UDHR and the ICCPR and ICESCR. Standard-setting is necessary for building the necessary international consensus on definition and for moving international human rights law forward. The commission, however, was not particularly interested in protecting human rights. Private complaints were buried and the council did its best not to offend states.[39]

The deference to states soon gave way to the Commission on Human Rights being used as a foreign policy tool by states in the East–West or the North–South conflict. When the commission did try to move toward protecting human rights, it was often for political reasons. The politicization of the commission, coupled with the double standards and inconsistencies in state policies, eventually led to it being discredited. Still, even though politicized and discredited, the commission did investigate those states engaged in gross violations of human rights.[40] It also advanced human rights by creating special and thematic procedures which allowed for working groups and increased cooperation with NGOs. Special rapporteurs and independent commissions were created to investigate specific human rights issues such as torture, religious discrimination, and forced disappearances. Sidebar 4.1 by Special Rapporteur Sergio Pinheiro explains why bodies such as the Commission on Human Rights will always be politicized. Politics is about promoting certain values and preferences, often at the expense of other values and preferences.

Sidebar 4.1 Special Rapporteur Paulo Sergio Pinheiro, the politicization of the CHR (Commission on Human Rights) and afterwards[41]

Many civil society organizations, since the CHR's 58th session in spring 2002, have intensely criticized the growing politicisation of the appointment process, in which the expertise of candidates sometimes appears to be secondary to their political acceptability. In a certain way it would be naïf to expect that hyper-politicised bodies such as the CHR and the HRC will renounce political criteria. The depoliticisation is a dream that will never be fulfilled in a system of states because, as Jeroen Gutter reminded us, "the implementation of human rights is not a politically neutral process that can be approached in an entirely legalistic, bureaucratic and scientific (rational) manner." We should remind ourselves that what happens with the implementation of human rights is permanently subjected to the limitations and existing contradictions of the current state of the world order and the present development of international relations which prevail in UN bodies. It is really a midsummer night's dream to expect that the new HRC room can be a spaceship – under that very appropriate new colorful cavernous ceiling painting featuring hundreds of hanging icicles – floating above reality full of righteous saviours rescuing victims of abuse, freed from politics and hypocrisy, moved by the sense of ethics.

During the last decade of the CHR it was common to see some member states accusing others that they were politicising the agenda and the debates in the commission. But invoking politisation has become a way to express disapproval without really saying what the speakers really have in mind. Considering that the HRC as well as the CHR is a multilateral body constituted by representatives of states which continue to protect their interests, the political nature of the HRC is an essential element for its functioning. In fact this reference to politicisation was not a rigorous interpretation of several processes much more complexes which were taking place inside the CHR and continue to prevail in the HRC. As the International Service for Human Rights once has suggested what has happened was what could be called a "political hijacking" of the agenda of the commission to promote their agendas or to protect their interests. In fact the commission was politicised immediately after its creation in 1946 and, particularly in the 1970s and 1980s, profoundly divided between the Western and socialist blocs. Since those times a growing abyss between the developed and developing countries became evident.

It would be naive to expect that this political behaviour of the member states would just change because the format of the body has been changed. We can see, observing the votes held in the HRC, that this division has survived and sometimes has become as crystallized or more than in the CHR. There is a generalised suspicion from the countries of the southern hemisphere towards the Western and European countries vis-à-vis any initiative from the regional Western and Others Group, WEOG, at the UN.

> Observing the behaviour of the members of the HRC, *plus ça change plus c'est la même chose* (the more things change the more they stay the same). I think that the division between the North and South continues to prevail in the very defensive practices of some regional groups *vis-à-vis* other groups.

Toward the end of its institutional life, the commission became even more politicized when states with exceptionally poor human rights records, such as Libya, Cuba, Zimbabwe, Sudan, and Saudi Arabia were elected to the commission. The commission had become a vehicle to shield member states and other rights-abusers form international criticism, not a credible advocate for international human rights and humanitarian principles.

At the 2005 World Summit, the member states of the UN took decisive action and agreed to abolish the Commission on Human Rights and create the HRC. At this time, the United States, under the George W. Bush Administration, had a very contentious relationship with the UN and its diplomacy reflected this. The 2003 decision of the US to invade Iraq without Security Council authorization was a disaster for US multilateral diplomacy. The deteriorating security situation in Iraq, the US mistreatment and abuse of Iraqi prisoners at the Abu Ghraib prison, the revelation of secret CIA detention camps, and the allegations of torture (termed by the administration as "enhanced interrogation techniques") all worked against any meaningful US leadership on human rights or humanitarian affairs.

Bush also appointed UN-skeptic John Bolton to be the US ambassador to the UN. Bolton's diplomatic skills, at best, were poor and he alienated even traditional US allies. Bolton opposed almost all reforms being proposed at the 2005 Summit, including the HRC. The proposed reforms were the product of years of preparatory work by states, UN officials, and civil society actors, including a high level panel of eminent persons that had been appointed by Secretary-General Kofi Annan. In spite of US intransigence and obstruction, member states did manage to agree to empower the General Assembly to create the HRC and left it to the General Assembly to decide on its mandate, membership, and procedures.

Not surprisingly, the HRC got off to a rocky start. The HRC differs from its predecessor in that election of the forty-seven council members (instead of fifty-three) was by a majority vote of the General Assembly rather than by the much smaller ECOSOC. Each region is allotted a certain number of seats to ensure a global, well-rounded representation. The United States opted not to stand for election in part because it wanted council members to be elected by a two-thirds majority. Critics point out that the Bush Administration was also worried the United States could not even muster a simple majority to get elected. The first round of HRC elections resulted in Algeria, China, Pakistan, Saudi Arabia, and Cuba joining the HRC as members. During its first year of operation, the HRC singled out only Israel for rebuke while Sudan, China, Zimbabwe, and Myanmar escaped serious scrutiny and formal criticism.

The HRC continued its disproportionate focus on Israel, criticizing Israeli policies in occupied territories fifteen times by 2008.[42] It did manage to criticize Myanmar once for its bloody crackdown on monks and protesters. President Barack Obama shifted the US stance on the HRC and the United States was elected in 2009. The HRC has since condemned violence in Libya and suspended its membership in the HRC. The gross violations of human rights in Syria, North Korea, and Iraq have been scrutinized and condemned and Sudan withdrew its candidacy for a HRC seat under intense diplomatic pressure.

While not entirely living up to its promise, the HRC does seem to be taking its responsibilities more seriously. This is due, in part, to the use of **Universal Periodic Review (UPR)** as a tool for challenging states to improve their own records. The UPR is a staggered peer review process where all 193 UN members report on the status of their domestic human rights and explain how they are meeting their obligations under international human rights law. As part of the UN reform process that led to the creation of the HRC, the UPR process also allows NGOs and other stakeholders, such as national human rights bodies, to contribute to the process by submitting information through a formalized process. The HRC is responsible for conducting the reviews and all states elected to the HRC have to undergo UPR during their term. The hope was that the UPR requirement would discourage states with demonstrably poor records from seeking a seat on the council and prevent the council from being too selective in terms of calling out certain states. The jury is still out as to whether UPR is an effective diplomatic tool encouraging states to improve their records. Analyses of the first full UPR cycle (2007–11) are just beginning to be published and any meaningful comparative data are scant because the HRC is only midterm during the second cycle (2012–14).

The politicization of multilateral human rights bodies seems to be inevitable since states are the embodiment of politics and, when they comprise multilateral bodies such as the HRC, choices and outcomes are political. States seem to recognize this and it is encouraging that the HRC has continued the use of special procedures (independent experts acting in their own personal capacity) to investigate, address, and report on human rights and humanitarian principles either thematically or in a country-specific context. Examples of special procedures include the use of special rapporteurs and independent commissions of inquiry (discussed in Chapter 5). By utilizing independent human rights experts who do not represent states, a more objective assessment of a situation can be made.

The regional multilateral architecture

Multilateral approaches to promoting and protecting international human rights and humanitarian principles has also occurred regionally. Regional bodies and law not only articulate rights and duties, but also establish commissions and courts to oversee and implement the law. Regional human rights bodies tend to be narrow in terms of formal state participation and are likely to employ independent experts. However, this does not necessarily mean they are more effective because without meaningful state commitment, promotion and protection of human rights and humanitarian principles are superficial at best. The regional multilateral human rights architecture generally follows the same blueprint: An IGO endorses and supervises the development of a regional human rights convention (and related laws). That law usually calls for a human rights commission (comprised of human rights experts) to administratively investigate complaints and a court to issue advisory opinions and adjudicate disputes arising under the law. While impressive on paper, not all states within a region are party to the treaty. Moreover, many commissions are not allowed to receive individual complaints and many states do not accept the jurisdiction of the regional court. As a result, human rights protection on a regional basis is uneven and, unfortunately, seems to be most effective in areas where there are already high levels of respect for human rights.

Europe. The multilateral human rights protection in Europe consists of overlapping organizations involving the **Council of Europe**, the **Organization** (once Conference) **for Cooperation and Security in Europe (OSCE)**, and the **EU**. Europe has the most comprehensive and effective regional human rights framework. It was developed by sovereign states and it has contributed to the integration of Europe. The evolution of the European human rights regime is noteworthy because European states have, over time, authorized relatively independent bodies to protect human rights regionally. The European project began with the creation of the Council of Europe in 1949 to promote cooperation in Western Europe. Initially, only ten states comprised the Council of Europe but it has since grown to include forty-seven members. The Council of Europe oversaw the creation of the **European Convention on Human Rights and Fundamental Freedoms** (1950) with its five additional protocols. The convention established a commission (now defunct) and the **European Court on Human Rights**. The court is authorized to issue binding judgments regarding state policies and individuals are allowed to petition the court.

The OSCE/CSCE was responsible for the breakthrough in human rights protection during the Cold War (see Chapter 2) and made progress on diplomatically protecting minorities during the post-Cold War instability. The OCSE remains important because its fifty-seven member states include Russia and Russian-allied states, and thus, is the preferred forum for resolving regional disputes involving these states. The central role of OSCE monitors and officials in mediating the current crisis in Ukraine demonstrates its continued relevance.

The twenty-eight-member EU has made the European Convention of Human Rights and Fundamental Freedoms the keystone treaty for rights in Europe and joining the EU means internalizing the treaty's provisions. The EU also created the European Court of Justice which is empowered to decide human rights cases alongside European Court of Human Rights. The defining feature of European human rights protection is that for EU citizens international human rights are the law of the land. This makes protection largely a technical issue and less of a political one. Other regions have not been as effective in institutionalizing human rights.

The Americas. The Americas have several regional organizations but most prominent is the **Organization of American States (OAS)**, a thirty-five-member IGO. The OAS also has a regional convention, commission, and court. Regional human rights are organized around the **American Declaration on the Rights and Duties of Man** (1948) and the **American Convention of Human Rights** (1969). The **InterAmerican Commission on Human Rights** was created in 1959 and it is charged with investigating human rights situations, but its decisions and findings are usually ignored. The **InterAmerican Court of Human Rights**, which was created in 1969 but did not become operational until 1980, may issue binding decisions regarding state policy for states that have agreed to give the court jurisdiction. Very few states have and even those that have, know that the court is reluctant to proceed with cases without their consent. Moreover, only states or the commission can present cases. Individuals do not have the right of private petition.

Several factors work against effective regional human rights protection in the Americas. First, many states privilege respect for state sovereignty, especially given the history of US political and military interventions in the region. Second, US exceptionalism means it has not been able to lead on human rights through its example. The United States has signed but not ratified the convention and it has not consented to the jurisdiction of the court. Third, the domestic human rights records of many OAS states are poor and a few states have even withdrawn from the treaty. Venezuela's denunciation of the convention in 2012 was a step backward in the region's human rights protection.

Africa and the Middle East. The states of Africa and the Middle East have established several regional or thematic IGOs including the **African Union (AU)** (and its predecessor the Organization of African Unity); the **League of Arab States** (comprising North African and Middle Eastern Arab States), and the **Organization of Islamic Cooperation** (OIC) (an association of Islamic states). While human rights are mentioned as part their mandates, their role in promoting and protecting international human rights is, at best, complicated. The AU human rights framework began under the auspices of the Organization of African Unity but it is not well developed largely because it is under-resourced and it has very little state political will supporting it.[43] The central human rights convention is the **African Charter on Human and Peoples' Rights** (Banjul Charter) which entered into force in 1986 and it is noteworthy because it includes collective rights such as self-determination and rights to natural resources. The Banjul Charter is considered a uniquely African approach to human rights because it reinforces sovereignty and contains collective rights. It calls for a commission but initially not a court.[44] The **African Court on Human and Peoples' Rights** was established in 1998 by the Protocol to the African Charter on Human and Peoples' Rights. The charter, commission, and court became main human rights mechanisms for the region when the AU succeeded the Organization of African Unity in 2002. The fifty-three member states of the AU, beginning in 2008, have streamlined regional judicial bodies by merging the African Court of Justice with the African Court on

Human and Peoples Rights. Initial optimism about better human rights protection in the AU soon gave way to skepticism when in 2014 AU member states decided to give heads of state immunity from war crimes and crimes against humanity prosecutions.[45] African states are experiencing a bit of buyer's remorse having initially supported the creation of the ICC, but then finding themselves as targets of ICC prosecutions with two African heads of state already indicted and other prominent political figures in the dock or under ICC investigation.

The twenty-two-member Arab League is a marginal IGO when it comes to promoting and protecting human rights among Arab states. The organizing regional law is the **Arab Charter on Human Rights** which was first adopted in 1994 but did not enter into force until 2008 after it was revised. The charter created **Arab Human Rights Committee** and, in 2014, Arab League members were considering the creation of a court. The charter has drawn criticism for containing anti-Zionist language, equating Zionism with racism, allowing for the death penalty for children, and not being consistent with international law relating to the rights of women.

Similarly the OIC, a fifty-six-member IGO of Islamic states, embraces a conception of human rights which is different from UN standards. In 1990, the OIC passed the **Cairo Declaration on Human Rights in Islam** and in 2012 created the **Independent Permanent Human Rights Commission**. The Cairo Declaration is problematic because it claims that human rights must be consistent with Sharia Law, which is not particularly protective of the freedom of expression, the rights of religious minorities, or women. Some criminal penalties found in Sharia Law are considered to be cruel and unusual. The OIC and the Arab League have taken strong stances against Western liberal human rights norms. For example, in 2006, a Danish newspaper published a political cartoon that depicted the Prophet Mohammed. The OIC and Arab League spoke out against the newspaper and helped organize protests that eventually became violent and left Danish embassies in flames around the Muslim world.[46] More recently, their member states have sought make the defamation of religion or expressions critical of Islam a form of hate speech and not protected by international human rights law.

Asia. In terms of developing a regional framework for the promotion and protection of human rights, Asia is just beginning. ASEAN is a ten-member state IGO which recently passed the controversial **ASEAN Declaration of Human Rights** (2012). The Declaration is widely criticized by human rights groups and UN officials as being deeply flawed. Besides being inconsistent with existing international standards, it fails to include important individual civil and political rights, like the freedom association. It also creates duties for individuals, raising concerns that if an individual fails to meet their responsibility, it would justify government violations of human rights.[47] ASEAN states also created the **ASEAN Intergovernmental Commission on Human Rights** in 2009, which drafted the ASEAN Declaration, and is working toward deepening human rights within the region. ASEAN is a small IGO and the only one focused on human rights in a very large and diverse area. Important Asian states such as China, Japan, and South Korea are not members of a regional human rights regime.

Conclusion

The proliferation of international human rights and humanitarian organizations and law shows that states care about these issues and are willing to devote a considerable portion of their multilateral diplomacy to defining and implementing human rights and humanitarian principles. The evolution of multilateral human rights and humanitarian diplomacy also demonstrates the states, as the principle duty-bearers under international law, fundamentally disagree about the definition and implementation of rights and principles. They disagree about how human rights and humanitarian principles should be prioritized and what is permissible and impermissible state action on behalf of those rights and principles. The regional architectures reflect the commitment of member states to "universal" rights and principles and that commitment is not particularly deep in many areas of the world. That is why the push and pull of human rights and humanitarian diplomacy is necessary for advancing rights and principles.

Key terms

Multilateral diplomacy, IGO diplomacy, first UN, second UN, third UN, the P-5, peacekeeping, first generation peacekeeping, second generation peacekeeping/peace enforcement, third generation peacekeeping/peacebuilding, Peacebuilding Commission, human security, Resolution 688, The International Criminal Tribunal for the former Yugoslavia (ICTY), Operation Turquoise, *genocidaires*, the International Criminal Tribunal for Rwanda (ICTR), the Independent International Commission on Kosovo, Responsibility to Protect (R2P), the International Commission on Intervention and State Sovereignty (ICISS), 2005 World Summit, preventative diplomacy, ad hoc international criminal tribunals, hybrid courts, Commission on Human Rights, Universal Periodic Review (UPR), Council of Europe, Organization for Cooperation and Security in Europe, EU, European Convention on Human Rights and Fundamental Freedoms, European Court on Human Rights, Organization of American States, American Declaration on the Rights and Duties of Man, InterAmerican Convention of Human Rights, InterAmerican Commission on Human Rights, InterAmerican Court for Human Rights, African Union, League of Arab States, Organization of Islamic Cooperation, African Charter on Human and Peoples' Rights, African Court on Human and Peoples' Rights, Arab Charter on Human Rights, Arab Human Rights Committee, Cairo Declaration on Human Rights in Islam, Independent Permanent Human Rights Commission, ASEAN Declaration of Human Rights, ASEAN Intergovernmental Commission on Human Rights.

> **Discussion questions**
>
> 1. Discuss the differences between IGO diplomacy and multilateral diplomacy.
> 2. Discuss the evolution and the role of UN peacekeeping in the evolution of human rights and humanitarian protection.
> 3. What is R2P and why is it a controversial norm in human rights protection?
> 4. Will multilateral human rights bodies ever become depoliticized?

Notes

1 Margaret P. Karns and Karen A. Mingst, "International Organizations and Diplomacy," in *The Oxford Handbook of Modern Diplomacy*, ed. Andrew F. Cooper, Jorge Heine, and Ramesh Thakur (Oxford: Oxford University Press, 2013), 142.
2 See Thomas G. Weiss, David P. Forsythe, Roger A. Coate, and Kelly-Kate Pease, *The United Nations and Changing World Politics*, 7th edition (Boulder: Westview Press, 2014), 14–15; Thomas G. Weiss, Tatiana Carayannis, and Richard Jolly, "The Third United Nations," *Global Governance*, 15:1 (2009), 123–142.
3 Jack Donnelly, *International Human Rights* (Boulder: Westview Press, 1993), 7–10.
4 Weiss et al., *The United Nations*, 62.
5 This discussion of UN peacekeeping is drawn from Kelly-Kate S. Pease, *International Organizations* (New York: Pearson Publishing, 2012), 118–119.
6 Paul Taylor, "The United Nations and International Organizations," in *The Globalization of World Politics: An Introduction to International Relations*, ed. John Bayliss and Steve Smith (Oxford: Oxford University Press, 1998), 280.
7 John MacKinlay and Jarat Chopra, "Second Generation Multinational Operations," in *The Politics of Global Governance: International Organizations in and Interdependent World*, ed. Paul Diehl (Boulder: Lynne Rienner Press, 1997), 174–200, 175.
8 United Nations Security Council Resolution S/RES/0688 (April 5, 1991).
9 United Nations Security Council Resolution S/RES/0819 (April 16, 1992).
10 The humanitarian impulse to "do something" because of media coverage is part of the "the CNN Effect." See Piers Robinson, *The CNN Effect: The Myth of Media, Foreign Policy and Intervention* (New York: Routledge, 2002).
11 United Nations Security Council Resolution, S/RES/0929 (June 22, 1994).
12 See Fiona Terry, *The Paradox of Humanitarian Action: Condemned to Repeat* (Ithaca: Cornell University Press), 155–215.
13 See International Criminal Tribunal for Rwanda, available at www.unictr.org/en/tribunal; and The ICTR Remembers: 20th Anniversary of the Rwandan Genocide at http://unmict.org/ictr-remembers/.
14 ICTR Remembers: 20th Anniversary of the Rwandan Genocide.
15 Press Release, SC/6659, "Security Council Rejects Demand for Cessation of Use of Force against Federal Republic of Yugoslavia," March 26, 1999, accessed August 29, 2014. www.un.org/News/Press/docs/1999/19990326.sc6659.html.

16 Steven Lee Myers, "Chinese Embassy Bombing: A Wide Net of Blame," *New York Times*, April 17, 2000, accessed August 28, 2014. www.nytimes.com/2000/04/17/world/chinese-embassy-bombing-a-wide-net-of-blame.html.
17 BBC, "Confrontation over Pristina Airport," March 9, 2000, accessed August 29, 2014, http://news.bbc.co.uk/2/hi/europe/671495.stm.
18 See United Nations International Criminal Tribunal for the Former Yugoslavia, *Case Information Sheet: Kosovo, Croatia, and Bosnia. Slobodan Milosevic*, accessed October 15, 2015. www.icty.org/x/cases/slobodan_milosevic/cis/en/cis_milosevic_slobodan_en.pdf.
19 United Nations, "Press Briefing on the Kosovo Commission," *Press Briefing*, October 23, 2000, accessed October 16, 2014. www.un.org/News/briefings/docs/2000/20001023.kosovobrfg.doc.html; also Independent International Commission on Kosovo, *Kosovo Report* (Oxford: Oxford University Press, 2001).
20 Kofi A. Annan, *We the Peoples: The Role of the United Nations in the 21st Century* (New York: United Nations, 2000), accessed October 4, 2015. www.un.org/en/events/pastevents/pdfs/We_The_Peoples.pdf.
21 International Commission on Intervention and State Sovereignty, *The Responsibility to Protect Report* (Ottawa: ICISSS, 2001), XI, accessed October 4, 2015. http://responsibilitytoprotect.org/ICISS%20Report.pdf.
22 United Nations General Assembly, A/RES/601, *2005 World Summit Outcome*, para. 139 (October 24, 2005), accessed October 15, 2014. http://unpan1.un.org/intradoc/groups/public/documents/UN/UNPAN021752.pdf.
23 For an overview, see Thomas G. Weiss, "The Responsibility to Protect (R2P) and Modern Diplomacy," in *The Oxford Handbook of Modern Diplomacy*, ed. Andrew F. Cooper, Jorge Heine, and Ramesh Thakur (Oxford: Oxford University Press, 2013), 763–778.
24 Abdullahi Boru Halakhe, "R2P in Practice: Ethnic Violence, Elections and Atrocity Prevention," *Global Centre for the Responsibility to Protect*, 3, accessed August 27, 2014. www.globalr2p.org/media/files/kenya_occasionalpaper_web.pdf.
25 See the International Coalition for the Responsibility to Protect, "The Crisis in Kenya," accessed October 15, 2014. www.responsibilitytoprotect.org/index.php/crises/crisis-in-kenya.
26 The International Federation of the Red Cross, "Myanmar: Cyclone Nargis 2008 Facts and Figures," May 3, 2011, accessed October 15, 2014. www.ifrc.org/en/news-and-media/news-stories/asia-pacific/myanmar/myanmar-cyclone-nargis-2008-facts-and-figures/.
27 David Rieff, "Humanitarian Vanities," *New York Times Magazine*, June 1, 2008, 13.
28 Alex J. Bellamy and Catherine Drummond, "Southeast Asia: Between Noninterference and Sovereignty as Responsibility," in *The Routledge Handbook of the Responsibility to Protect*, ed. W. Andy Knight and Frazer Ergeton (New York: Routledge, 2012), 245–256, 250.
29 Bellamy and Drummond, "Southeast Asia," 250.
30 Rebecca Barber, "The Responsibility to Protect and the Survivors of Natural Disaster: Cyclone Nargis, a Case Study," *Journal of Conflict and Security Law*, 12:1 (2009), 3–34.
31 Security Council SC/10200, "Security Council Approves Fly Zone, Authorizing 'All Necessary Measures' to Protect Civilians by a Vote of 10 in Favour and with 5 Abstentions," 17 March, 2011, accessed October 4, 2015. www.un.org/News/Press/docs/2011/sc10200.doc.htm.

32 Owen Jones, "Libya is a Disaster We Helped Create: The West Must Take Responsibility,"*Guardian*, March 23, 2014, accessed October 15, 2014. www.theguardian.com/commentisfree/2014/mar/24/libya-disaster-shames-western-interventionists.
33 The UN News Centre, "Removal of Syria's Chemical Weapon's Material Complete, announces OPCW-UN Mission," June 23, 2014, accessed July 2, 2014. www.un.org/apps/news/story.asp?NewsID=48103#.VAkEUY10zmQ.
34 United Nations General Assembly Resolution 1761 (November 6, 1962): A/RES/1761.
35 See United Nations General Assembly Resolution 3201, "Declaration on the Establishment of a New International Economic Order" (May 1, 1974): A/RES/S-6/3201. The right to development was formally recognized by United Nations General Assembly Resolution A/RES/41128 (December 4, 1986).
36 David P. Forsythe, *Human Rights in International Relations* (Cambridge: Cambridge University Press, 2000), 66.
37 "At the Opening of the Thematic Dialogue of the General Assembly on the Responsibility to Protect," July 23, 2009, accessed August 15, 2014. www.un.org/ga/president/63/statements/openingr2p230709.shtml.
38 United Nations General Assembly Resolution 3379 (November 10, 1975): A/RES/3379.
39 Weiss *et al.*, *The United Nations*, 210.
40 James H. Lebovic and Eric Voeten, "The Politics of Shame," *International Studies Quarterly*, 50:4 (2006), 861–888.
41 Excerpt from Paulo Sergio Pinheiro, "Being a Special Rapporteur: A Delicate Balancing Act," *International Journal of Human Rights*, 15 (2011), 168–169. Reprinted with permission from Taylor and Francis Group.
42 Weiss *et al.*, *The United Nations*, 213.
43 Philip Alston and Ryan Goodman, *International Human Rights: The Successor to International Human Rights in Context: Law, Politics and Morals* (Oxford: Oxford University Press, 2013), 1025.
44 David P. Forsythe, *Human Rights in International Relations*, 2nd edition (Cambridge: Cambridge University Press, 2006), 146.
45 Mike Pflantz, "African Union Leaders Give Themselves Immunity from War Crimes Prosecution," *Telegraph*, July 2, 2014, accessed September 13, 2014. http://www.telegraph.co.uk/news/worldnews/africaandindianocean/10940047/African-leaders-vote-to-give-themselves-immunity-from-war-crimes-prosecutions.
46 Kelly-Kate Pease, *International Organization*, 5th edition (New York: Pearson, 2012), 33.
47 Human Rights Watch, "Civil Society Denounces Adoption of Flawed ASEAN Human Rights Declaration," accessed October 1, 2014. www.hrw.org/news/2012/11/19/civil-society-denounces-adoption-flawed-asean-human-rights-declaration.

5
IGO diplomacy and the international civil service

Complementing, and often conflicting with, multilateral human rights and humanitarian diplomacy is **IGO diplomacy**. Officials from IGOs also engage in diplomatic activities designed to: galvanize international attention; educate, mobilize, and pressure states; provide expertise; and coordinate the human rights and humanitarian activities of states, NGOs, and other IGOs. IGO diplomacy focuses on the **international civil service** that consists of agencies and their employees who are, for the most part, independent of states. This means that officials are not state representatives and do not take their instructions from a specific government. At the same time, the agencies they work for are dependent on states for financing, logistics, and sometimes even protection.

Like most bureaucracies, the international civil service, often referred to as the **secretariat**, is hierarchically structured. Individuals are hired for their expertise and promoted because of merit (although some patronage does exist). International civil servants are expected to exude a neutral competence and put the agency's mission or mandate first. At the nexus between member states and the international civil service are high-ranking IGO officials who, directly or indirectly, report to a secretary-general. These officials cannot run afoul of states and their staff must recognize the delicate and ever-changing balance between state interests and agency mandates. This chapter examines IGO diplomacy by looking at how high-ranking and lower level international civil servants seek to promote and protect international human rights and humanitarian principles by bargaining and negotiating with states, as well as non-state actors.

The United Nations Secretary-General

The United Nations Secretary-General is the chief diplomat of the UN and head of the UN secretariat. The secretary-general is elected to a five-year, renewable term where the Security Council makes a recommendation to the General Assembly which then must approve the nominee with a two-thirds majority. Informally, candidates for secretary-general cannot be nationals of one of the P-5. Yet, they must be acceptable to the P-5 and are chosen on a rotational regional basis. The position invariably involves pleasing the more powerful states, while not appearing to be an extension of those states. Regardless of values, goals, and good intentions, the secretary-general cannot be effective if they run afoul of important states. As a result, once assuming the office, most secretaries-general engage in quiet diplomacy, or use their "**good offices**," to try to resolve human rights and humanitarian situations. They must be more public servant than independent actor and leave the more public human rights and humanitarian diplomacy to subordinates, member states, and NGOs. Early secretaries-general did not publicly, or in any meaningful way, promote or demonstrate a commitment to international human rights.[1] If they did, it was because human rights or humanitarian principles were directly linked to security situations or peacekeeping operations.

Beginning with UN Secretary-General **Boutros Boutros-Ghali** (1992–96) and his groundbreaking *An Agenda for Peace* (1992), human rights were explicitly linked to positive peace. Actively promoting and respecting human rights and humanitarian principles become a central UN strategy for developing friendly relations among states and avoiding violent conflict. More notably, Boutros-Ghali was able to move member states of the General Assembly to create the OHCHR to better coordinate UN human rights activities. The OHCHR was perhaps the most important outcome of the Vienna World Conference on Human Rights and actualizing the OHCHR required diplomatic compromise. The vast majority of developing countries had long resisted its creation because of fears it would be biased toward Western notions of political and civil rights; however, when Western countries moved toward recognizing the human right to development, the necessary consensus was reached to enable the creation of the OHCHR.[2] Boutros-Ghali eventually fell out of favor with states, especially the United States, for expanding the mandate of peacekeeping operations in Bosnia on his own authority. States began to withhold peacekeeping contributions and that nearly bankrupted the UN. The United States, under the Clinton Administration, effectively vetoed Boutros-Ghali's second term.[3]

Secretary-General **Kofi Annan** was the first to make human rights and humanitarianism top priorities for the office. He assumed office in 1997 but his prior position was that of head of UN peacekeeping, which included overseeing the disastrous missions in Rwanda and Bosnia. As such, he was keenly aware of the human costs of Security Council paralysis and the consequences of failing to take meaningful action to back up strong diplomatic words. He also was aware that the existing "standard operating procedures" of UN diplomacy were contributing to the inability of the UN to confront genocide and gross violations of human rights. Trying not to offend governments committing genocide was part of the problem, not necessarily part of the solution.

Annan was instrumental in developing of the evolving norms of human security and R2P. It was Annan who appointed the International Commission on Intervention and Sovereignty in 2001, which coined the phrase "responsibility to protect" and negotiated the norm's adoption at the 2005 World Summit. He also appointed the High Level Panel on Threats, Challenges and Change which in 2004 produced the groundbreaking *A More Secure World: Our Shared Responsibility*.[4] This report provided key recommendations for UN reform, including the creation of the HRC and the Peacebuilding

Commission. Annan articulated the **"human-rights based"** approach in *In Larger Freedom: Toward Security, Development and Human Rights for All*.[5] Implementing a human-rights based approach generally centers on building the capacity of states, organizations, and individuals to actualize and advance human rights. Annan asked that all UN agencies mainstream human rights in their programs and activities.

Relatedly, Annan was also central to organizing the private, for-profit sector as partners in promoting human rights. Under the moniker, **Global Compact**, the UN called upon corporations to embrace universal principles and consider their responsibility to their employees and the community.[6] Annan recognized that businesses and business practices can threaten (or enhance) the enjoyment of international human rights and that companies need to be educated and prodded to respect human rights. At some point, businesses might actually become advocates for human rights and humanitarian principles, not just in their philanthropy, but in their essential operations. Annan's overtures to the private, for-profit sector and the Global Compact has coalesced around the norm of CSR, which encourages companies to mainstream human rights in their operations. Annan's commitment to international human rights and humanitarian principles placed him at the forefront of human rights and humanitarian diplomacy at the UN. Upon leaving office, he has continued to serve as an important diplomat for human rights informally in his personal capacity and formally as a special envoy for different IGOs trying to address humanitarian needs in complex emergencies.

Whether Annan's tenure sets a lasting precedent for future secretaries-general remains to be seen. Annan's successor, **Ban Ki-moon**, has kept a lower profile on human rights and to many human rights activists, he has been somewhat of a disappointment. He did not oppose or criticize the execution of Saddam Hussein, stating that "the issue of the capital punishment is for each and every member state to decide."[7] This was especially discouraging given the "second" UN's long-standing policy of opposing the death penalty. Since then, however, Secretary-General Ban has been publicly critical of human rights violations in places like Syria, Sudan, Kenya, and Libya. Notable diplomatic accomplishments include getting Sudan to consent to a large UN peacekeeping mission in Darfur, which has saved thousands of lives, and for coordinating the humanitarian response to the crisis in Cote d'Ivoire. Ban's low-key quiet diplomacy is a stark departure from Annan's more public profile; however, member states appear to prefer it. Ban was elected to a second term in 2012.

The United Nations High Commissioner for Human Rights

The position of **United Nations High Commissioner for Human Rights** was created in 1993 and is the official head of the OHCHR. The launch of any new agency or institution within an existing larger framework is always beset with problems related to defining responsibility centers and reporting lines. When the OHCHR was created, its mandate was ill-defined and vague; and it was uncertain what authority it had in promoting human rights vis-à-vis other UN human rights and humanitarian agencies and states.[8] Hence, initial High Commissioners were formative in shaping the OHCHR and had a defining impact in the evolution of human rights protection at the UN.

Formally speaking, the selection of the UN High Commissioner for Human Rights is straightforward: The UN Secretary-General nominates an individual who has a proven track record promoting human rights, strong diplomatic skills, and a global reputation. Then, the General Assembly approves the appointment through a majority vote. However, other criteria and qualifications are less clear and more fluid. Informally, candidates must be acceptable to important member states (who can pressure the secretary-general regarding appointments and reappointments). Candidates must also be willing to keep OHCHR operations in-line with other UN priorities set by the secretary-general. Increasingly, finding a suitable candidate also involves soliciting input from civil society, which has decried the lack of transparency in the selection process.[9] Many human rights NGOs continue to express concern that political considerations are too determinative in the selection process. Needless to say, the selection of a candidate requires extensive behind-the-scenes consultations and informal diplomacy.

Constraints are imposed on the high commissioner by a number of different actors, including the secretary-general and member states, all of whom may have conflicting agendas. Member states often lack consensus regarding human rights priorities and are therefore unable or unwilling to provide the funding to implement human rights strategies. In addition, states dislike public shaming. Even if they could agree with human rights norms, they are generally not enthusiastic about the possibility of being publicly criticized.[10] The high commissioner must find the appropriate diplomatic balance to pursue the protection of human rights and set the human rights agenda against the backdrop of these political pressures.

Each high commissioner has had a different diplomatic style and many have left under a diplomatic cloud. Secretary-General Boutros Boutros-Ghali appointed the first high commissioner, **Jose Ayala-Lasso**, in 1994. Ayala-Lasso preferred the use of quiet diplomacy and his style alleviated the fears of many member states, particularly from the Global South, that they would be "targets" of the OHCHR.[11] Ayala-Lasso did not complete his term and resigned in 1997 to become the foreign minister of Ecuador. He is credited for defining and promoting inter-agency cooperation among UN human rights agencies and the development of field missions. He was criticized, however, for not confronting state violations of human rights.[12]

Mary Robinson, the former president of Ireland, was appointed the second High Commissioner for Human Rights in 1997. She continued to build on the human rights field missions that Lasso started, and expanded the UN presence to many other countries including Cambodia, the Central African Republic, the Democratic Republic of the Congo, El Salvador, Gaza, Guatemala, Indonesia, Liberia, Malawi, Mongolia, Sierra Leone, and areas in southern Africa and southeast Europe.[13] Missions on the ground brought the United Nations to act on matters considered to be domestic affairs, which drew considerable criticism from many member states, especially those that view international human rights as aspirational and an internal matter for individual states to decide. Robinson was also unpopular with the United States because of her use of public diplomacy in speaking out against violations occurring in Israeli occupied territories, and her unwillingness to challenge attacks on Israel and Zionism at the 2001 World Conference Against Racism, Racial Discrimination, Xenophobia and Related Intolerance in South Africa. Even though the notorious "Zionism Equals Racism" General Assembly resolution was rescinded in 1991, the UN has had difficulty shaking its anti-Israeli bias. Its resurgence at this conference drew widespread criticism.

The United States was also unhappy with Robinson's pointed criticism of US policies during its "War on Terror." Robinson managed to alienate Russia over its actions in Chechnya and China over its policies toward the Muslim Uighers in the contested Xinjaing province of China. Toward the end of her tenure in 2002, the United States was actively lobbying for her ouster.[14] Human rights advocates point to the unhappiness of the world's great powers as evidence that Robinson was doing something right; however, alienating important states also means becoming ineffective as a UN diplomat and being shown the door.

Subsequent high commissioners have continued to use different means of human rights diplomacy to balance multiple and competing interests. After Robinson, Secretary-General Kofi Annan appointed Brazil's **Sergio Vieira de Mello** as high commissioner. He had extensive UN experience and was seen as possessing more honed diplomatic skills than his predecessor. He had good relations with the United States and relied heavily on quiet diplomacy. He had been particularly effective at deftly negotiating the independence of East Timor from Indonesia when he was head of the UN mission there from 1999–2002.

Vieira de Mello was also willing to engage gross violators of human rights in often-vain attempts to change their brutal policies.[15] After only eight months as high commissioner, he was appointed by the secretary-general to become the UN representative in Iraq, partly because of his good relations with the United States, and partly because the secretary-general desired to reassert UN relevance in international security matters.[16] His life was cut short in 2003 when he was killed, along with twenty-one others, by a suicide bomber at the lightly fortified UN headquarters in Iraq. Termed the "UN's 9/11," this attack was a serious setback for UN–US relations and left the OHCHR in disarray. Acting High Commissioner **Bertrand Ramcharan** spent his brief tenure trying raise agency morale and keeping respect for human rights and humanitarian principles front and center for states engaged in violent conflict.

The life and death of Vieira de Mello highlights a couple of dilemmas for UN human rights diplomacy: "What compromises must the U.N. make to alleviate suffering in countries where warlords or dictators rule? A second dilemma concerns the U.N.'s place in big power politics: Can the institution's representatives play an autonomous role in crises where its strongest member states have important stakes, or will U.N. officials ultimately end up serving those states' interests?"[17] The answers to these questions are invariably subject to worldview interpretations and explain why human rights and humanitarian diplomacy is a necessary part of world politics.

In 2004 **Louise Arbour** assumed the position of high commissioner. A former prosecutor for the International Criminal Tribunals for Yugoslavia and Rwanda, she made legal history by being the first to indict a sitting head of state (Serbia's Slobodan Milosevic). She was also a Canadian Supreme Court Justice with extensive diplomatic experience prior to becoming high commissioner. She began her post relying on quiet diplomacy, but as she continued in her role, she became more outspoken. This led her to clash with the United States when she rebuked US policies regarding arbitrary detention and "enhanced" interrogation techniques (which many observers say amounted to torture).[18] Arbour resigned after the end of her four-year term and did not seek to be reappointed.

Navanethem (Navi) Pillay succeeded Arbour in 2008 and was particularly strident in calling attention to human rights abuses occurring worldwide. She labeled the violence in the Congo as a "possible genocide" and called out Rwanda for its policy of militarily supporting Congolese militias. This was a difficult step given the already complicated relationship between the UN and Rwanda as a result of UN actions and inactions during the 1994 genocide. Pillay was very outspoken about the rights of the LGBTQ community which unsettled many states, especially in Africa and the Middle East. She was also considered to be the leading advocate for decisive international action to curb the carnage resulting from the Syrian civil war. Pillay was a practitioner of quiet, behind-the-scenes diplomacy and appreciated the importance of the civil society in the diplomatic process. Sidebar 5.1 features High Commissioner Pillay, in her own words, discussing the intricacies and dilemmas of human rights diplomacy. Pillay's initial term officially ended in 2012 but her appointment was extended for two additional years, making her the longest serving high commissioner since the position's inception.

Sidebar 5.1 Statement by Navanethem Pillay, United Nations High Commissioner for Human Rights[19]

Human rights diplomacy: An oxymoron?
Cambridge, Massachusetts, 28 October 2009
Ladies and Gentlemen,
I am very pleased to be here today and to speak again at my US alma mater. My address is entitled: "Human Rights Diplomacy: An Oxymoron?" I hope that I will manage to inspire many of the students here to take up human rights advocacy, on a pro bono basis if you pursue other career paths in the legal profession.

As both a former judge and a former activist I have alternated between the deliberate pace of legal proceedings and the passion of public advocacy. As High Commissioner for Human Rights, I pursue both. I am also finding my way through a third course of action, which is private diplomacy. Unlike legal proceedings and public advocacy, diplomacy often takes place behind the scenes. It is a powerful tool, but often its power is not visible. Today I want to share with you a few preliminary reflections on the role of diplomacy in the protection and promotion of human rights.

Last year we celebrated the sixtieth anniversary of perhaps the greatest achievement of human rights diplomacy, that is, the Universal Declaration of Human Rights. We look back with admiration at the determination that led to the formulation and adoption of the Universal Declaration in 1948. All too often, however, we underplay the intense negotiations, the well-honed diplomatic skills, the hotly debated options and quietly found compromises, and ultimately, the intergovernmental efforts and willingness to find common ground that ultimately sustained international agreement on the Declaration.

Since then, human rights diplomacy has pursued two very different, but mutually reinforcing paths: on the one hand, we have witnessed the development of international law through which States willingly assumed human rights obligations and the formulation and continuing expansion of a system of human rights monitoring including by treaty bodies, special procedures mandate holders, complaint procedures, and now the Universal Periodic Review procedure of the Human Rights Council. On the other hand, we have seen the growth and impact of the international human rights movement, which through committed advocacy has often been instrumental in pressing recalcitrant governments to embrace in law, and implement in practice, internationally recognized human rights principles.

At times, this advocacy has been conducted behind the scenes by civil society groups, including human rights defenders and international organizations, as well as through the peer pressure of sympathetic governments. This quiet diplomacy operates on the principle of engagement, with persuasion and sometimes the prospect of more public advocacy as its primary tools.

Sometimes human rights nongovernmental organizations and other champions of the human rights cause have adopted a highly visible strategy of "naming and shaming" those who commit human rights violations. Some would regard this strategy and diplomacy as antithetical. But there is no doubt that exposing human rights violations and calling perpetrators to account publicly has produced remarkable results, often engendering positive change both domestically and internationally. Public advocacy can work independently of or in tandem with quiet diplomacy, as well as with judicial and quasi-judicial human rights mechanisms.

To better put into context how human rights diplomacy in all its articulations has developed in the last few decades, allow me to discuss briefly the historical background that shaped it. The end of the cold war in the early 1990's had fuelled hopes for a "gentler, kinder" world in international relations. Yet subsequently, in fact within a mere three-year span, war in the former Yugoslavia, in Somalia, and the Rwandan genocide in 1994 shattered those hopes.

The 1990s was also the decade that witnessed a radical transformation in the conduct of war, and indeed the "privatization" of conflict. Rather than confrontations among States, most of the so-called small wars of the decade were marked by the violent internal competition between either State forces and well-armed rebels, or conflict between different militia of non-state actors in control of large swaths of territory, natural resources and weapons. The suppliers of weapons and the beneficiaries of profits from natural resources fuelling some of these wars were also private individuals or businesses that were callously unconcerned with the human rights record and the rapacity of their customers. Tragically, the victims of these conflicts were increasingly also "private" individuals, civilians caught between the contenders or deliberately targeted by belligerents. Widespread, gross and systematic human rights violations recurred in virtually all of these conflicts. Crimes against humanity, ethnic cleansing, war crimes and even genocide also tragically marked that decade.

But these were also the years in which large-scale humanitarian and human rights-oriented advocacy campaigns led by like-minded States, international organizations and nongovernmental activists were launched in response to the atrocities. Such campaigns included the movement to ban landmines and the use of child soldiers, and to control the misuse and proliferation of small arms and light weapons. At that time, the framework for international justice developed significantly, with the creation of the tribunals for the former Yugoslavia and Rwanda, and ultimately with the campaign that led to the establishment of the International Criminal Court. I was privileged to serve in the Rwanda Tribunal and the ICC, in both cases from their first days of infancy, thrown into action and trying desperately to meet the great challenges and high expectations surrounding their creation. And it is well-known that these groundbreaking advances in international criminal justice are largely due to the efforts of civil society.

It is against this background that the post of the High Commissioner for Human Rights was created in 1993, much as a result of public human rights advocacy at the Vienna World Conference on Human Rights, and since then the Office of the High Commissioner has progressively expanded its operations. With regard to diplomacy, our efforts have unfolded both "internally" and "externally"; both proactively and reactively; both publicly and quietly; and both as a stand-alone outreach strategy and in partnership.

As you probably know, human rights are enshrined in the UN Charter as a fundamental purpose of the organization. Every department and agency in the UN system has its own unique mandate and focus, but all share a stated commitment to common values, including human rights and gender equality. The World Summit of 2005 articulated the need to promote human rights, development and security simultaneously. Embracing such recognition, in the same year the World Summit doubled the OHCHR budget empowering us to expand our areas of intervention and strengthen our ranks and advocacy.

Indeed, we have come a long way in terms of mainstreaming human rights within the UN system. There has been notable progress in the peace and security pillar, in terms of human rights components of UN integrated missions for peacekeeping, and in the emergence of the "responsibility to protect" doctrine from the 2005 World Summit which enjoins States to protect civilians from the worst abuses. When the concept of responsibility to protect was first enunciated against the backdrop of the Rwandan genocide and the war in the former Yugoslavia, there was widespread reluctance to embrace it. Doubts were raised about the legitimacy of the ways and means of external intervention to be carried out, possibly against the wishes of a sovereign State. Objections, however, could not persuasively counter the inherent soundness of this concept which is anchored in the fundamental notion of civilian inviolability. As a result, the concept continued to make significant inroads in international thought, and it was finally endorsed by the World Summit. Norms and pledges, however, are good only if their full implications are understood and effectively applied in practice. There is no doubt that the full potential of the protection norm is still far from being realized. In that doctrine UN institutions have an important role to play, in interpreting and applying the norm, and in helping States to discharge their responsibility.

Increased interaction with the UN Security Council is of vital importance to promote and protect human rights. In particular, it is crucial that the Security Council – in its efforts to prevent conflict, re-establish peace and security, guide peace negotiations and post-conflict peace building and recovery processes – envisages the effective integration of the protection of human rights in all phases of a transition. These phases span from peace negotiations to the restoration of normalcy, to the creation of institutions and the provision of justice. In this regard, OHCHR has assisted and will continue to support the efforts of the international community.

Equally important is progress in the development pillar in order to build capacity and effective institutions on the ground. This requires a committed and far-sighted active engagement by all concerned partners. An increasing number of agencies have adopted human rights-based approaches and integrated human rights into their policies and programmes. In so doing, they have brought a sharper focus on human rights into UN-supported national development efforts, and are thus better equipped to understand the needs and rights of the most marginalised and excluded. The recent food, financial and economic crises starkly highlighted the critical vulnerabilities that stem from violations of human rights, including economic, social, and cultural rights.

Many if not most of the UN Development Assistance Frameworks developed by UN country teams and endorsed by the respective Governments in recent years have reflected "nationally owned" and internationally recognised human rights to maximize results. Program implementation has also benefited from the adoption of a human rights-based approach, particularly with regard to the attainment of economic, social and cultural rights, including access to food, water, housing, health and education. While progress remains uneven, these achievements deserve recognition.

To be sure, the universal membership, multilateral character, neutrality and legitimacy of the United Nations provide unique comparative advantages in this field, helping to address recipient countries' fears that human rights are merely another form of donor "conditionality."

But in all honesty I must tell you that this mainstreaming of human rights is not always easy. I am often astonished at the resistance to and fear of human rights. From the Security Council to the UN Country Teams that operate on the ground, there is an ongoing reluctance to embrace human rights mainly driven by perceived need to accommodate the sensitivities of member states. We must address this head on if we are to make significant progress.

A potentially invaluable vehicle for the enhancement of UN synergy is the Human Rights Council, which is the intergovernmental body created in 2006 as a successor to the Commission on Human Rights, which had attracted growing criticism. The Council is virtually a standing body. The frequency of its meetings – both in formal and informal gatherings – may thus create more opportunities to better hone operations and responses to both chronic human rights conditions and sudden crises. This may also help to build a firmer ground of understanding among the Council's members than sporadic or less frequent interactions allowed for. An example of this added value is offered by the thematic and country-specific special sessions of the Human Rights Council, which help throw a timely light on situations of concern.

Crucially, the new Universal Periodic Review of the Human Rights Council, designed to examine the human rights record of all States, seeks to overcome the perceived selectivity and regional confrontations of the former Commission on Human Rights when considering national human rights situations. As the experience of the review has shown, States have conscientiously prepared their national reports through broad consultations with relevant stakeholders, including civil society. To date, 80 States have been reviewed. As result of this process, various countries under review firmly pledged to strengthen implementation of human rights standards at the national level, as well as their cooperation with human rights mechanisms. If used effectively, the UPR can help address implementation gaps and contribute to building capacity on the ground.

My Office services the human rights mechanisms, such as special procedures and human rights treaty bodies. The former are entrusted to examine, investigate, monitor, advise and publicly report on human rights situations worldwide. Through their direct contacts with Governments, their public statements, their reports to the Human Right Council and to the General Assembly, as well as informal briefings, the special procedures experts can offer invaluable information for identifying both preventive and corrective measures to address situations of concern and enhance practical implementation strategies on the ground. Through their recommendations, the treaty bodies provide states with guidance for national implementation of their obligations. Their work, including general comments on various provisions of the treaties, is also used by courts and other judicial bodies in the development of jurisprudence on international human rights law, as well as providing important substantive information for consideration in the UPR process.

It is easy to get caught up in the world of the United Nations, yet I believe that we must always be guided in our priorities and all our efforts to promote and protect human rights by conditions on the ground, where violent conflict, discrimination, poverty, injustice and repression persist in too many parts of the world. Indeed, no country can claim a spotless record on human rights. Moreover, long-standing or emerging global problems, such as climate change, epidemics, shortages of resources including water and food, as well as the current financial crises and economic recession compound situations of entrenched vulnerability and hardship that preclude the full enjoyment of rights. The measure of our success in my view is the difference we make in the lives of women and men around the world.

In my current role as High Commissioner for Human Rights, as I mentioned earlier, I am now called on to be a diplomat and to use the power of diplomacy to further human rights. I find myself often in a highly politicized context that contrasts starkly with my experience as a judge. I have carried over into my diplomatic endeavors all my judicial instincts. I do not rank rights and I use my office as a venue where everyone will be given a fair audience. I have called publicly, repeatedly, for a single standard of human rights to which all states should be held equally accountable. In the United Nations this is a challenge, but as I believe that the credibility of my Office depends on impartiality, I believe the credibility of other human rights undertakings similarly depends on impartiality. What I find is that when you move from treaty bodies, comprised of experts serving in their individual capacity, to bodies such as the Human Rights Council, comprised of political representation, ensuring that political considerations do not enter into the dialogue is a great challenge.

It certainly helps to have a system such as the Universal Periodic Review, which ensures that each country will be examined, but I have seen some countries undergoing review stack the list of speakers in their support. In contrast, some states have welcomed the opportunity to openly discuss their internal challenges as well as their achievements, and I am hopeful that their vision of this review process ultimately prevails. In this context there is much room for quiet diplomacy.

A case in point, and in fact a case-study, in such human rights diplomacy was the review conference against racism, racial discrimination, xenophobia and related intolerance which took place in April 2009 in Geneva. The conference wrapped up with wide agreement in which 182 States undertook to prevent, prohibit and respond to all manifestations of racism and intolerance. But such consensus was hardly a foregone conclusion. A number of voices advocated a boycott of the review conference for well over a year, long before a single word was put to paper. This opposition was for the most part based on fears that the Geneva meeting would trigger a repetition of the virulent anti-Semitic activities of some non-governmental organizations at the margins of the 2001 World Conference in Durban. The odious actions of a few had tainted the reputation of the entire process from Durban in 2001 to the conference in Geneva in 2009. In the end, ten UN Member States, including the United States, decided to stay away from the Geneva gathering which the UN General Assembly had called to review the implementation of the Durban Declaration and Programme of Action, the final document of the 2001 conference.

From the outset, rather than focussing on the surrounding political controversies, my Office sought to engage all Member States by providing technical input and specific proposals. These were grounded in the well-established jurisprudence and practice of human rights mechanisms, such as Treaty Bodies and Special Procedures. At the same time, we began a wide range of consultations to gather the views of governmental and nongovernmental interlocutors, at the national, regional and international level. We did so at each and every phase of the drafting, negotiating and the deliberating processes involving the outcome document, the final say of the review conference. My Office played a role in facilitating resolution of the difficult issue of "defamation of religion" by organizing a workshop six months before the conference to look at the provisions of the Covenant on Civil and Political Rights, Articles 19 and 20 on incitement to racial hatred, as an alternative framework, based on international law, a framework that ultimately prevailed and was adopted in the Outcome Document.

We also honed and stepped up our communications strategies by reaching out to wider audiences and empowering them to be informed and have a say well in advance of events. Our communications strategy succeeded because it was intrinsically linked to our substantive initiatives and was effective in countering misinformation. We also offered victims opportunities to speak directly of their plight and thus inform the general public. Nongovernmental organizations were given a credible, open and democratic platform to express their views with zero tolerance for disrespectful outbursts. Despite some isolated instances of intemperate behaviour on the part of a handful of NGOs, there was no repetition of the odious slurs and confrontation that had marked the Durban conference.

In the end, the Durban Review Conference provided a platform for a new beginning. The few States that chose to stay away should now evaluate the Outcome Document adopted by the conference on its own merit and substance. Many of these States participated in its drafting and were part of the emerging consensus up until the very eve of the conference. This is why I am hopeful that they will rejoin international efforts to combat racism and intolerance worldwide.

Let me conclude by saying that I have found diplomacy to be an effective and for me a new component to what is I believe a more holistic approach to human rights protection. In addition to building a rapid response capacity for human rights crises, which may often require public advocacy, I think much more can be done to develop a long term prevention strategies that include a focus on the institutional capacity of states to respond when human rights are at risk. I am a firm believer in speaking out. I have and will continue to speak out strongly against human rights violations wherever they occur. At the same time, in my capacity as UN High Commissioner for Human Rights, I look forward to greater dialogue and engagement with states, and will do my best to master the art of diplomacy to this end.

Thank You

In 2014, Prince **Zeid al-Hussein**, a seasoned Jordanian diplomat and respected human rights advocate, replaced Pillay. Zeid al-Hussein assumed the post at a time when Middle East violence had become a wider regional war and respect for internationally recognized human rights and humanitarian principles seemed almost non-existent. The humanitarian situations in Syria and Iraq constitute two of the worst humanitarian crises facing the international community today. As the high commissioner, he, like his predecessors, will have to decide between public and quiet diplomacy, given the human rights situation on the ground and the politics at play in the first UN. He will also have to juggle the diverse demands of NGOs about what to do about those situations.

The diplomacy of the high commissioner is somewhat easier in that their central responsibility is to advance respect for international human rights and humanitarian principles. The OHCHR does not have the same interests or concerns as states. At the same time, the OHCHR knows that states have different conceptions and priorities regarding human rights and needs to find common ground in order to move forward. As such, the diplomatic position of the OHCHR is to maintain human rights that are interdependent, indivisible, and universal and then try to move other actors toward that ideal through advocacy and programming.

The OHCHR operations and staff.[20] The mandate of the OHCHR involves enhancing the level of protection and respect for human rights internationally. It is also the UN body that helps states fulfill their human rights obligations by providing more objective assessments of human rights challenges, including identifying and developing responses to human rights situations. The work of the OHCHR centers on standard-setting and capacity building, as well as implementing and monitoring international human rights. It maintains a network of partnerships with other UN agencies, governments, NGOs, regional IGOs, and businesses to assist and guide human rights protection. It advises governments on technical issues, such as setting up national ombudsman offices, and helping states incorporate international human rights in their domestic judicial and legislative systems. In addition to supporting the HRC, it also assists with the treaty monitoring bodies/committees and helping states meet their treaty obligations.

The OHCHR spearheads the mainstreaming of human rights throughout the UN system and for articulating a "rights-based" approach to UN activities. This means putting respect for human rights at the forefront of UN actions. More importantly, the OHCHR uses IGO diplomacy to improve on and advance international human rights standards. The OHCHR has a staff of over 1,000 people including 250 human rights officers stationed with field missions, regional offices, and UN peacekeeping missions. The staff run field missions; write and disseminate human rights reports; liaise with civil society groups; and educate the public and state officials. These functions help to build national capacity because it involves training national officials and civil society actors in the areas of justice administration, legislative reform, electoral process, and other tactics necessary to implement internationally recognized human rights standards on the ground.

The regional offices and centers also liaise with regional IGOs such as the AU and the Arab League to bridge the gaps between regional and global standards/perspectives. In addition to having a long-term presence in countries and regions, the OHCHR is ready to deploy human rights advisors and rapid response personnel to analyze specific human rights situations or crises. They gather evidence, find facts, and support commissions of inquiry.

The OHCHR engages in comprehensive human rights education. Its publications inform governments, national institutions, civil society, the general public, and the media about international human rights standards and raise awareness of human rights situations. It produces human rights training manuals, fact sheets, and reference guides that contribute to the growing global human rights consensus. This comprehensive education empowers others to contribute to that consensus. The more actors use the same "playbook," the easier it is to find common ground and move forward.

The OHCHR is also integrally involved in supporting, loosely coordinating, and checking other UN human rights bodies, especially the **charter-based** and **treaty-based bodies** (discussed below). The charter-based bodies include the multilateral HRC and the accompanying UPR. Charter-based bodies also include the "special procedures" of the HRC and independent commissions of inquiry appointed by the HRC. The treaty-based bodies are the committees and monitoring bodies that oversee the implementation of international human rights law. These human rights bodies provide unique dimensions of human rights and humanitarian diplomacy because they utilize independent experts who are neither UN nor state employees. These independent experts can function as a buffer between IGOs and states and bring additional influence to bear on behalf of human rights and humanitarian principles.

Special procedures: rapporteurs

The HRC (as did its defunct predecessor the Commission on Human Rights) utilizes "special procedures" to investigate and report on human rights situations and violations. This involves appointing independent human rights experts (individuals or a small panel) to help the inherently political HRC assess situations and arrive at recommendations objectively. The OHCHR recommends and supports these independent experts, called **special rapporteurs**. Special rapporteurs investigate country-specific and thematic issues relating to human rights or humanitarian situations. The first special rapporteur was appointed in 1979 by the Commission on Human Rights to investigate and report on human rights abuses in Chile. The first thematic rapporteur was appointed in 1982 to examine summary and arbitrary executions and remains active today.

The HRC has continued the commission's tradition of special procedures. Table 5.1 illustrates the extensive and comprehensive nature of the mandates supported by the OHCHR. Mandate-holders engage in a wide range of activities including fact-finding and meeting with public officials, NGOs, and persons at-risk. They make recommendations to governments and issue public statements. The work of these independent experts serve as valuable inputs to multilateral and IGO human rights and humanitarian diplomacy. Rapporteurs also have a normative impact by educating and socializing both state and non-state actors.

The decision to appoint a rapporteur and the actual selection process is, of course, politicized since the decision lies with member states of the HRC. Therefore, prior to appointments, the high commissioner, council members, and affected states need to engage in extensive quiet diplomacy to reach a decision and then savvy public diplomacy in order "sell" the decision to relevant domestic and international constituencies. Still, states can ignore rapporteur recommendations. For example, the United States rejects, and therefore ignores, the authority of the HRC and its thematic rapporteur on extrajudicial, summary, and arbitrary execution because the rapporteur has called into question the US use of drones to kill terror suspects in other countries.[21] The questionable legality of the drone program, both domestically and internationally, coupled with the questionable status of the combatants, creates a political minefield that the special rapporteur must consider. Rapporteurs must also define and navigate their own professional relationships with the UN and states as to how to best promote and protect human rights.[22]

Special rapporteurs do not receive compensation for their missions and are only reimbursed for travel and mission-related expenses. This is to ensure their independence and autonomy. They have fewer constraints than typical UN officials, but are still expected to follow the same code of conduct. If human rights abuses are verified, rapporteurs usually act first by communicating with the concerned government(s) and making recommendation regarding corrective measures.[23] They often issue detailed reports and propose strategies for improving the protection of human rights, especially in relation to thematic issues.

Table 5.1 Special procedures: thematic and country mandates

Name	Year established	Year extended	Name and country of origin of mandate holder(s)
Special Rapporteur on adequate housing as a component of the right to an adequate standard of living, and on the right to non-discrimination in this context	2000	2007	Ms. Leilani Farha (Canada)
Working Group of Experts on People of African Descent	2002	2003	Ms. Mireille Fanon Mendes-France (France)
Working Group on Arbitrary Detention	1991	1997	Mr. Mads Andenas (Norway)
Special Rapporteur on the sale of children, child prostitution and child pornography	1990	2008	Ms. Maud De Boerbuguicchio (Netherlands)
Special Rapporteur in the field of cultural rights	2009	2012	Ms. Farida Shaheed (Pakistan)
Independent expert on the promotion of a democratic and equitable international order	2011		Mr. Alfred de Zayas
Special Rapporteur on the rights of persons with disabilities	2014		TBA
Special Rapporteur on the right to education	1998	2008	Mr. Kishore Singh (India)
Independent Expert on the issue of human rights obligations relating to the enjoyment of a safe, clean, healthy and sustainable environment	2012		Mr. John Knox
Working Group on Enforced or Involuntary Disappearances	1980	2007	Mr. Ariel Dulitzky (Argentina/USA)
		2011	Mr. Oliver de Frouville (France), Ms. Jasminka Dzumhu (Bosnia and Herzegovina)
		2014	Ms. Houria Es Slami (Morocco), Mr. Osman El-Hajje (Lebanon)
Special Rapporteur on extra judicial, summary or arbitrary executions	1982	2011	Mr. Christof Heyns (S. Africa)
		2014	
Special Rapporteur on extreme poverty and human rights	1998	2011	Mr. Philip Alston (Australia)
		2014	

Table 5.1 (cont)

Name	Year established	Year extended	Name and country of origin of mandate holder(s)
Special Rapporteur on the right to food	2000	2010, 2013	Ms. Hilal Elver (Turkey)
Independent Expert on the effects of foreign debt and other related international financial obligations of States on the full enjoyment of all human rights, particularly economic, social and cultural rights	2000	2008	Mr. Juan Bohoslavsky (Argentina)
Special Rapporteur on the rights to freedom of peaceful assembly and of association	2010	2013	Mr. Maina Kiai (Kenya)
Special Rapporteur on the promotion and protection of the right to freedom of opinion and expression	1993	2008, 2011, 2014	Mr. David Kaye (USA)
Special Rapporteur on freedom of religion or belief	1986	2007, 2010, 2013	Mr. Heiner Bielefeldt (Germany)
Special Rapporteur on the right of everyone to the enjoyment of the highest attainable standard of physical and mental health	2002	2010	Mr. Dainius Puras (Lithuania)
Special Rapporteur on the situation of human rights defenders	2000	2008, 2011, 2014	Mr. Michel Forst (France)
Special Rapporteur on the independence of judges and lawyers	1994	2008, 2011, 2014	Ms. Gabriela Knaul (Brazil)
Special Rapporteur on the rights of indigenous peoples	2001	2010, 2013	Ms. Victoria Lucia Tauli-Corpuz (the Philippines)
Special Rapporteur on the human rights of internally displaced persons	2004	2010, 2013	Mr. Chaloka Beyani (Zambia)

Mandate	Established	Mandate holder	Year
Working Group on the use of mercenaries as a means of violating human rights and impeding the exercise of the right of peoples to self-determination	2005	Ms. Patricia Arias (Chile) Ms. Anton Katz (S. Africa) Ms. Elzbieta Karska (Poland) Mr. Gabor Rona (USA/Hungary) Mr. Saeed Mokbil (Yemen)	2010 2013
Special Rapporteur on the human rights of migrants	1999	Mr. François Crépeau (Canada)	2008 2011 2014
Special Rapporteur on minority issues	2005	Ms. Rita Izsák (Hungary)	2008 2011 2014
Independent Expert on the enjoyment of all human rights by older persons	2013	Ms. Rosa Kornfeld-Matte (Chile)	
Special Rapporteur on the promotion of truth, justice, reparation and guarantees of non-recurrence	2011	Mr. Pablo De Greiff (Colombia)	
Special Rapporteur on contemporary forms of racism, racial discrimination, xenophobia and related intolerance	1993	Mr. Mutuma Ruteere (Kenya)	2008 2011 2014
Special Rapporteur on contemporary forms of slavery, including its causes and its consequences	2007	Ms. Urmila Bhoola (S. Africa)	2010 2013
Independent Expert on human rights and international solidarity	2005	Ms. Virginia Dandan (Philippines)	2008 2011 2014
Special Rapporteur on the promotion and protection of human rights while countering terrorism	2005	Mr. Ben Emmerson (UK and N. Ireland)	2010 2013
Special Rapporteur on torture and other cruel, inhuman or degrading treatment or punishment	1985	Mr. Juan Ernessto Mendez (Argentina)	2008 2011 2014

Table 5.1 (cont)

Name	Year established	Year extended	Name and country of origin of mandate holder(s)
Special Rapporteur on the implications for human rights of the environmentally sound management and disposal of hazardous substances and wastes	1995	2011 2012	Mr. Baskut Tuncak (Turkey)
Special Rapporteur on trafficking in persons, especially women and children	2004	2008 2011 2014	Ms. Maria Grazia Giammarinaro (Italy)
Working Group on the issue of human rights and transnational corporations and other business enterprises	2011	2014	Mr. Michael K. Addo (Ghana) Mr. Puvan J. Selvanathan (Malaysia) Ms. Alexandra Guaqueta (Colombia/USA) Mr. Pavel Sulyandziga (Russia) Ms. Margaret Jungk (USA)
Special Rapporteur on the human right to safe drinking water and sanitation	2008	2011	Ms. Catarina de Albuquerque (Portugal)
Working Group on the issue of discrimination against women in law and in practice	2010	2013 2013	Ms. Frances Raday (Israel/UK) Ms. Emna Aouij (Tunisia) Ms. Eleonora Zielinska (Poland) Ms. Kamala Chandrakirana (Indonesia) Ms. Alda Facio (Costa Rica)
Special Rapporteur on violence against women, its causes and consequences	1994	2008	Ms. Rashida Manjoo (S. Africa)

Source: Compiled from www.ohchr.org.

The special rapporteur's country visits consist of fact-finding and investigating alleged human rights violations. Country visits are generally short, usually lasting no longer than fifteen days. Rapporteurs meet with victims and consult with human rights NGOs (which are valuable sources of quality data and information). They offer recommendations and quietly urge governments to take corrective action. Rapporteurs realize that government officials are much more receptive and responsive to quiet diplomacy. After the country visit, the special rapporteur issues a final report. In Sidebar 5.2 former Special Rapporteur Paulo Sergio Pinheiro provides a first-hand account of the rapporteur's role and challenges. At the end of the day, Pinheiro remains concerned about the overall impact of special rapporteurs because they have no way of holding states accountable.[24]

Sidebar 5.2 Special Rapporteur Paulo Sergio Pinheiro: the independence of special rapporteurs[25]

Special rapporteurs take pains to maintain their independence, impartiality, and objectivity; to weigh the information on human rights provided by governments and civil society groups; and to report fully on the progress made and obstacles faced. Special rapporteurs perform a delicate balancing act. They must discharge their duties with thoroughness and sobriety, bearing in mind their essential role of protecting the interests of victims. But the mandate of the special rapporteurs has an intrinsic and almost insolvable contradiction. On the one hand, as our title says – this French word very strange in English and in many languages, apparently suggested by Bertrand Rancharam inspired by similar mandates at International Labour Office (ILO) – we are supposed *rapporter*, to prepare rapports, report (but we cannot be just *reporters* in the media meaning), accurate depictions of the situation of human rights in the countries or the state of the theme under our responsibility.

Special rapporteurs cannot limit their activities to denouncing, name and shaming or embarrassing states: roles commonly played by non-governmental organisations (NGOs). The role of a special rapporteur goes well beyond that of NGOs because we work closely with all parties interested in improving the status of human rights, especially the state. As suggested earlier, there is room for different styles of engagement – indeed, vocal and visible criticism and behind-the-scenes negotiations are complementary and often mutually reinforcing. Even if undeniably there is an inescapable tension between impartial fact-finding and clear and sound public assessments.

On one side, the special rapporteur is supposed to report about human rights violations. But on the other hand, you have always to interact with the government because if you are not able to talk to governments, there is no meaning in having a mandate of the HRC. As a country rapporteur I had determined that I had the added responsibility of "engaging" within the country in focus. I had a good relationship with the government of Myanmar during the first four years of my mandate. What was a challenge lay in engaging with a sort of new leadership not very prone, to say the least, to be engaged with the UN mechanisms on the world stage. In the beginning the NGOs thought that I was too soft with the military junta but at the end had been praised. Given the need to keep the regime as a partner, even reluctantly, I treated its government officials like those of any other UN member state. Objective fact-finding does not mean neutrality; special rapporteurs will sometimes be required to denounce abuses for which there is evidence.

…

Special rapporteurs, much more than other actors in the international community, are compelled, I would say condemned, to navigate under the determinations of insolvable contradictions.

We must serve as voices for the voiceless and as spokespersons for the victims, but our effectiveness depends on maintaining a dialogue with host countries and concerned capitals around the world, most especially with the permanent members of the Security Council. An essential aspect of the job description is to foster contacts with other countries concerned with a particular human rights crisis. During the Burundi assignment, I sought to fathom the views from all countries with an interest in the area, including the Great Lakes region and Europe. It was essential for my mandate to maintain dialogue within the extended diplomatic community. In both Africa and Asia, I have sought systematically to solicit the views of neighbouring countries in each region in order to cross-check my own intuition and analyses. During my missions to Myanmar, for instance, I have attempted to understand and learn from the perceptions of China, India and Southeast Asian countries – and especially from Japan, Malaysia, Singapore, and Thailand.

Usually, but not always, constructive dialogue has resulted, but independence remains paramount. For instance, I assumed a critical stance *vis-à-vis* economic sanctions imposed on Burundi by its nine neighbours at the Great Lakes region, arguing that economic sanctions mostly affect poor peoples and leave elites largely untouched. My views found a certain resonance in the Security Council, which never approved the regional sanctions.

The best answer for that contradiction intrinsic to the mandate is to go beyond the role of rapporteur, of fact-finders, and to try to build some kind of "principled engagement." In Myanmar, I have sought to maintain that "principled engagement" between the special rapporteur and the host government. We should demonstrate eagerness to listen, learn, and understand. We should not merely point fingers. However, discretion sometimes has its advantages. Special rapporteurs are appointed by the CHR's member states, but they are not emissaries of any country or group of countries. Sometimes we have to remind state officials of that. Owing to their close working relations with member states, special rapporteurs often encounter highly ambiguous reactions from observers and feel certain ambivalence even among ourselves.

The recommendations of special rapporteurs are often used by the OHCHR as a rationale to send country teams to follow up on situations. These reports also inform HRC decisions regarding whether to extend mandates. Special rapporteurs need to create and maintain contacts in mandate countries and to cultivate a good working relationship. According to Pinheiro, special rapporteurs would not exist if it were not for the media.[26] The media allow special rapporteurs to engage in "**megaphone diplomacy**" to reach a wider audience.[27] Megaphone diplomacy advances human rights and humanitarian principles by building public awareness and informing the public debate. It has the indirect benefit of allowing rapporteurs to build a network of contacts. Still, even though technically they are not UN employees, special rapporteurs must have their press communications vetted by the UN before making them public.

A special rapporteur must balance advocating/protecting the interests of the victims of human rights violations with fully reporting on their findings (which may compromise their ability to advocate and protect, especially if they run afoul of states).[28] Moreover, they must also be careful not to draw too much attention to their office. Discretion allows them increased access to authorities and others that might otherwise be unobtainable.

Independent commissions of inquiry

The OHCHR also supports the work of **commissions of inquiry** which are appointed on an ad hoc basis by the HRC to investigate gross violations of human rights. Commissions often work with special rapporteurs to establish facts, collect evidence, assess responsibility, and issue reports and recommendations. Comprised of a small number of independent human rights experts (usually between three and five members), commissions work with the other UN bodies and NGOs to interview refugees and witnesses and take testimony. Since the HRC became operational in 2006 it has appointed thirteen fact-finding and commissions of inquiry. Three of the more recent inquiries are ongoing, investigating human rights violations and war crimes in North Korea, Syria, and Gaza. Commissions are central for providing states and judicial bodies with the quality information and reliable evidence necessary to hold those responsible for crimes accountable. Unfortunately, these commissions cannot make states act or force them to follow up on their findings. Sometimes, it is more politically expedient to move on from crises rather than revisit atrocities, especially if follow-up action causes more harm than good.

United Nations treaty monitoring bodies

The treaty monitoring bodies are committees of independent human rights experts who supervise state implementation of ratified treaties. The committees serve an important diplomatic role because they interact with state officials, encouraging and

Table 5.2 Diplomacy: treaty monitoring bodies

Treaty monitoring bodies	Consideration of individual complaints	Conduct inquiries	Adoption of general comments
Human Rights Committee (CCPR)	Yes	No	Yes
Committee on Economic, Social and Cultural Rights (CESCR)	Yes	No	Yes
Committee on the Elimination of Racial Discrimination (CERD)	Yes	No	Yes
Committee on the Elimination of Discrimination against Women (CEDAW)	Yes	Yes	Yes
Committee against Torture (CAT)	Yes	Yes	Yes
Committee on the Rights of the Child (CRC)	Yes	Yes	Yes
Committee on Migrant Workers (CMW)	Yes	No	Yes
Committee on the Rights of Persons with Disabilities (CRPD)	Yes	Yes	Yes
Committee on Enforced Disappearances (CED)	Yes	Yes	Yes
The Subcommittee on Prevention of Torture and other Cruel, Inhuman or Degrading Treatment or Punishment (SPT)	No	No	No

Source: Compiled from www.ohchr.org.

prodding states to conform to international human rights standards. **Committee diplomacy** takes several forms.[29] First, all committees are authorized to receive and review reports submitted by state parties. These reports explain how states are putting human rights provisions into practice at home. After receiving reports and feedback from relevant sources, committees will then generate questions for states to answer. This starts a public dialogue with states and members of civil society are encouraged to participate.[30] The committees will issue "concluding observations" which usually consist of recommendations for state parties and corresponding deadlines. Second, some committees, but certainly not all, receive and consider individual petitions and complaints. This quasi-judicial function represents a legal evolution because it gives individuals the procedural right to seek protection and redress for human rights violations. Third, and relatedly, some committee are authorized to conduct inquiries into human situations. Finally, all the committees issue "general comments" which amount to independent, expert interpretations of treaty provisions and articulate new directions for human rights protection. Table 5.2 lists treaty monitoring bodies supported by the OHCHR and their range of committee diplomacy.

The impressive structure and range of activities of the treaty monitoring bodies mask several challenges of committee diplomacy in advancing international human rights. Many states are noncompliant and fail to submit reports. Many of the reports submitted are vague, incomplete, and poorly written. While some committees might be authorized to receive individual petitions and conduct inquiries, it is often allowed only on a state-by-state basis. Committees still need state consent, which many states have withheld in treaty "reservations." Even if a state party has consented to a committee's authority to conduct inquiries, the committee is not going to get very far without the cooperation of the target state.

Regardless of these challenges, the procedures of the treaty monitoring bodies have several diplomatic benefits.[31] Reporting requirements lead countries to more carefully consider human rights domestically and assess how they measure up to international standards. The intent of "concluding comments" is not to criticize but to enter into a constructive dialogue with states and provide concrete strategies for improving human rights. The procedures also allow for civil society engagement which helps strengthen and educate human rights NGOs. Whether these processes make a significant difference on the ground is unclear.[32] What is clear is that various actors (states, treaty monitoring bodies, and NGOs) engage in negotiations in order to monitor, report, implement, and improve respect for international human rights.

The United Nations High Commissioner for Refugees (UNHCR)

The UNHCR is responsible for protecting and assisting refugees, IDPs, and stateless persons. The position was created in 1950 by the General Assembly, initially with a narrow three-year mandate to respond to the post-World War II European refugee crisis. Its mandate has evolved and been extended by the General Assembly since. The General Assembly also called upon member states to support the work of the UNHCR by becoming parties to and implementing the relevant international covenants.[33] The **1951 Convention Relating to the Status of Refugees** sets out the legal definition of a refugee and articulates the principle of *nonrefoulement* (or no return). A refugee is defined as someone who "owing to a well-founded fear of being persecuted for reasons of race, religion, nationality, membership of a particular social group or political opinion, is outside the country of his nationality, and is unable to, or owing to such fear, is unwilling to avail himself of the protection of that country; or who, not having a nationality and being outside the country of his habitual resident as a result of such events, is unable or, owing to such fear, in unwilling to return to it." *Nonrefoulement* protects refugees because signatories are legally obligated not to return individuals with refugee status, or those seeking such status, back to a situation of persecution. It is through *nonrefoulement* that refugees and asylum-seekers are ultimately protected.

While only states grant asylum, the UNHCR seeks to find durable solutions to the plight of refugees through three mechanisms. The first is **voluntary repatriation** whereby UNHCR officials mediate the safe return of individuals to their home country. This is quite difficult because the conditions in the refugee's country of origin are not likely to have changed in the short term. Moreover, both the individual and the government must agree. The second mechanism is **resettlement** in a third country. Resettlement is at the discretion of states, so UNHCR officials must engage in ongoing diplomacy to encourage other states to permanently resettle refugees. **Assimilation** in the country of first asylum is the last, and most likely, solution. States are very sensitive about their borders and a mass influx of asylum-seekers can be destabilizing. A great deal of UNHCR diplomacy is geared toward encouraging countries of first asylum to at least provide temporary safe haven and to be generous in granting asylum.

Unfortunately, the legal definition of a refugee is quite narrow because it applies only to *individuals* who can demonstrate that they have a well-founded fear of persecution. In other words, they must show that they are individual targets of persecution. Individuals fleeing foreign occupation, civil war, or generalized violence do not necessarily qualify as a refugee because these are conditions that affect the general population as a whole. Also, those unable to cross an international border technically do not qualify. Most states reserve the right to make refugee and asylum determinations and, therefore, tend to embrace the legally narrow, individualistic definition when making such determinations.

One of the central diplomatic issues complicating refugee protection is that the UNHCR mandate has evolved to assist those who flee "refugee-like" situations while the legal definition of a refugee and corresponding state obligations have not. The evolution of the UNHCR mandate is clear. In 1957, the General Assembly authorized the UNHCR to assist with the mass influx of Chinese asylum-seekers into UK-controlled Hong Kong, even though they did not meet the statutory definition of a refugee.[34] The UNHCR mandate expanded further to include those fleeing generalized violence when the General Assembly authorized the agency to assist 80,000 Algerians who had fled to neighboring countries in 1958.[35] This anticolonial rebellion and France's brutal counterinsurgency campaign created the first mass forced migration that would come to characterize the decolonization process. In 1972, the UNHCR was called upon to assist those unable to flee Turkey's invasion of Cyprus. This created a new category of persons assisted by the UNHCR, **internally displaced persons (IDPs)**.

The scale of UNHCR activities increased dramatically with the post-Cold War crises in the former Yugoslavia, Rwanda, Sudan, Congo, Liberia, Afghanistan, Iraq, and Syria. The UNHCR is usually one of the first-responders to complex emergency situations and provides lifesaving assistance such as food, water, shelter, and medical care. So while the mandate of the UNHCR has been extended and expanded, the legal framework formalizing state obligations has barely budged. Other than the **1967 Protocol**, which removed the temporal and geographic limitations of the 1951 Convention, international law has not developed to address new realities. UN efforts to create legal obligations regarding IDPs have been abandoned and states resist the idea that they are legally obligated to provide humanitarian assistance. Thus, IGO diplomacy regarding refugees and those in refugee-like situations involves moving states beyond their narrow legal obligations and to assume more responsibility for protecting those likewise-assisted by the UNHCR. It involves financing UNHCR humanitarian activities and finding more effective strategies for managing current complex emergencies. In 2014 the UNHCR estimated that the world population of refugees, asylum-seekers, and IDPs exceeded fifty million people. The current high commissioner is **António Guterres** and he heads an agency staff of more than 8,600 members who operate in 126 countries.[36]

The UNHCR was one of the first UN agencies to use **celebrity diplomacy** to increase its visibility and raise awareness of refugee and IDP populations worldwide. By appointing celebrities, such as the American actor Angelina Jolie, as **Goodwill Ambassadors**, the UNHCR can build global support for its activities. It also adds an element of populism to traditional forms of diplomacy.[37] Some observers caution that the use of celebrities for diplomacy can be tricky because it adds a high profile agent, who often has unprecedented access to key decision-makers, to the already complicated mix of negotiations.[38] Celebrities also tend to be more oriented to Western values thereby giving these values a higher profile.[39] The UNHCR avoids this by maintaining that its values are global and encouraging diversity among Goodwill Ambassadors. Current Goodwill Ambassadors include the popular Chinese actor Yao Chen and Turkish singing star Muazzez Ersoy.[40]

The Office for the Coordination of Humanitarian Affairs (OCHA)

The OCHA is the department responsible for coordinating UN humanitarian relief activities worldwide and organizing state, UN, and NGO actors' responses to emergency situations. Originally, the international relief functions of the United Nations were originally composed of two separate bodies, the Department of Humanitarian Affairs and the UN Disaster Relief Office, but in 1998, the separate entities were restructured to become OCHA.[41] OCHA is headed by an undersecretary general, called the **Emergency Relief Coordinator (ERC)**. **Jan Egeland** did much to define the ERC in its role as head of OCHA and was one of Kofi Annan's closest advisors. In his capacity as ERC, he was responsible for coordinating the massive humanitarian relief efforts during the Indian Ocean Tsunami (2004) and the Darfur crisis (2004). Like many human rights and humanitarian diplomats, Egeland has held many positions with government, such as State Secretary in the Norwegian Ministry of Foreign Affairs and NGOs, such as Human Rights Watch and the Norwegian Refugee Council.

In 2010, Secretary-General Ban Ki-moon appointed the current ERC, **Valerie Amos**. Amos has spent a considerable amount of her time as ERC negotiating humanitarian access to Syrian civilians and mediating tensions when NGOs delivered humanitarian aid without UN coordination or Syrian government consent. After Syria threatened to attack unapproved convoys, she successfully lobbied Security Council members to authorize the delivery of UN humanitarian aid without state consent. The ERC works not only with other UN bodies, such as the UNHCR, the World Health Organization (WHO), and the World Food Program, but also coordinates with the thousands of humanitarian NGOs operating outside the UN. The delivery of humanitarian assistance is decentralized because no one is really in charge, and as a result, efforts can become confused and duplicated.[42] The OCHA uses a **Cluster Coordination** approach in order to enhance coordination, predictability, and accountability when managing humanitarian crises. Key accountable humanitarian organizations are identified in advance to be mobilized during emergencies.[43] The organization has nearly 2,000 staff members who work to facilitate humanitarian aid in four continents.[44] These individuals work through regional and country offices and these offices are headed by a humanitarian coordinator who manages operations.

The diplomacy necessary for coordinating and delivering humanitarian aid is manifold. Sometimes ceasefires need to be negotiated and humanitarian corridors established. Overflight rights need to be secured. States need to be prodded to provide funding and materiel or to follow through on their pledges. The logistics of delivery can involve foreign militaries, local and national officials, private companies, and NGOs, all of which can cause bottlenecks that must be overcome.[45] Humanitarian workers are often at risk in conflict zones so their personal security must also be negotiated. UN personnel must be careful not to run afoul of states or they will find themselves unwelcome. In 2006 Jan Egeland's plane was not allowed to land by Sudan even though he was invited to visit the Darfur region and UN special envoy Jan Pronk was declared PNG for his comments about the conduct of Sudanese military.

The regional civil service

The bureaucracies and independent experts that support regional human rights regimes tend to be organized around three entities: A high commissioner; a committee/commission; and a court. Europe also has treaty monitoring bodies. The effectiveness of these entities depends in large part on the commitment of the states comprising the regional IGO. As discussed in Chapter 4, Europe has taken great strides in internalizing international human rights as defined by the international bill of rights, while others either lag behind or have decided to define and prioritize human rights and humanitarian principles in a way more acceptable to their members. Europe has embraced the global UN regime because it reflects its values and most European states were instrumental in creating it. Europe may even be the vanguard of the UN regime.

With the other regional bodies, it is unclear whether regional IGO diplomacy has had much of an effect on states in fulfilling their obligations for a number of reasons. First, the bodies are in their nascent stages. Second, regional treaty obligations are increasingly and significantly different than the UN regime. Third, many states have not allowed regional IGO officials a great deal of independence. It is difficult to gage whether these human rights experts embrace UN norms and law or are chosen because they actually see regional norms as preferable. They very well could use their independent expertise to try bridge the gap between human rights and human rights perspectives. The political commitment and will of regional member states are fundamental to the effectiveness of regional bureaucracies created to support human rights bodies and initiatives.

Regional commissioners of human rights

The Council of Europe is the only regional organization with a high commissioner, which was established in 1999. The commissioner is an independent and impartial institution within the Council of Europe, mandated to promote human rights within the member states. The primary goal of the commissioner is to advise governments on implementing human rights as outlined in European and international instruments.[46] The commissioner also supports the work of the European treaty monitoring bodies. The treaty monitoring bodies include:

- European Committee for the Prevention of Torture and Inhuman or Degrading Treatment or Punishment;
- European Committee of Social Rights;
- Advisory Committee on the Framework Convention for the Protection of National Minorities;
- European Commission against Racism and Intolerance;
- Group of Experts on Action Against Trafficking in Human Beings.

The European treaty monitoring bodies cooperate informally with their UN counterparts.[47]

Regional human rights commissions

The European Commission is now defunct and has been replaced by a high commissioner. The InterAmerican Commission for Human Rights is a seven-member, independent body charged with promoting and protecting human rights within the OAS system and also serves as the treaty monitoring body for the 1969 American Convention on Human Rights. This commission does not have a particularly noteworthy record largely because OAS states have not empowered the commission. In spite of being hamstrung by states, the commission's seven members are diverse and have distinguished human rights records. The commission has also drawn attention to the rights of indigenous peoples and the persistent problem of domestic violence against women.[48]

The African Commission on Human and Peoples' Rights supervises the implementation of the African Charter on Human and Peoples' Rights (Banjul Charter). The commission is an eleven-member body that is elected by the AU assembly from a slate of experts nominated by states.[49] The commission has set up special rapporteurs, committees, and working groups on several human rights topics although most of these mechanisms have not been particularly effective because they lack resources and the political backing of states.

When the Arab Charter on Human Rights entered into force in 2008, the corresponding Arab Human Rights Committee became operational. The committee consists of seven independent experts elected by states parties. The charter requires state parties to submit progress reports to the committee and the committee will offer recommendations. The Organization of Islamic Conference created the Independent Permanent Human Rights Commission in 2012 and it consists of eighteen independent experts, with six coming from Arab member states, six from Asian states, and six from African states.[50] It is charged with assessing human rights in the context of Islam; however, as of yet, it does not have a track record to assess. The ASEAN Intergovernmental Commission on Human Rights is an eleven-member body appointed by member states. Like its regional counterparts, it is in the early stages of development but, unlike them, it is designed as a multilateral body representing states rather than an independent body comprised of experts.

Regional human rights courts

The European Court of Human Rights was established in 1959 by the European Convention for the Protection of Human Rights and Fundamental Freedoms. The court was the first international court established to make determinations on human rights matters and has created more human rights jurisprudence than any other international system.[51] All member states of the Council of Europe are parties to the Convention and therefore fall under the court's jurisdiction. The European Court of Human Rights hears complaints about member states and these complaints can be brought by individuals, groups, NGOs, and other states. Parties bringing claims before the court must first exhaust domestic remedies before the complaint can be heard. The court can also issue advisory opinions on human rights issues that can help bridge the gap between multiple interpretations. The Commissioner for Human Rights uses court judgments and advisory opinions to form recommendations for member states. The European Court of Justice, the EU court, also may hear human rights cases and it complements the work of the European Court of Human Rights.

The InterAmerican Court of Human Rights also does not have the same level of acceptance as its European counterparts. It was created by OAS indirectly when it adopted the American Convention on Human Rights which called for the creation of a court to adjudicate disputes arising under the treaty. When the treaty entered into force in 1979, it was a time when forced disappearances, executions, and torture were commonplace and there was an ambivalence toward inter-American institutions.[52] It still has not gained much traction as a force for the protection of international or regional human rights.

The African Court on Human and Peoples' Rights was established in 1998 by the Protocol to the African Charter on Human and Peoples' Rights. Only twenty-six states are parties to the Court and it did not issue is first judgment until 2009.[53] AU members have since merged this court with the African Court of Justice to try to better improve protection. ASEAN and the OIC do not have human rights courts nor are other regional courts empowered to hear human rights cases.

Conclusion

Human rights and humanitarian principles are advanced by IGO diplomacy, especially when multilateral state diplomacy provides for and supports IGO officials, civil servants, and independent experts in their independent promotion and protection efforts. These efforts involve helping to develop, define, implement, and monitor international human rights standards. The uneven application of human rights across agencies and regions suggest that considerable disagreement still exists among relevant actors regarding the definition and implementation of human rights and humanitarian principles. Human rights and humanitarian diplomacy by IGOs reflects two dimensions of human protection. When there is general consensus among member states regarding the priority of competing interest and values, such as in Europe, IGO human rights protection can push the status of human rights forward. However, where major states resist or reject existing standards (or do not make human rights a priority), IGO diplomacy is geared more toward building consensus on an ad hoc basis and coordinating international action. The regional frameworks for IGO human rights protection are ineffective at best and, at worst, reflect a fracturing of the fragile consensus surround international human rights and humanitarian principles.

Key terms

IGO diplomacy, international civil service, secretariat, good offices, Boutros Boutros-Ghali, Kofi Annan, human-rights based approach, Global Compact, Ban Ki-moon, United Nations High Commissioner for Human Rights, Jose Ayala-Lasso, Mary Robinson, Sergio Vieira de Mello, Bertrand Ramacharan, Louis Arbour, Navanethem (Navi) Pillay, Zeid al-Hussein, charter-based and treaty-based bodies, special rapporteurs, megaphone diplomacy, commissions of inquiry, 1951 Convention Relating to the Status of Refugees, *nonrefoulement*, voluntary repatriation, resettlement, assimilation, internally displaced persons (IDPs), 1967 Protocol, António Guterres, celebrity diplomacy, Goodwill Ambassadors, Emergency Relief Coordinator (ERC), Jan Egeland, Valerie Amos, Cluster Coordination.

Discussion questions

1. Discuss the human rights and humanitarian IGO diplomacy conducted by the UN Secretary-General. What innovations have different secretaries-general brought to human rights and humanitarian diplomacy?
2. Discuss the roles of the OHCHR and UNHCR in promoting and protecting human rights and humanitarian principles.
3. Discuss the role of independent experts in multilateral and IGO diplomacy.
4. What are some of the positive and negative diplomatic consequences of the development of regional human rights bodies?

Notes

1 David P. Forsythe, "The UN Secretary-General and Human Rights," in *The Challenging Role of the UN Secretary-General: Making "The Most Impossible Job in the World" Possible*, ed. Benjamin Rivlin and Leon Gordenker (Westport: Greenwood Press, 1993), 211–232.
2 See "First UN High Commissioner for Human Rights Named," *Africa Report*, 39:1 (March–April 1994), 10–12.
3 For details of the troubled relationship see Boutros Boutros-Ghali, *Unvanquished: A U.S.- U.N. Saga* (New York: Random House, 1999).
4 High Level Panel on Threats, Challenges and Change, *A More Secured World: Our Shared Responsibility*, 2004, accessed October 5, 2014. www.un.org/en/peacebuilding/pdf/historical/hlp_more_secure_world.pdf.

5 Kofi Annan, *In Larger Freedom: Toward Security, Development and Human Rights for All*, accessed October 5, 2014. www.un.org/en/events/pastevents/pdfs/larger_freedom_exec_summary.pdf.
6 See *The United Nations Global Compact*, accessed September 5, 2014. www.unglobalcompact.org/.
7 Julia Preston, "New U.N. Chief Invites Controversy by Declining to Oppose Hussein Execution," *New York Times*, January 3, 2007, accessed October 15, 2014. www.nytimes.com/2007/01/03/world/middleeast/03nations.html?fta=y&_r=0.
8 Charles J. Brown, "The Limits of Institutional Diplomacy," *Freedom Review*, 25:4 (April 1994), 31–33.
9 Neil MacFarquhar, "Open Search Urged for U.N. Rights Job," *New York Times*, June 10, 2008, A9, accessed October 15, 2014. http://query.nytimes.com/gst/fullpage.html?res=9A03EED71639F933A25755C0A96E9C8B63.
10 David P. Forsythe, *Human Rights in International Relations* (New York: Cambridge University Press, 2006), 69.
11 Thomas G. Weiss, David P. Forsythe, Roger A. Coate, and Kelly-Kate Pease, *The United Nations and Changing World Politics*, 7th edition (Boulder: Westview Press, 2014), 207.
12 Philip Aston, "Neither Fish nor Fowl: The Quest to Define the Role of the UN High Commissioner for Human Rights," *European Journal of International Law*, 8:2 (1997), 321–335, 321.
13 Weiss *et al.*, *The United Nations*, 208.
14 Clare Kapp, "Brazilian Diplomat Moves Into the Hot Seat," *The Lancet*, 360 (September 21, 2002), 93.
15 Samantha Powers, "The Envoy," *The New Yorker*, **83**:42 (January 7, 2008), 42–55, 42. For a detailed account of the life of Sergio Vieira de Mello, also see Samantha Powers, *Chasing the Flame: Sergio Vieira de Mello and the Fight to Save the World* (New York: Penguin Press, 2009), especially Chapter 14.
16 Powers, "The Envoy," 42.
17 Richard Gowan, "Diplomatic Fallout: Vieira de Mello and the Dark Side of U.N. Diplomacy," *World Politics Review*, 1 (August 12, 2013), accessed September 21, 2014. www.worldpoliticsreview.com/articles/13156/diplomatic-fallout-vieira-de-mello-and-the-dark-side-of-u-n-diplomacy.
18 See Ruth Blakeley, "Dirty Hands, Clean Conscience? The CIA Inspector General's Investigation of 'Enhanced Interrogation Techniques,' in 'The War on Terror and the Torture Debate,'" *Journal of Human Rights*, 10:4 (October–December 2011), 544–561; M. Cheriff Bassiounit, "The Institutionalization of Torture Under the Bush Administration," *Case Western Reserve Journal of International Law*, 37:2/3 (2006), 389–425.
19 Available at www.ohchr.org/EN/NewsEvents/Pages/DisplayNews.aspx?NewsID=9569&LangID=e. Accessed October 4, 2015.
20 Much of the description of OCHCR field operations and staff is drawn from the website www.ohchr.org/EN/Countries/Pages/WorkInField.aspx, accessed October 5, 2015.
21 Philip Alston, Jason Morgan-Foster, and William Abresch, "The Competence of the UN Human Rights Council and Its Special Procedures in Armed Conflicts: Extrajudicial Executions and the War on Terror," *European Journal of International Law*, 19 (2008), 183–209.

22 Joanna Naples-Mitchell, "Perspectives of UN Special Rapporteurs on their Role: Inherent Tensions and Unique Contributions to Human Rights," *International Journal of Human Rights*, 15:2 (February 2011), 232–248.
23 Rosa Freedman, *The United Nations Human Rights Council: A Critique and Early Assessment* (New York: Routledge, 2013), 111.
24 Paulo Sergio Pinheiro, "Being a Special Rapporteur: A Delicate Balancing Act," *International Journal of Human Rights*, 15 (2011), 169.
25 Reprinted with permission from publisher. Pinheiro, "Being a Special Rapporteur," 162–171. *Journal of Human Rights* , 15 (2011)
26 Pinheiro, "Being a Special Rapporteur," 168.
27 Pinheiro, "Being a Special Rapporteur," 168.
28 Pinheiro, "Being a Special Rapporteur," 168.
29 Michael O'Flaherty, "The United Nations Human Rights Treaty Bodies," in *Human Rights Diplomacy: Contemporary Perspectives*, ed. Michael O'Flaherty, Zdzisław Kędzia, Amrei Müller, and George Ulrich (Leiden: Martinus Nijhoff Publishers, 2011), 157.
30 O'Flaherty, "The United Nations Human Rights Treaty Bodies," 161.
31 O'Flaherty, "The United Nations Human Rights Treaty Bodies," 159.
32 O'Flaherty, "The United Nations Human Rights Treaty Bodies," 161.
33 United Nations General Assembly Resolution 428 (v), December 14, 1950, accessed October 5, 2015. www.un.org/documents/ga/res/5/ares5.htm.
34 Leon Gordenker, *Refugees in International Politics* (London: Croom Helm, 1987), 39–48.
35 Gil Loescher, *Beyond Charity: International Cooperation and the Global Refugee Crisis* (Oxford: Oxford University Press, 1996), 72.
36 The UNHCR, "Governance and Organization: How the UNHCR is Structured," accessed October 15, 2014. www.unhcr.org/pages/49c3646c80.html.
37 Mark Wheeler, "Celebrity Diplomacy: United Nations' Goodwill Ambassadors and Messengers of Peace," *Celebrity Studies*, 2:1 (2011), 6–18.
38 Andrew F. Cooper, *Celebrity Diplomacy* (Boulder: Paradigm Publishers, 2008).
39 Mark D. Alleyne, "The United Nations' Celebrity Diplomacy," *SAIS Review of International Affairs*, 25:1 (2005), 175–185.
40 "Goodwill Ambassadors," accessed October 5, 2014. www.unhcr.org/pages/49c3646c3e.html.
41 Weiss *et al.*, *The United Nations*, 222–225.
42 Weiss *et al.*, *The United Nations*, 224.
43 For more information about Cluster Coordination, see United Nations Office for the Coordination of Humanitarian Affairs, "Cluster Coordination," accessed September 1, 2014. www.unocha.org/what-we-do/coordination-tools/cluster-coordination.
44 United Nations Office for the Coordination of Humanitarian Affairs, "Who we are," accessed September 1, 2014. www.unocha.org/about-us/who-we-are.
45 Jan Egeland, "Humanitarian Diplomacy," in *The Oxford Handbook of Modern Diplomacy*, ed. Andrew F. Cooper, Jorge Heine, and Ramesh Thaur (Oxford: Oxford University Press, 2013), 356–357.
46 The Council of Europe, "Commissioner for Human Rights," accessed September 4, 2014. www.coe.int/en/web/commissioner/mandate.

47 For more information, see "The European Union and International Human Rights Law," accessed October 15, 2014. www.europe.ohchr.org/Documents/Publications/EU_and_International_Law.pdf.
48 Alanis Olivares and Efren C. Goettingen, "Indigenous Peoples' Rights and the Extractive Industry: Jurisprudence from the Inter-American System of Human Rights," *Journal of International Law*, 5:1 (2013), 187–214; Paula Spieler, "The Maria da Pheha Case and the Inter-American Commission on Human Rights: Contributions to the Debate of Domestic Violence Against Women in Brazil," *Indiana Journal of Global Legal Studies*, 18:1 (2011), 121–143.
49 "About ACHPR," accessed October 5, 2014. www.achpr.org/about/.
50 "OIC Human Rights," accessed October 5, 2014. https://oichumanrights.wordpress.com/category/independent-permanent-human-rights-commission-iphrc/.
51 Philip Alston and Ryan Goodman, *International Human Rights: The Successor to International Human Rights in Context: Law, Politics and Morals* (Oxford: Oxford University Press, 2013), 891.
52 Alston and Goodman, *International Human Rights*, 980.
53 African Union: A United Strong Africa, "The African Court on Human and Peoples' Rights," accessed September 4, 2014. www.au.int/en/organs/cj.

6
NGO diplomacy

Global civil society, depending on definition, consists of hundreds of thousands of private civic actors including NGOs and private individuals. Many conceptions of "**civil society**" distinguish between private, nonprofit organizations (such as NGOs) and private, for-profit organizations (such as national and multinational corporations), with the former being principled organizations, and therefore, part of civil society; and the latter being self-interested, and therefore, not a civil society actor.[1] This chapter is devoted to exploring NGO human rights and humanitarian diplomacy. Often referred to as track 2 diplomacy, NGOs participate in diplomacy through their advocacy, their role as subcontractors, and as vehicles for citizen diplomacy.[2] This chapter also provides an overview of some of the more prominent NGOs and their contributions to human rights and humanitarian diplomacy. Recall that there are important distinctions between human rights and humanitarian affairs, and therefore, important differences between human rights NGOs and humanitarian NGOs. Both types of NGO often operate within the same geographical and diplomatic space, but under separate legal frameworks: international human rights law and IHL. Both use the same advocacy tools, but in times of conflict and war, humanitarian NGOs are far more judicious in how they use information gathered in the field. They are more likely to use quiet diplomacy in their negotiations with governments and other actors so they can gain access to populations at-risk. Humanitarian NGOs have to balance immediate human needs on the ground with longer-term advocacy goals. A cost–benefit analysis is a must before deciding whether to speak out publicly against belligerents.

NGO diplomacy or advocacy?

NGOs are relevant actors in international diplomacy because they gather, evaluate, and disseminate information; set standards; advocate; and lobby on behalf of human rights and humanitarian principles.[3] When conceptualizing NGO human rights and humanitarian diplomacy, it is difficult, if not impossible, to distinguish between diplomacy and advocacy. One definition of human rights diplomacy holds that it "refers to the use of the range of persuasive negotiation-based diplomatic tools available to states and intergovernmental organizations for the specific purpose of promoting and protecting human rights."[4] This narrow definition assumes that states and IGOs are the only diplomatic actors. Yet NGOs are part of the equation because they encourage and pressure states and IGOs to respect human rights and humanitarian principles. They also help states and IGOs implement policy and play a crucial monitoring role. Recall that the International Federation of the Red Cross and other humanitarian aid organizations refer to "humanitarian diplomacy" as the process whereby NGOs are involved with "persuading decision makers and opinion leaders to act at all times in the interests of vulnerable people and with full respect for fundamental humanitarian principles."[5] NGOs engage in human rights and humanitarian diplomacy as a part of their advocacy. They do this by lobbying state and IGO officials and brokering relationships between diplomats. They use indirect lobbying techniques such as mobilizing public support or encouraging grassroots activism.

Some of this diplomacy is geared toward creating new human rights norms. Some norms need to be codified (for example, the rights of LGBTQ persons). Some internationally recognized human rights and humanitarian principles need greater attention or compliance (for example, the rights of women and children).[6] The operational gap between codification, ratification, and implementation of human rights and humanitarian principles means that NGOs play an instrumental role in shaping the diplomatic agenda and how human rights and humanitarian principles are negotiated and applied. Their diplomacy also helps create human rights and humanitarian law. Once created, law forms the diplomatic foundation upon which states, IGOs, and NGOs can continue to build respect for human rights and humanitarian principles.

NGOs spend a considerable amount of time and energy collecting and disseminating information about specific human rights abuses and humanitarian situations. They employ highly qualified experts and maximize their influence by using different channels to reach stakeholders. They calculate whether to seek media coverage, meet with government officials, or attempt to mobilize the public.[7] Government and IGO officials need quality, reliable data regarding human rights and humanitarian situations in order to improve public policy. This information can also help to clarify issues and reduce uncertainties, making it easier for problem-solving and negotiation. The credibility and efficacy of NGOs depends on the accuracy of their reporting. A discredited and unreliable actor simply cannot be effective in diplomacy. However, when credible NGOs push for official action on human rights, they give greater legitimacy to international efforts to address those issues.[8]

NGOs are often catalysts for human rights and humanitarian diplomacy by exposing abuses and conditions. They push for more effective human rights protection by governments. NGOs also work with like-minded governments and, therefore, can have a direct role in human rights diplomacy. Peggy Hicks of Human Rights Watch states that, "through our consistent engagement on human rights issues, NGOs develop strong relationships with policy makers that come into play at the entry level of decision making. Policy makers consult with NGO experts to get advice concerning policy options and views as to how particular approaches would be seen."[9]

NGO experts are often involved in policy-making through being voting members on policy-setting commissions and participating in working groups. This is evidenced by the campaign to adopt the Convention on Cluster Munitions and the Convention on the Right of Persons with Disabilities.[10] NGO experts also move into government and IGO positions and can directly affect policy. In this regard, NGOs serve as a talent bank for states seeking experts to fill government positions. NGOs also benefit from the experience of ex-government and IGO officials once they leave office.

Another advocacy related aspect of NGO diplomacy relates to norm creation, promotion, and agenda-setting by participating in transnational advocacy networks.[11] NGOs helped generate the shared norms and public pressure necessary to move states to create the ICC.[12] NGOs formed the Coalition for the International Criminal Court which was essential in starting ICC treaty negotiations.[13] Coalition members participated in preparatory meetings and conferences and they also worked to build a global network. The Coalition umbrella eventually covered more than 500 civil society organizations including a network of human rights, international law, humanitarian, religious, and women's NGOs. This network helped craft the working draft of the ICC statute by delivering working papers, meeting with government delegations, and lobbying. The Coalition was essential in providing supporting documentation and information to governments, media, and other NGOs.[14] NGOs also were able to bring the necessary expertise and grassroots pressure to bear on the diplomatic process to move many states to embrace the treaty.

NGOs as subcontractors

States and IGOs often turn to NGOs to help them carry out public policy.[15] States and IGOs rely on NGOs to deliver emergency humanitarian assistance to vulnerable populations experiencing war, violent conflict, or natural disasters. NGOs work on a continuous basis with people in extreme poverty, providing food, water, education, skills training, and medical services with funding provided by states.[16] How policy is implemented is as important as arriving at the policy itself in the real world actualization of human rights and humanitarian principles. The partnership between states on the one hand, and between NGOs on the other, is essential to the promotion and protection of human rights and humanitarian principles.

The partnership between states and NGOs is always evolving and fraught with difficulties. One difficulty is the **securitization of aid**, which means that the security interests of donor states often determine NGO relief activities. This can compromise the legitimacy and neutrality of NGOs and affect their ability to negotiate **humanitarian space**.[17] Another difficulty is that NGOs can be viewed as agents of foreign powers and, therefore, become targets of belligerents. In civil conflicts, NGO assistance in rebel-held territory means the NGOs could be viewed as agents of the opposition, aiding terrorist organizations, or giving comfort to the enemy. The subcontracting role of NGOs is tricky and can put NGO personnel in jeopardy.

NGOs as vehicles for citizen diplomacy

The concept of **citizen diplomacy** came into vogue during the Cold War and it meant that citizens have a responsibility to be unofficial ambassadors for their countries.[18] The private, unofficial dialogue between citizens is a potent way to further a society's political and cultural values, especially as they relate to human rights and humanitarian principles. During the Cold War, the US government established exchange programs such as the Peace Corps and the Fulbright Program to foster US citizen diplomacy throughout the world. After the Cold War, the definition of citizen diplomacy evolved to mean the process by which ordinary people can shape the values and norms of society, whether their own or global civil society's. In this regard, citizen diplomacy is multidirectional and NGOs become a vehicle for individuals to participate to shape human rights and humanitarian policies at home and abroad.

The International Campaign to Ban Landmines (ICBL) illustrates the concept of contemporary citizen diplomacy.[19] The ICRC was one of the first NGOs to draw attention to the indiscriminate nature of anti-personnel landmines. These weapons explode on contact, maiming or killing victims. In the 1970s, doctors became alarmed about the growing number of civilian and noncombatant victims of these weapons in places like Cambodia, Afghanistan, and Mozambique. The ICRC worked closely with military officials and physicians treating victims to document that most of the victims were civilians and not belligerents. They built a credible public relations case to show that the weapons were indiscriminate and, therefore, in violation of IHL.

Anti-personnel mines gained more attention in the 1990s with the end of the Cold War and the easing of East–West tensions. US Senator Patrick Leahy was a catalyst for the creation of the **International Campaign to Ban Landmines (ICBL)** after meeting a disabled boy in a Central American hospital in the 1980s. He led the congressional effort to create the War Victims Fund which provided millions annually for landmine victims.[20] His actions inspired Thomas Gebauer of Medico International and Bobby Muller of Vietnam Veterans of America Foundation to discuss the possibility of a campaign to ban anti-personnel landmines. In 1992, a group of six NGOs came together to found the ICBL. These NGOs included: Handicap International (France); Human Rights Watch (US); Medico International (Germany); Mines Advisory Group (UK); Physicians for Human Rights (US); and Vietnam Veterans of America Foundation (US). Working with like-minded governments and under the leadership of Canada's Foreign Minister Lloyd Axworthy, the diplomatic process for what would become the **Convention on the Prohibition and the Use, Stockpiling, Production, and Transfer of Anti-Personnel Mines and on their Destruction** (also known as the **Ottawa Treaty** or **Mine Ban Treaty**) began in 1996. The coalition of NGOs along with small and middle ranked states who formed the core of the landmine initiative within the international organizations established the "human security network."[21] The treaty gained the requisite number of signatures to enter into force in 1998. The critical mass necessary to create the political will to make this important contribution to IHL was, in large part, the result of citizen diplomacy.

Celebrity diplomacy also played an important role in the campaign when Princess Diana of the UK became concerned with the effects of landmines. She generated global publicity by visiting victims of landmines in Angola and famously walked across a minefield wearing a flak jacket and helmet. Those images, coupled with her celebrity, brought considerable attention to the cause. Sadly, her death (from a car accident in Paris) in 1997 generated additional awareness and may even have helped influence states to become party to the treaty. Major military powers, such as the United States, Russia, China, Israel, and India have not signed the treaty, but they are outliers given that 161 states have adopted the treaty. The international community, led by citizen diplomacy, has taken important steps for controlling these horrific weapons.

Human rights NGOs

Relatively few (approximately 250) NGOs consider the advancement of human rights and humanitarian principles to be their primary focus.[22] Human rights NGOs, such as Amnesty International and Human Rights Watch, perform several interrelated diplomatic functions that are part and parcel of their human rights advocacy, including fact-finding, monitoring, lobbying public officials, and shaping public opinion. These organizations were chosen for this text because they are two of the more reputable human rights NGOs. While their differences are highlighted, they also pursue many of the same agenda items and work together on occasion to release joint human rights statements and reports on important matters. They have worked together on issues such as sustainable development, drones, and media restrictions in South Sudan.

Amnesty International. Amnesty International began after British lawyer Peter Beneson launched a worldwide campaign called "Appeal for Amnesty 1961."[23] The campaign started when the *Observer* newspaper published Beneson's article, "The Forgotten Prisoners," about two students imprisoned in Portugal for criticizing the government. The article was reprinted all over the world and was the catalyst for the NGO's creation. In its first few years, Amnesty International used **letter-writing campaigns** to advocate for the release of prisoners of conscience. Letter-writing campaigns are a grassroots technique designed to bring direct pressure on those committing human rights violations. These campaigns also pressure state decision-makers to encourage their foreign counterparts to cease the offending behavior and protect human rights.

Amnesty International is comprised of over three million members worldwide and has regional hubs that carry out research and advocacy activities.[24] It enjoys consultative status at the UN which allows it to observe public UN business, distribute reports, submit written statements on UN agenda items, make oral statements, receive UN documents, and work on international legal instruments.[25] Amnesty International is funded solely by members and voluntary donations. It does not receive funding from national governments, nevertheless, it does try to maintain good relationships with government officials.

Amnesty International is an important vehicle for citizen diplomacy because its members contribute financially and participate in letter-writing campaigns.[26] Amnesty International uses its loyalty to human rights, along with its independence and impartiality, to not only criticize governments publicly, but at the same time, to work with authorities regarding specific cases of abuse.[27] Amnesty International's agenda has since evolved to include not only prisoners of conscience but also the establishment of preventative norms for issues such as torture, capital punishment, violence against women, and targeted killings.

Amnesty International has a solid reputation for providing accurate, unbiased information. While it may have organizational incentives to exaggerate allegations (such as obtaining funding and garnering media attention) Amnesty International appears to value credibility over popularity.[28] Credibility allows it to document and highlight violations and use that information to publicize the lag between human rights principles and practice. The data collected on human rights violations support Amnesty International's public campaigns and help to build the necessary public consensus to influence public policy.[29] Amnesty International is known for high levels of accuracy and diligent fact-checking. The trade-off for this accuracy is that considerable time is spent verifying information and this makes the exposure of abuses slower.[30] Today, Amnesty International is the world's largest grassroots human rights organization and has won the Nobel Peace Prize for advancing human rights.[31]

Human Rights Watch. Human Rights Watch began in 1978 as Helsinki Watch, an organization whose mission was to help citizen groups monitor Soviet compliance with international human rights standards and the Helsinki Accords. By using the tactic of publicly "naming and shaming" human rights abusers, Helsinki Watch arguably contributed to democratic transformations in the Soviet Union and Eastern Europe in the 1980s (see Chapter 2). Several other regional "Watch Committees" were also created and, in 1988, they were all combined into today's Human Rights Watch.

According to its mission statement, "Human Rights Watch is dedicated to protecting the human rights of people around the world. We stand with victims and activists to prevent discrimination, to uphold political freedom, to protect people from inhumane conduct in wartime, and to bring offenders to justice. We investigate and expose human rights violations and hold abusers accountable. We challenge governments and those who hold power to end abusive practices and respect international human rights law. We enlist the public and the international community to support the cause of human rights for all."[32] Human Rights Watch today is one of the most widely known human rights NGOs. It is a legitimate player in the field and its reports garner significant media attention. In Sidebar 6.1 Bill Frelick, Director of Human Rights Watch Refugee Rights Program, describes his organization's use of public diplomacy on behalf of Iraqi refugees in Jordan to illustrate the utility of Human Rights Watch reports in pressuring governments into taking action.

Sidebar 6.1 Bill Frelick – Human Rights Watch

In my work as the director of Human Rights Watch's Refugee Rights Program I have had the opportunity to engage in human rights diplomacy at various times and in different ways. Often our first objective is to make policymakers aware of and to acknowledge the existence of a human rights problem. For example prior to our November 2006 report, *The Silent Treatment: Fleeing Iraq, Surviving in Jordan*, Iraqi refugees were virtually invisible. Displaced Iraqis were rarely formally recognized as refugees either by the UN refugee agency (UNHCR) or by governments; they received virtually no humanitarian assistance; and most lived as illegal immigrants, subject to exploitation and abuse.

First, we needed to document the problem. Our report, aptly titled *The Silent Treatment*, featured scores of accounts of Iraqi refugees living in the shadows in Jordan, allowing them to step out just enough to talk about the abuses they faced. We also provided legal analysis to show that these Iraqis could not be presumptively dismissed as economic migrants, but that they had compelling claims for refugee status and needed protection, particularly against deportation or rejection at the border with Iraq.

To maximize the impact of the report, we timed its publication to coincide with President George W. Bush's visit to Amman, Jordan, holding a press conference to release the report the day before his arrival. The entire US presidential press entourage was in Amman looking for stories to cover. Our press conference was packed, in part, because the Jordanian government, in what it miscalculated as a preemptive move, denounced our report the day before, which created front-page headlines before we had said a word. In addition to the press conference, we placed op-ed pieces relating to the report in the *Jordan Times* and *International Herald Tribune*. The major press attention it garnered made it impossible for the Jordanian and US governments on the occasion of their summit and the wider international community to continue to ignore the plight of Iraqi refugees.

The Silent Treatment, and the NGO advocacy that grew from it, also had a significant impact on UNHCR. First, it emboldened the UN refugee agency to recognize asylum seekers from south and central Iraq as refugees on a prima facie basis and to take stronger advocacy positions on their behalf. Our work, together with that of our many NGO partners, also paved the way for UNHCR to seek – and receive – far more humanitarian assistance for displaced Iraqis than it could have dreamed of asking for before NGOs and the media brought such wide attention to their needs. UNHCR increased its donor appeals by 900 percent between 2006 and 2008. In 2006, prior to our first report, it only asked for $29 million, and had received less than half that amount from donor states. In January 2007 it more than doubled the appeal to $60 million. Having fully met that goal, it more than doubled the appeal again to $123 million in July 2007. In January 2008, UNHCR increased the appeal once more, asking for $261 million. These increased funds put more protection officers on the ground, expedited the processing of asylum applications, and improved the capacity to meet the humanitarian needs of displaced Iraqis.

We followed *The Silent Treatment* with another report, *From a Flood to a Trickle: Neighboring States Stop Iraqis Fleeing War and Persecution*, whose release coincided with an April 2007 conference on Iraqi refugees called for by UNHCR. That report provided a vital reality check on the back-patting rhetoric of the 104 states gathered in Geneva and forced the delegates to answer our charge – based on solid evidence gathered in the field – that Jordan, Syria, and Egypt were closing their doors to Iraqis seeking asylum at their borders and that the rest of the international community was failing to give these states the support they needed to accept more refugees.

Although governments began donating more to UNHCR for Iraqi refugees, offers to resettle Iraqi refugees moved at a snail's pace. We engaged publicly and privately with members of the US Congress and US State Department officials to spur them to take greater responsibility for the humanitarian consequences of the US military intervention in Iraq. In a July 9, 2007 letter to the editor of the Washington Post, I wrote:

In her July 5 letter, "Two Refugee Flows That Aren't Alike," Assistant Secretary of State Ellen R. Sauerbrey said that Iraqi refugees are arriving in the United States and that "their numbers will increase sharply in the months ahead." The United States admitted one Iraqi refugee in each of the months of April and May. In June, it admitted 63. That does indeed constitute a sharp increase, but one of little consequence to 2 million Iraqi refugees and another 2 million displaced inside Iraq.

Ms. Sauerbrey also said that the United States has funded 30 percent of the appeal for $60 million by the U.N. High Commissioner for Refugees. Not quite true. Of the $18 million Washington promised, the UNHCR has received only $12 million so far. Meanwhile, The Post reported that the United States is shelling out $592 million to build its embassy in Baghdad ["Construction Woes Add to Fear at Embassy," front page, July 5].

Ms. Sauerbrey said that we are "welcoming the persecuted and standing by our friends." Standing by seems to be the only thing the United States is doing as Iraqis continue to be forcibly displaced.

Within days of the publication of this letter, the State Department more than doubled its commitment to UNHCR, bringing its contributions to a total of $37 million. It also increased Iraqi resettlement from only 202 Iraqi refugees admitted in 2006 to 1,608 in 2007, and by 2008 pledged to admit 12,000. As of December 31, 2013, the US had admitted 108,224 Iraqi refugees (and Iraqi interpreters with special immigrant visas), since October 1, 2006.

It is always a challenge to assess the impact of human rights diplomacy, and modesty in making claims is prudent. If nothing else, we can say with confidence that our report on Iraqi refugees in Jordan and related advocacy marked a turning point: from that time onward no one could deny their existence and their plight.

Human Rights Watch is not without its critics, especially because it has the reputation of being slow to act against US interests.[33] Human Rights Watch lacks the same kind of credibility as Amnesty International because it is not a membership-based organization. As one human rights expert puts it, "one could say that it was elitist, non-democratic, non-transparent, and unaccountable."[34] Aside from Amnesty International, most human rights NGOs are not mass membership organizations and do not hold elections for their leaders.[35] Still, Human Rights Watch reports are widely respected and used by NGOs, IGOs, and governments as advocacy and lobbying tools.

NGO human rights diplomacy: strategy and tools

Many Western liberal democracies have effectively joined with NGOs, albeit tacitly, to monitor and promote human rights.[36] This also has the added effect of projecting Western liberal values relating to human rights. Fact-finding and monitoring are essential for furthering human rights and for engaging and prodding other actors, whether behind the scenes or publicly. NGOs are more likely to be seen as "honest brokers" because the promotion of human rights is considered their primary purpose and motivation.[37] States, on the other hand, clearly have other interests that often take precedence over the promotion and protection of human rights abroad. The lobbying of governmental and intergovernmental public officials can be both direct and indirect. Obviously, not all governments permit lobbying, especially by "foreign agents," but where lobbying is permissible (usually in liberal democracies) human rights NGOs can be found. This involves contacting public officials attempting to convince them of a specific policy position. NGOs often have an indirect effect on policy through their expert testimony before legislative and executive bodies.

Often, NGOs will turn to national courts in order to affect policy, especially when they lack the resources or the contacts to properly lobby legislative and executive officials. They do this by becoming party to a case, which in the United States can be difficult because of the "**standing**" issue. Standing means that in order to bring a case in court, petitioners have to show harm. For example, Amnesty International (along with other NGOs) sued the US government to challenge the constitutionality of warrantless wiretaps in the United States because such searches, they argued, harmed their ability to confidentially communicate with human rights advocates abroad. In 2013, the US Supreme Court ruled in ***Clapper v. Amnesty International USA*** that Amnesty International did not have standing to sue because it could not show that it was likely to be targeted and, therefore, harmed.[38] The standing requirement means NGOs must find other ways to influence public policy through the courts. One strategy is to provide legal representation to those directly harmed, which has the benefit of not only helping individuals directly but, if successful, in establishing a legal precedent that places respect for international human rights as a guiding legal principle. Another strategy involves filing ***amicus curiae*** (friend of the court) briefs. The *amicus curiae* brief serves to educate national and international lawyers and judges by providing them with the legal reasoning for potentially deciding a case using international human rights or humanitarian law.

Shaping public opinion is part and parcel of NGO lobbying and important in its own right. NGOs can help to influence the debate by consistently taking positions that are supportive of human rights. They also shape the debate by pointing out the human rights implications of broader topics.[39] Mobilizing at the grassroots level and influencing public opinion is at the heart of this process. Traditional methods of shaping public opinion include letters-to-the-editor, op-eds, open letters, and expert news commentary. Sidebar 6.2 includes an open letter to the UN from Amnesty International and Human Rights Watch calling for a transparent and consultative process for the selection of a new High Commissioner for Human Rights after the resignation of Louise Arbour in 2008. This letter illustrates how society actors publicly try to influence public policy.

Sidebar 6.2 Open letter to the United Nations[40]

17 March 2008
Open Letter to the United Nations
Following the resignation of Louise Arbour last week, Amnesty International and Human Rights Watch have called on the UN Secretary-General Ban Ki-moon to implement a transparent, consultative process for selecting a strong, independent and outspoken new High Commissioner for Human Rights.

Dear Secretary-General,

The UN High Commissioner for Human Rights, Louise Arbour, has set a high standard in promoting and protecting human rights throughout the world. As you begin to look for the next High Commissioner, we are writing to emphasize the high expectations which our organizations have for the successor to this important office. Appointing an extremely capable and highly qualified High Commissioner is crucial at this time when fundamental principles of human rights are challenged and the independence of the High Commissioner's Office is under attack. We appreciate the strong statement you made in Geneva, supporting the High Commissioner's Office as well as its independence, and we urge you to continue to defend vigorously the office's ability to operate without interference from any source.

Criteria /Qualifications for appointment

Our organizations believe that the new High Commissioner must be a person of the highest international standing and integrity, and have a proven track-record of public advocacy for human rights. She or he must be a human rights champion ready to be outspoken and independent in fulfilling the office's mandates. The High Commissioner must be a strong leader with a clear vision for the protection of all human rights, and bring dynamism, courage and commitment to the position. She or he must be able to inspire those working for the promotion and protection of human rights and the broader international community. In addition, the next High Commissioner should be someone with proven management skills and the ability to navigate effectively within a complex human rights community which comprises governments, civil society and other stakeholders.

We urge you to look at candidates from all countries and to select an exceptionally well-qualified candidate who would be able to meet the demands of this important post from the moment he or she assumes the post.

Selection process

The selection process will be very important in ensuring that the best qualified candidate for the position of High Commissioner is identified. You have stressed the importance of accountability, professionalism and transparency for the United Nations, and we urge that you apply these principles as well to the selection of the new High Commissioner. We recommend the following:

- A formal description of the qualifications you are seeking in the next High Commissioner should be formulated relying on the qualities set out above, and should be made public. This description would assist in the identification of candidates and facilitate your assessment of their competencies.
- The process must be transparent and include wide consultation with all stakeholders, governmental and nongovernmental, including civil society, notably NGOs dealing with human rights.
- There should be a set timetable for nominations, shortlists and final selection to provide a framework for the selection process that ensures transparency and accountability.

The appointment processes for both the current UN High Commissioner for Refugees and the Administrator of UNDP provide useful guidance in this regard. In both cases, the shortlist of candidates was made public, an important step in ensuring that the Secretary-General had the broadest possible input in making those appointments. A similar process would greatly enhance the credibility of your ultimate appointment, and assist you in selecting the most outstanding candidate for this crucial post.

Human rights, with peace and security and development, are one of the three pillars of the United Nations. It is vital that the next holder of this position be a compelling leader for human rights within the United Nations system and throughout the world. In this year of the 60th anniversary of the Universal Declaration of Human Rights, we urge you to put in place a process that reflects

> the gravity and significance of this appointment to human rights victims and defenders worldwide.
> Yours sincerely,
>
> Irene Khan   Kenneth Roth
> Secretary General   Executive Director
> Amnesty International   Human Rights Watch

Another strategy afforded to human rights NGOs is "**naming and shaming.**" By publicly calling out gross violators of human rights, governments and other actors are pushed to change their policies and behaviors. In the case of genocide, naming and shaming has been effective at reducing the severity of atrocities.[41] Even the threat of naming and shaming can help ameliorate human rights violations because governments want to move quickly to blunt criticism. Amnesty International was founded on the principle that governments respond to public opinion and they can be made to respond to violations by being embarrassed. Human rights reports frame the debate and put violators in the position of having to respond to allegations of violations.

NGOs are now using different technologies in conjunction with their traditional methods to reach a broader audience. Human Rights Watch increasingly uses the Internet and social media to disseminate reports and press releases. They update and educate their readers and the general public on human rights issues and government responses to reports of violations.[42] While Internet and social media technology affords many advantages like communicating a precise message, it also can compartmentalize audiences and allow members of the audience to pick and choose what they wish to view and read. This means human rights NGOs may end up "preaching to the choir" rather than educating those in need of conversion. The censorship of the Internet and social media means NGOs are limited in their ability to reach citizens in oppressive states. These technologies also provide a medium for others to quickly respond to and counter the message of human rights NGOs. The result can be a public relations battle where the "truth" becomes muddied or even lost.[43]

Humanitarian NGOs

Humanitarian NGOs aim to reach populations that are affected by conflict, disaster, and crisis by coordinating efforts from their headquarters and distributing aid in the field. A large part of their work centers on raising money and finding supplies to ensure that resources are available when a crisis hits. The ICRC and MSF are two of the larger, more respected humanitarian NGOs with global reach. These organizations advocate and protect differently. The ICRC uses confidentiality to enhance its ability to negotiate access, while neutrality and impartiality enables the MSF to provide health care almost anywhere in the world.

The International Committee of the Red Cross. The ICRC was established in 1863 to provide humanitarian assistance to those who are affected by armed conflict and promote laws to protect the "victims of war." Henry Dunant, a Swiss businessman, started the movement after witnessing the aftermath the Battle of Solferino (1859) where over 40,000 soldiers were killed or wounded. Dunant observed that both sides of the conflict had veterinarians on hand to tend to the battle horses but no medical personnel to care for the wounded. He abandoned his business trip to help the wounded and then went home to write the *Memory of Solferino*, where he described the suffering and advocated for relief services. He then began a committee that eventually became the ICRC.

The ICRC is an independent and neutral organization based in Geneva, Switzerland. Its mandate is derived from the Geneva Conventions of 1949 and it is principally involved with assisting the victims of war (POWs, the wounded, civilians, and other noncombatants). Today, the organization is comprised of 12,000 people in eighty countries. National societies and the International Federation form the **International Red Cross and Red Crescent Movement**. In situations of armed conflict the ICRC coordinates the response of its national partners. It plays a formal humanitarian role in most armed conflicts because it has special rights and duties provided by the Geneva Conventions and Protocols. It is also means that the ICRC has a permanent international mandate for its work. The ICRC works with states to expand legal protections for victims of war and limit human suffering. It is also the only non-state actor working for human rights and humanitarian affairs that has been granted observer status in the UN General Assembly. The ICRC also meets monthly with the Security Council because of its close working relationships with governments experiencing armed conflict.[44]

The ICRC responds to humanitarian needs by visiting detainees, protecting civilians, restoring family links, ensuring economic security, and providing water, housing, and health care. The ICRC also works to build respect for IHL and contribute to its development. The ICRC generally does not use publicity to pressure states, opting for quiet diplomacy instead. The ICRC has built a reputation for meticulously precise statements about the treatment of POWs and other victims of armed conflict. The ICRC will not comment unless its delegates in the field can directly verify facts. One human rights expert could not find one example of the ICRC providing a false public statement regarding humanitarian conditions.[45]

ICRC confidentiality is essential for gaining access to the victims of war. The ICRC uses confidentiality to build trust with relevant stakeholders and data collected from field operations is shared discretely with appropriate authorities. In addition, the ICRC seals its archives for forty years (after which it makes the archives available to researchers). This means that, in time, its reputation can be affected, but not until long after the fact.[46] For example, the depth of ICRC knowledge of the conditions in German concentration camps (and the existence of deaths camps) during World War II did not become widely known until the 1990s. This has spurred debate about the moral and ethical obligations of the ICRC when faced with mass atrocities.[47]

The ICRC is often criticized for not speaking out on certain issues, especially when there is insufficient progress in achieving humanitarian objectives. The ICRC is careful to not appear to be complacent when abuses are taking place; however, the ICRC maintains that its discretion is essential for protecting victims of war. The main focus of the ICRC is to gain access and improve conditions for those affected, regardless of their role in the conflict. If ICRC delegates find evidence of abuse when visiting detainees, they take their concerns to the appropriate national authorities or responsible parties as opposed to releasing the information in a report to the public.[48]

The ICRC does speak out at times, especially if public authorities publish parts of its reports without its consent. The ICRC reserves the right to publish the entire report to prevent inaccurate and incomplete interpretations.[49] The ICRC will also "go public" if, after repeated requests, it is denied access to prisoners and has exhausted all other diplomatic avenues.[50]

Médecins Sans Frontières. MSF is a humanitarian NGO that delivers emergency aid to people affected by armed conflicts, natural disasters, and complex emergencies and operates under the principles of neutrality, impartiality, and medical ethics.[51] It is comprised of thousands of medical and logistical professionals working in over seventy countries. MSF was created in 1971 in the midst of the Biafra crisis when a small group of ICRC doctors (including Bernard Kouchner, who later became the Foreign Minister of France and vocal advocate of R2P) were appalled by the ICRC's complacency in the face of mass atrocities committed by the Nigerian Army. Hospital staff, volunteers, and civilians were routinely targeted and murdered. French physicians responding to the crisis started their own organization which emphasized victims' rights over neutrality and confidentiality.

The three main goals of MSF are to: offer humanitarian aid; bear witness and speak out; and offer quality medical care. It conducts its own assessment of people's needs and strives for neutrality and nondiscrimination. It assists victims of armed conflict, regardless of race, nationality, gender, religion, or their culpability in contributing to the conflict. It seeks to provide the best possible health care and raise public awareness to help confront diseases such as malaria. The original MSF charter (1971) stated that the organization would refrain from "any interference in State's internal affairs" and from "passing judgment or publicly expressing an opinion – either positive or negative – regarding events, forces or leaders who accepted their assistance." In 1978, the president of MSF announced that its staff would be "reporting human rights violations and unacceptable events they witnessed to the bureau … The bureau will then make the executive decision on whether to inform the public, in cases where MSF was the sole witness."[52] MSF is now regarded as the leading advocate for human rights-based humanitarianism.[53] In Sidebar 6.3 Hosanna Fox of MSF describes how civil society engaged authorities in the lead poisoning epidemic in northern Nigeria that caused the death of hundreds of children and sickened thousands. Her experience highlights the difficulties NGOs encounter while trying to remain neutral and impartial, yet providing a voice to the voiceless.

Sidebar 6.3 Hosanna Fox – civil society engagement

In 2012, I worked in an advocacy role in northern Nigeria with medical humanitarian organization, Médecins Sans Frontières/Doctors Without Borders (MSF). One of our key medical activities there was an emergency intervention in response to an unprecedented epidemic of lead-poisoning, during which 400 children died in the first months. One of the particularities of this response was that medical treatment for children could not begin until the village in which they lived had undergone the process of environmental remediation, which removed the lead contamination from their home environments. As part of the initial emergency response in 2010, MSF had actively advocated for the remediation of all eight affected villages. Seven out of eight of the villages underwent remediation and over 2000 children received medical treatment. Remediation in the eighth village, however, was not completed due to a delay in the release of funds, and as a result, severely lead-poisoned children were unable to receive urgently needed medical assistance. In 2012, I was deployed as a Humanitarian Affairs Officer to support advocacy activities focused on the release of funds promised by the government so that MSF could finally deliver medical assistance.

Our advocacy strategy employed a range of modes and tactics, which included both intensive bilateral engagement and public pressure tactics. One notable – and particularly successful aspect – of our strategy was the engagement of civil society groups.

Traditional humanitarian diplomacy activities such as bilateral meetings with a variety of stakeholders behind closed doors were complemented by civil society engagement – or social mobilisation. This decision had several motivations.

Firstly, while the value of social mobilisation around accountability focusing on government responsibility to the community affected was acknowledged, it was felt that these activities were not appropriate for a humanitarian agency – not only would it compromise our perceived neutrality, but it wasn't really our place to participate in the political landscape of a country we worked in. It was, however, our place to advocate for accountability on behalf of our patients and to endorse activities that would amplify the effects of our own humanitarian diplomacy.

The second motivation was to foster a broader range of voices, so that the "humanitarian diplomacy voice" was not an isolated voice but rather part of a chorus. Moreover, it was decided that empowering civil society groups who knew the local context better and were social media savvy would result in a higher quality outcomes.

With this in mind, we collaborated with a group of Nigerian social responsibility activists, who started a campaign called Follow The Money, which called for transparency and accountability from the Nigerian government in the immediate release and responsible expenditure of the funds for the remediation of the last lead-contaminated village.

The primary platform for the Follow The Money campaign was their website, which included petitions targeting key decision makers, social media links, a graphic tracking the progress of the remediation, transparency information on the remediation budget, a tracker showing recent news stories and background information on the lead poisoning crisis.

In addition to their extensive youth network, their understanding of the local political landscape, their ability to exploit social media and their ability to interact with the stakeholder group productively, Follow The Money was also able to engage the community concerned in ways that we could not. They have nurtured solid and productive relationships with the community and community leaders and continue to engage them in empowerment and awareness-raising exercises in ways that have benefited the community and creative a positive environment for humanitarian activities once they started. In all these regards, the more traditional humanitarian diplomacy activities were significantly reinforced and then amplified.

It's also worth noting that not only was the civil society engagement very effective in the short term achievement of the immediate goals, but it ended up being one of the most sustainable successes of the advocacy campaign. Not only did the lead organisation exceed expectations for the campaign, but their activities also laid the foundation for the establishment of a permanent registered NGO, with an international trusteeship and funding to continue and broaden its accountability and transparency activities.

In summary, here were the lessons learned that I took away from this experience as a humanitarian diplomat:

- Humanitarian and Human Rights Diplomats – as those who have taken on the responsibility of giving a voice to the voiceless – need to be prepared to engage stakeholders in flexible and innovative ways, including being aware of and willing to exploit and/or access informal and less visible power structures.
- Nuanced cultural and religious understanding of the contexts in which we work and how our actions are perceived in these environments can only increase our ability to act and speak on behalf of those we represent. However, we will only ever be outsiders and this should be acknowledged. Engaging civil society actors can address this inherent limitation.
- Building strategic partnerships with other actors can increase the reach and therefore effectiveness of diplomatic efforts exponentially. Whether to amplify our voice or provide a proxy voice, collaborating and coordinating with the full range of stakeholders or empowering local actors leads to a richer humanitarian/human rights diplomacy practice.

As a field practitioner, I've no doubt taken liberties with traditional understandings of diplomatic theory – and there are no doubt those that would argue that

> engagement with civil society as described here is not strictly humanitarian diplomacy. And they may well be right, but it's also worth considering where the needs we represent are not being met by current practice.
>
> While traditional diplomacy often happens at the "higher" levels of the political landscape and often involves elite power-holders, social mobilisation means engaging with a sector of society that is often perceived as either powerless and/or outside spaces where traditional diplomacy takes place. Perhaps this is a vestige of colonial notions of power and how it is wielded or perhaps this is simply a miscalculation or lack of innovation on the part of contemporary humanitarian and human rights diplomats. In any case, if humanitarian and human rights diplomacy truly seeks to use negotiation and bargaining to promote and protect human rights and humanitarian principles, then seeking engagement outside of the traditional corridors of power – both literally and figuratively – can be extremely effective. Where we are blind to where and how diplomacy is taking place in its many ad hoc and imperfect forms, we neglect to take into account how decisions are actually being made, where power actually resides and thusly we remain unaware of the full range of options to influence.
>
> Moreover, broadening diplomatic engagement address one of the darker sides of both humanitarian and diplomatic practice, which is to broker power outside the view and or reach of those directly concerned.
>
> Finally, it is worth considering to what and to whom we are responsible. If humanitarian and human rights diplomats are indeed responsible for giving a voice to the voiceless, this is a lofty strategy that demands pragmatic tactics. Much of diplomacy happens well away from the theory presented in textbooks. While the theoretical underpinnings are important as a foundation for practice, in order to bring the practice off the page, humanitarian and human rights diplomats must be able to translate theory into the real world where diplomacy happens.
>
> This, indeed is the challenge for mud-boot practitioners!

Bearing witness to abuses and the threat of wider publicity can prod belligerents to exercise restraint. MSF has to decide whether speaking out would yield greater benefits than keeping quiet, especially when the cost might involve being denied access to vulnerable populations. One negotiating tactic used by MSF is to exert media and diplomatic pressure. While operating in Ethiopia (2007–08), MSF experienced considerable difficulty with local authorities. MSF had few official contacts and its operations were insufficient and poorly organized.[54] MSF held a series of diplomatic meetings with main donors and concerned parties, as well as a press conference. It condemned the government's refusal to allow MSF access. Human rights violations were documented by the Dutch section of the organization, and those abuses where then reported by international media.[55] Donors then provided the necessary resources in order for MSF to act.

Conversely, in Sri Lanka, MSF decided not to go public regarding the atrocities committed by the government in putting down the Tamil rebellion. This regime was eager to appear to the world, and its own people, as the guarantor of a rule of law and democratic values. At the end of the day, MSF opted for the lesser evil, choosing to improve the conditions of the survivors of an all-out war that no political power seemed capable of checking.[56]

Conclusion

Without reputable NGOs, states and IGOs would have very little impartial information regarding human rights abuses occurring around the world. NGOs spend a considerable amount of their energy on collecting and disseminating information about human rights abuses and humanitarian situations. This expert information can help clarify issues and reduce uncertainties, making it easier for diplomatic negotiators to improve their bargaining position. NGOs use various tactics in human rights and humanitarian diplomacy to advocate for improved conditions. They bear witness and, at times, speak out. Human Rights Watch and Amnesty International make it a priority to publish reports that document atrocities and to provide these reports to policy-makers for use in higher level diplomacy. Other organizations, such as the ICRC and MSF, prefer to remain neutral, if at all possible, in order to provide aid and protection to at-risk populations. Paradoxically, their silence is their best negotiating tool, allowing them to provide services without hostile interference. NGOs are also at the cutting edge of advancing rights and principles. Clear examples of NGO influence include the ICC Statute and the ICBL. States sometimes work hard to disprove NGO claims or attempt to bar their entry. States would not go to such great lengths if NGOs were irrelevant to advancing human rights and humanitarian principles.[57]

Key terms

Civil society, securitization of aid, humanitarian space, citizen diplomacy, International Campaign to Ban Landmines (ICBL), Convention on the Prohibition and the Use, Stockpiling, Production, and Transfer of Anti-Personnel Mines and on their Destruction, letter-writing campaigns, standing, *Clapper* v. *Amnesty International USA, amicus curiae*, naming and shaming, the International Red Cross and Red Crescent Movement.

Discussion questions

1. How do human rights and humanitarian NGOs differ in their diplomatic approach?
2. What are the diplomatic functions of human rights NGOs? What kinds of strategies and tools to the use?
3. How does quiet diplomacy help and hinder the activities of humanitarian NGOs?
4. How useful is NGO network diplomacy if major states reject the aims and goals of diplomacy?

Notes

1 See for example Kathryn Hochstetler, "Civil Society," in *The Oxford Handbook of Modern Diplomacy*, ed. Andrew F. Cooper, Jorge Heine, and Ramesh Thakur (Oxford: Oxford University Press, 2013), 176–191.
2 David P. Forsythe, *Human Rights in International Relations* (New York: Cambridge University Press, 2006), 188.
3 Claude E. Welch, Jr, "Introduction," in *NGOs and Human Rights: Promise and Performance*, ed. Claude E. Welch (Philadelphia: University of Philadelphia Press, 2001), 1–24, 4–7.
4 George Ulrich, "Framework for the Analysis of Human Rights Diplomacy," in *Human Rights Diplomacy: Contemporary Perspectives*, ed. Michael O'Flaherty, Kedzia Zdislaw, Amerie Muller, and George Ulrich (Leiden: Martinus Nijhoff Publishers, 2011), 19–49, 25–28.
5 See the International Federation of the Red Cross and Red Crescent Societies, "Humanitarian Diplomacy," accessed December 26, 2013. www.ifrc.org/en/what-we-do/humanitarian-diplomacy/humanitarian-diplomacy-policy/.
6 Hochstetler, "Civil Society," 179.
7 David P. Forsythe, "Human Rights," in *The Oxford Handbook of Modern Diplomacy*, ed. Andrew F. Cooper, Jorge Heine, and Ramesh Thakur (Oxford: Oxford University Press, 2013), 668–669.
8 Peggy Hicks, "Human Rights Diplomacy: The NGO Role," in *Human Rights Diplomacy- Contemporary Perspectives*, ed. Michael O'Flaherty, Kedzia Zdislaw, Amerei Muller, and George Ulrich (Leiden: Martinus Nijhoff Publishers, 2011), 217–222, 220–222.
9 Hicks, "Human Rights Diplomacy," 220.
10 Hicks, "Human Rights Diplomacy," 220.
11 Margaret E. Keck and Kathryn Sikkink, *Advocacy Beyond Borders: Advocacy Networks In International Politics* (Ithaca: Cornell University Press, 1998).
12 Helen Durham, "The Role of Civil Society in Creating the International Criminal Court Statute: Ten Years On and Looking Back," *International Humanitarian Legal Studies*, 3 (2012), 3–42, 8.
13 Claude E. Welch, Jr. and Ashley F. Watkins, "Extending Enforcement: The Coalition for the International Criminal Court," *Human Rights Quarterly*, 33:4 (November 2011), 927–1032.

14 Durham, "The Role of Civil Society," 12.
15 Kelly-Kate Pease, *International Organizations*, 5th edition (Upper Saddle River: Longman, 2012), 36.
16 Iram Ejaz, Shaikh Babar, and Rizvi Narjis, "NGOs and Government Partnership for Health Systems Strengthening: A Qualitative Study Presenting Viewpoints of Government, NGOs and Donors in Pakistan," *BMC Health Services Research*, 11:1 (2011), 122–128; Michelle Keck, "State Funded NGO in Civil Wars: The US Case," *BMC Health Services Research*, 17:4 (December 2011), 411–427.
17 Roisin Shannon, "Playing with Principles in the Era of Securitized Aid: Negotiating Humanitarian Space in Post 9–11 Afghanistan," *Progress in Development Studies*, 9:1 (January 2009), 15–36.
18 Sherry Mueller, "The Nexus of U.S. Public Diplomacy and Citizen Diplomacy," in *Routledge Handbook of Public Diplomacy*, ed. Nancy Snow and Philip M. Tayler (New York: Taylor & Francis, 2009), 101–110, 101–102.
19 The network of governments and NGOs which formed a coalition to work on the landmine campaign was referred to as "citizen diplomacy" by Jody Williams and Stephen Goose. For more information see John English, "The Ottawa Convention on Anti-Personnel Landmines," in *The Oxford Handbook of Modern Diplomacy*, ed. Andrew F. Cooper, Jorge Heine, and Ramesh Thakur (Oxford: Oxford University Press, 2013), 797–808, 801; see also Jody Williams and Stephen D. Goose, "Citizen Diplomacy and the Ottawa Process," in *Banning Landmines: Disarmament, Citizen Diplomacy, and Human Security*, ed. Jody Williams, Stephen D. Goose, and Mary Wareham (Plymouth: Rowman & Littlefield, 2008), 181–198.
20 English, "The Ottawa Convention," 798.
21 Williams and Goose, "Citizen Diplomacy," 188.
22 Forsythe, *Human Rights in International Relations*, 188.
23 Amnesty International, "The History of Amnesty International," accessed October 6, 2014. www.amnesty.org/en/who-we-are/history.
24 Amnesty International, "Who We Are," accessed September 1, 2014. www.amnesty.org/en/who-we-are/about-amnesty-international.
25 Anne Marie Clark, *Diplomacy of Conscience: Amnesty International and Changing Human Rights Norms* (Princeton: Princeton University Press, 2001), 124.
26 Forsythe, "Human Rights," 669.
27 Clark, *Diplomacy of Conscience*, 12–13.
28 Daniel W. Hill, Jr., Will H. Moore and Bumba Mukherjee, "Information Politics Versus Organization Incentives: When are Amnesty International's 'Naming and Shaming' Reports Biased?" *International Studies Quarterly*, 57:2 (June 2013), 219–232.
29 Clark, *Diplomacy of Conscience*, 37.
30 Morton E. Winston, "Assessing the Effectiveness of International Human Rights NGOs: Amnesty International," in *NGOs and Human Rights: Promise and Performance*, ed. Claude E. Welch, Jr. (Philadelphia: University of Philadelphia Press, 2001), 25–54, 36–38.
31 Amnesty International, "Our Mission," accessed October 22, 2013. www.amnestyusa.org/about-us/our-mission.
32 Human Rights Watch, "About Us," accessed October 4, 2015. www.hrw.org/about.
33 Kean Bhatt, "The Hypocrisy of Human Rights Watch," *NACLA Report on the Americas*, 46:4 (Winter 2013), 54–48; Gerald M. Steinberg, "Human Rights Watch Protects Arab Tyrants," *Middle East Quarterly*, 20:3 (Summer 2013), 49–58.
34 Forsythe, *Human Rights in International Relations*, 191.

35 Forsythe, *Human Rights in International Relations*, 191.
36 Kishan S. Rana, *21st Century Diplomacy: A Practitioner's Guide* (New York: The Continuum International Publishing Group, 2011), 25.
37 Michael O'Flaherty, Kedzia Zdislaw, Amerie Muller, and George Ulrich, *Human Rights Diplomacy: Contemporary Perspectives* (Leiden: Martinus Nijhoff Publishers, 2011), 6–7.
38 For an overview of the case see Liz Clark Rinehart, "Clapper v. Amnesty International USA: Allowing the FISA Amendment Act of 2008 to Turn Incidentally in Certainly," *Maryland Law Review*, 73:3 (2014), 1018–1048.
39 Hicks, "Human Rights Diplomacy," 219.
40 Available at www.amnesty.org/en/latest/news/2008/03/open-letter-united-nations-20080317. Accessed October 5, 2015.
41 Matthew Krain, "J'accuse! Does Naming and Shaming Reduce the Severity of Genocides or Politicides?" *International Studies Quarterly*, 56:3 (September 2012), 574–589.
42 Widney Brown, "Human Rights Watch: An Overview," in *NGOs and Human Rights: Promise and Performance*, ed. Claude E. Welch, Jr. (Philadelphia: University of Philadelphia Press, 2001), 72–84, 80.
43 See James M. Russell, "The Ambivalence about the Globalization of Telecommunications: The Story of Amnesty International, Shell Oil Company, and Nigeria," *Journal of Human Rights*, 1:2 (September 2002), 405–416, 405.
44 Forsythe, "Human Rights," 667.
45 Forsythe, *Human Rights in International Relations*, 193.
46 Forsythe, "Human Rights," 669.
47 Sabastien Farre, "The ICRC and the Detainees in Nazi Concentration Camps (1942–1945)," *International Review of the Red Cross*, 94:888 (2012), 1381.
48 The International Committee of the Red Cross, "Confidentiality: Key to the ICRC's Work but Not Unconditional," accessed October 15, 2014. www.icrc.org/eng/resources/documents/interview/confidentiality-interview-010608.htm.
49 The International Committee of the Red Cross, "Confidentiality."
50 The International Committee of the Red Cross, "Confidentiality."
51 Médecins Sans Frontières, "About MSF," accessed November 27, 2013. www.msf.org/about-msf.
52 Fabrice Weissman, "Silence Heals … From the Cold War to the War on Terror, MSF Speaks Out: A Brief History," in *Humanitarian Negotiations Revealed: The MSF Experience*, ed. Clare Magone, Michael Neuman, and Fabrice Weissman (New York: Columbia University Press, 2011), 178.
53 David G. Chandler, "The Road to Military Humanitarianism: How Human Rights NGOs Shaped a New Humanitarian Agenda," *Human Rights Quarterly*, 23 (2001), 696.
54 Laurence Binet, "Ethiopia: A Fool's Game in Ogaden," in *Humanitarian Negotiations Revealed: The MSF Experience*, ed. Clare Magone, Michael Neuman, and Fabrice Weissman (New York: Columbia University Press, 2011), 39.
55 Binet, "Ethiopia," 36.
56 Fabrice Weissman, "Sri Lanka: Amid All-Out War," in *Humanitarian Negotiations Revealed: The MSF Experience*, ed. Clare Magone, Michael Neuman, and Fabrice Weissman (New York: Columbia University Press, 2011), 20.
57 For more information, see Forsythe, "Human Rights," 670.

7
The human rights and humanitarian professional

Human rights and humanitarian diplomacy takes place on many different levels and through a variety of channels. Previous chapters have explored how states, IGOs, and NGOs institutionally conduct diplomacy to advance human rights and humanitarian principles. Prominent individuals working for these institutions, or who have taken high profile public stances, have been discussed in tandem to show the importance of individuals in defining and advancing respect for international human rights and principles. This chapter is devoted to the human rights and humanitarian professionals (the professionals) who are on the front lines of diplomacy. The diplomacy of average human rights and humanitarian workers has only recently received scrutiny.[1] They lack the power and profile of other actors, yet realizing and implementing human rights and humanitarian principles simply would not be possible without them. In the day-to-day conduct of **field diplomacy**, these individuals negotiate and bargain for access to at-risk populations and provide aid and protection. They are also the ones implementing the human rights and humanitarian policies of their governments or international organizations. They have to make quick decisions and think on their feet because agreements reached at the highest levels often have little or no bearing to events on the ground.

This chapter also details the "**professionalization**" of human rights and humanitarian work and, relatedly, the nuts and bolts of human rights and humanitarian negotiations. It also examines who the professionals are, with special attention paid to human rights officers, lawyers, and detention monitors. The professionals have the most direct and tangible impact in preserving and improving human dignity – the principal objective of human rights and humanitarian diplomacy. The work of the professional is complemented by those from other professions, such as artists, journalists, and academics who also seek to advance human rights and humanitarian principles.

The professionalization of human rights and humanitarianism

The concept of the human rights and humanitarian "professional" has received considerable attention in recent years. Generally speaking, professions are groups of individuals who possess certain kinds of formal educational and experiential credentials. Many professions are also defined by ethical codes of conduct and professional guidelines (or best practices) that guide the behavior of their members. The professionalization of the human rights and humanitarian work is evidenced by the proliferation of handbooks, codes, and guidelines issued by states, IGOs, and NGOs. These documents are used in on-the-job training programs and circulated widely to build a collective professional identity and shared intellectual community. Listed below are some of the more influential and readily accessible handbooks, along with their institutional authors:

- *Professional Standards for Protection Work Carried Out by Humanitarian and Human Rights Actors in Armed Conflict and Other Situations of Violence* (ICRC, 2013);[2]
- *Handbook and Guidelines on Procedures and Criteria for Determining Refugee Status under the 1951 Convention and the 1967 Protocol Relating to the Status of Refugees* (UNHCR, 2011);[3]
- *Guiding Principles for Human Rights Field Officers Working in Conflict and Post-Conflict Environments* (Human Rights Law Centre, University of Nottingham, 2008);[4]
- *Statement of Ethical Commitments of Human Rights Professionals* (Human Rights Law Centre, University of Nottingham, 2008);[5]
- *UNHCR Manual on Refugee Protection and the European Convention on Human Rights* (UNHCR, August 2006);[6]
- *Manual on Human Rights Monitoring* (OHCHR, 2001);[7]
- *Human Rights Training: A Manual on Human Rights Training Methodology* (OHCHR, High Commissioner for Human Rights Centre for Human Rights, 2000);[8]
- *The Code of Conduct for the International Red Cross and Red Crescent Movement and Non-Governmental Organizations (NGOs) in Disaster Relief.* Geneva (ICRC, 1994).[9]

Important differences exist in terms of specific standards because the issuing organizations confront different kinds of human rights and humanitarian problems; however, all have respect for universal human rights and humanitarian principles and the relevant international law in common. They all seek to provide aid and protection in a nondiscriminatory and apolitical way.

The collaborative research project convened by Michael O'Flaherty and George Ulrich deserves special mention because it has gone a long way in defining the hard work of promoting and protecting human rights as a profession.[10] They have assembled their research findings into guidelines and principles that are widely applicable to those working in a human rights or humanitarian capacity. Specific principles include: the authority of international human rights and humanitarian law; respect for organizational mandates; accurate reporting, monitoring, and advocating; building capacity and partnerships in the field; doing no harm; and acting with integrity.[11] International human rights and humanitarian law contributes to the "professionalization" of the human rights and humanitarian worker because it provides a common standard that diverse organizations and individuals can reference. Ethical codes-of-conduct are more developed for human rights and humanitarian field workers providing medical and legal services because they involve other professions (medicine and law) that already have institutionalized ethics associated with their professions. Those ethics are increasingly being refined for the field.[12] The 2008 Statement of Ethical Principles for Human Rights Professionals includes eighteen ethical guidelines and principles to ensure that professionals "undertake their work with truthfulness, humility, and compassion."[13] This statement represents an important step in creating a professional identity among human rights and humanitarian workers, and can be found in the Appendix.

Field diplomacy: the art of negotiation

Negotiation is an essential aspect of human rights and humanitarian diplomacy. This includes negotiating access, which has several related dimensions. First, human rights and humanitarian organizations almost always need state consent in order to enter and establish themselves within a state's territory. The physical presence of IGO, NGO, or foreign state personnel within the territory of a state is the product of extensive negotiations at the highest levels. Second, human rights and humanitarian professionals will need visas in order to enter and work in the country. Just because matters may have been decided at upper levels, it does not mean the decision has trickled down to the bureaucrats issuing transit, entry, work, business, and resident visas. Third, once in-country, the professionals need to reach populations in need of assistance and protection. This involves either going to the people or having the people come to them. In more stable situations, negotiations center on this **freedom of movement**.[14] In conflict zones, this sometimes means creating humanitarian corridors and safe areas. Fourth, the professionals need protection themselves. This means state and irregular military forces must want to provide safe passage and respect the integrity of the negotiated humanitarian space.

Negotiating access can be especially problematic. Getting public officials and other actors to respect human rights and humanitarian principles is not easy. To convince them to allow outsiders to do it means these actors are effectively conceding that they are unable or unwilling to do so themselves. The professional must be able to persuade, make promises, provide incentives, and even make threats (for example, going public about violations), all while keeping the other party engaged in negotiations.

The nuts and bolts of negotiation involves a specific skill set and few professionals are trained specifically to engage in human rights and humanitarian diplomacy. As a remedy, human rights and humanitarian IGOs and NGOs have created handbooks to help guide negotiations in the field. Several publications are noteworthy. In 2004, Deborah Mancini-Griffoli and Andre Picot of the Center for Humanitarian Dialogue published *Humanitarian Negotiation: A Handbook for Securing Access, Assistance and Protection for Civilians of Armed Conflict* and it has become the "go-to" reference for negotiating basics and strategies.[15] The stakes are quite high in complex emergencies because compromises, concessions, and missteps may lead to death and increased suffering among populations.

Mancini-Giffoli and Picot identify several key phases to successful humanitarian negotiations.[16] The "analysis" phase involves defining humanitarian objectives, identifying the right negotiating counterparts, and determining the forms of **leverage** available. Human rights and humanitarian professionals have several different kinds of leverage: **quiet advocacy** (persuasion); **loud advocacy** (denunciation); **material assistance** (substitute); **professional expertise** (support); and **allies** (mobilizing those who can exert influence).[17] The second phase centers on developing a negotiating "strategy." This includes selecting the negotiating team, defining the starting point, and choosing tactics. The third phase is the actual "face-to-face" negotiations. The team must build rapport with their counterparts, manage cultural differences, and pay particularly close attention to language. Once an agreement is reached, the final stage of negotiation involves "follow-through" whereby ongoing negotiations and the actual agreement are monitored. The specific details of each phase will vary depending on the type of humanitarian negotiation and the extent to which all sides stand to benefit.

Another useful guide is *Humanitarian Negotiations Revealed: The MSF Experience*.[18] This edited volume explains the consequences of "shrinking humanitarian space" and the "grubby" negotiations necessary to operate effectively in conflict zones. It uses stories contributed by field professionals to illustrate how to gain leverage, negotiate what seems to be non-negotiable, and interact with gross violators of human rights and humanitarian principles. Similarly, Gerard McHugh and Manuel Bessler of the UN OCHA provide *Humanitarian Negotiations with Armed Groups: A Manual for Practitioners*.[19] This valuable resource overviews the same stages of negotiations as Mancini-Giffoli and Picot but also explains how IHL can help frame the negotiations. It also shows how to set the ground rules that will govern the interactions of humanitarian professionals and armed groups in conflict zones.

The human rights officer

Direct, routine human rights diplomacy is often conducted by **human rights officers**. The human rights officer usually is employed either by governments or by IGOs and even may be an intern or volunteer. Within the UN system, they are often spearheading the "human rights-based approach" to UN agency operations. Human rights officers perform a variety of tasks and duties depending on the terms of their employment. These include:

- working with peacekeeping missions;
- investigating human rights complaints;
- identifying human rights violations;
- interviewing victims and public officials;
- monitoring demonstrations;

- observing local judicial and court proceedings;
- writing reports;
- inter-agency and governmental liaising.

Just as lawyers and physicians have codes of conduct regardless of where they are working, human rights officers confront many personal and professional challenges, as well as conflicts of interest. Moreover, they are often deployed in situations where resources are scarce and the security situation is, at best, fluid. Human rights officers are better positioned to avoid bias and criticism by maintaining the highest professional and ethical standards. The nature of this job invariably brings human rights field officers into conflict with host governments, local police forces, and even peacekeeping missions. For example, UN human rights field officers routinely clashed with military officials (national as well as international) over the use of detention and how to best protect minorities in Kosovo.[20] While considerable agreement existed that these were important human rights issues, officials disagreed on how they should be implemented, especially in a conflict zone with uncertain public authority and deep-seated ethnic animosities. Human rights officers must negotiate the always-complex political landscape to keep human rights as a priority in the minds of public authorities. At the same time, they must avoid offending host governments. Being expelled or being PNG'd does little to push human rights forward.[21]

The monitoring and reporting role of human rights and humanitarian officers complements multilevel diplomacy because it provides negotiators with the necessary information to form strategy and make good decisions. The professional gathers testimony, statistics, and evidence which then prompts states and IGOs to act. This information also forms the basis for policy recommendations and can be used to raise awareness, generate public support, and raise money. Compiling detailed, accurate, and reliable information in fluid human rights situations is also an important tool for holding those who violate those rights and principles accountable, criminally and civilly. Courts, commissions, and lawyers use the data as evidence, to corroborate testimony, or to aid in their own investigations. Reports detail human rights violations and provide recommendations on how the human rights conditions can be improved. They also indirectly pressure responsible public authorities to pay attention to and improve respect for human rights. They also prompt other states to consider human rights and humanitarian situations in areas where their national interests are not directly engaged.

Lawyers

Lawyers have a complicated relationship with international human rights and humanitarian principles. On the one hand, lawyers specializing in international human rights and humanitarian law provide the legal expertise that helps states, IGOs, and NGOs create, implement, and enforce international human rights and humanitarian law. These lawyers also tend to be well versed in other areas of international law including international diplomatic law and international law regarding the recourse to war. This makes them essential to the conduct of human rights and humanitarian diplomacy. On the other hand, they have an ethical duty to their clients (states, IGOs, NGOs, or individuals) and to uphold the law. This can be problematic because client interests can conflict and laws at the local, national, and international levels are often contradictory. Just because treaties have been ratified at the international level does not mean those legal provisions have been included in domestic laws or embraced at the local level. Little attention is paid regarding how to reconcile the ethical challenges faced by lawyers with the international legal requirements and internal domestic constraints.[22]

International human rights and humanitarian lawyers serve in a variety of capacities. Professionally, they serve in government and IGO agencies advising public officials and creating policy. They represent their organizations in legal proceedings and advance missions. When lawyers work for states, a large part of their job is formulating legal arguments that ideally will inform state human rights and humanitarian policies and mainstream human rights into other policy areas. However, lawyers often find that they need to construct legal arguments to justify existing policy or legitimize political decisions. Lawyers also populate national human rights and ombudsman offices. The human rights ombudsman investigates and addresses alleged human rights violations, often through administrative oversight and direct protection.[23] Ideally, national human rights commissions and ombudsmen should be independent, neutral, and work to resolve complaints through recommendations or mediation. This provides the benefits of avoiding formal legal proceedings, cost effectiveness, and a quicker resolution to the dispute. Quiet mediation also can help keep the complaint out of the media, which is a major incentive for states.

International human rights and humanitarian lawyers advise and serve as IGO officials. They are important parts of IGO staff and act as special rapporteurs and serve on independent commissions of inquiry. They engage in a form of committee diplomacy when they participate in charter and treaty monitoring bodies. Recall that many of these bodies investigate complaints and formulate general comments and recommendations. Within the UN system, lawyers also comprise the **International Law Commission (ILC)** which is responsible for the progressive development of international law. The ILC is made up of thirty-four legal experts[24] nominated by member states who produce treaty drafts and legal research on substantive questions related to international law. The ILC has worked on treaty drafts related to the ICC and statelessness and worked informally with the ICRC and UNHCR on legal analyses related to war crimes and asylum, respectively.

International human rights and humanitarian lawyers are critical for the operation of international and hybrid criminal courts. Lawyers draft court statutes detailing the geographic and temporal jurisdiction of the courts, the types of crimes investigated and prosecuted, and rules of procedure and evidence. Statutes detail legal liability for crimes, affirmative defenses, sentences and penalties, and rules for detention. Crafting of a court statute, whether international or hybrid, involves the blending of different legal traditions and procedures, as well as reconciling domestic and international law. Once the court is established, lawyers serve as judges, prosecutors, and defense counsels (or on their respective staff). They research legal questions, formulate strategy, take depositions, and conduct investigations. They work with local and state officials in identifying crime scenes, collecting evidence, and interviewing witnesses, as well as prepare pre-trial documents, draft legal arguments, and write legal appeals. The role of the defense in international criminal prosecutions should not be overlooked as they defend the human rights of the accused. This poses special challenges since those accused are assumed to bear the most responsibility for grievous crimes: genocide, war crimes, and crimes against humanity. Yet, the right to legal counsel and a fair, impartial hearing are important rights of the accused. International and hybrid criminal courts are uniquely "legal" diplomatic tools requiring the expertise of human rights and humanitarian lawyers.

Within NGOs, human rights and humanitarian lawyers often serve the organization's immediate legal needs and also represent those the organization seeks to protect, such as asylum-seekers, detainees, and political prisoners incarcerated for other crimes. They also represent individuals from groups that traditionally have had difficulty in actualizing their rights: women, children, migrants, indigenous peoples, stateless persons, and members of the LGBTQ community. They serve as legal counsel for individuals seeking to actualize specific rights such as the rights to work, to work for a fair wage, for equal pay, for marriage equality, for an education, or simply for the security of the person. They also advocate for individuals as part of a class or group. Lawyers write and file *amicus curiae* briefs. These lawyers have a direct role in advancing the rights of their clients and, indirectly, they can foster the internalization of international human rights and humanitarian law in domestic law and legal proceedings.[25]

In addition to lawyering, lawyers are also independent advocates in that they use the law and their expertise to advance respect human rights and humanitarian principles. Known as **cause lawyers**, these politically motivated lawyers formulate and advance social and political causes.[26] The cause can be the advancement of internationally recognized human rights and humanitarian principles. It could also involve advocating for changes in national or local laws and using the language of international human rights to advance specific aspects of policy. One "cause" in need of cause lawyers is the security of human rights and humanitarian lawyers in states that do not have independent, professional judiciaries.[27] In societies that lack a commitment to the rule of law and where the judiciary is hyper-politicized, human rights and humanitarian lawyers are on the front lines trying to build the necessary legal structures in order for law to be useful for promoting and protecting human rights. That makes them targets of states and other actors that fear the political consequences of the rule of law and concerted domestic efforts to advance human rights. The international news is replete with stories of human rights and humanitarian lawyers under siege with threats to their lives, their families' lives, and their livelihoods. All too often this news is that they have been murdered. Even in societies where international human rights and principles are generally embraced and consequences are not personally dire, cause lawyers are often pressured and intimidated by governments, especially when they defend unpopular individuals such as terror suspects or adult males migrating from troubled areas of the world.

Lawyers are often the champions of human rights and humanitarian principles, and sometimes, they are the martyrs. But law by its nature is conservative and designed to preserve certain values, preferences, and privileges. Lawyers that defend and advance international human rights and humanitarian principles are often met by other lawyers that defend and advance other rights and principles. Today, it seems implausible that lawyers would argue for formal racial segregation, but gender segregation or discrimination is tolerated even by some human rights lawyers. The family rights of members of LGBTQ community are not embraced by many human rights lawyers (save for LGBTQ cause lawyers), especially in non-Western societies. A lawyer whose expertise is human rights or humanitarian law often encounters lawyers from other specializations such as employment law, family law, and corporate law who have little or no understanding of international human rights and humanitarian law. Hence, the "mainstreaming" of human rights within bar associations and legal professions would engage *all* lawyers in furtherance of human dignity, not just human rights and humanitarian lawyers.[28] By asking all lawyers to consider the human rights and humanitarian implications of their lawyering, fewer lawyers might be willing to make legal arguments that justify torture, systemic discrimination, or deference to those who engage in gross violations of human rights.

Detention monitors

Detention monitors (or delegates) are specialized professionals who perform the unenviable task of protecting individuals who are being detained or incarcerated against their will. This population is particularly vulnerable because they are widely perceived by well-meaning people as imminent threats, and the conditions of confinement can lead to callous, predatory, and depraved behavior by detention officials, as well as other detainees. Detention facilities are often the loci of torture and other cruel and unusual punishments, hence local, national, and international monitoring is essential to uphold the human dignity. Persons who are detained as a result of armed conflict (POWs and interned civilians) comprise one category and are monitored by the ICRC, as well as other international and national entities. Another category includes migrants, asylum-seekers, and those fleeing natural disaster or civil unrest as they are often subject to detention. Moreover, every state operates some kind of domestic prison system for punishing and rehabilitating those convicted of domestic crimes, and they constitute a third category of detainee.

The ICRC has the most institutionalized presence relating to detention visits because this ICRC role is prescribed by the Geneva Conventions. In 2012, the ICRC visited 540,000 detainees in ninety-seven countries.[29] The ICRC delegate may interview detainees, restore family links, promote respect for international humanitarian law, and assess detainee health.[30] IHL facilitates the diplomacy necessary in order for

ICRC delegates to gain access to facilities and ICRC quiet diplomacy and neutrality reinforces a cooperative dynamic with state officials (and other belligerents) during situations of armed conflict. On the ground, detention delegates follow similar procedures. "Delegates start by meeting the person in charge of the detention facility. This is an opportunity to present the objective of the visit and discuss both the general situations and the implementation of previous ICRC recommendations. Together with personnel from the detaining authority, the delegates then visit all areas used by and or for detainees such as cells, barracks, interrogation rooms, kitchens, latrines, exercise yards, and infirmaries."[31]

The ICRC is often criticized for being too quiet in its approach because of its long-standing practice of taking concerns and violations directly to the relevant public authorities and not making public inhumane conditions or treatment. The ICRC rarely goes public and, when it does, it is quite circumspect. The ICRC presence also can be used by government officials to make claims that detainees are well-treated and any additional oversight by NGOs or other actors is unnecessary.[32] Some of the ICRC's greatest challenges are not just in troubled areas of the world such as Rwanda, Somalia, and Iraq, but with the US government in its "war on terror." The ICRC has visited known US detention facilities in Cuba, Iraq, and Afghanistan; however, leaked reports of top secret CIA interrogation and detention facilities around the world have raised serious humanitarian concerns regarding the conditions and treatment of those detainees.

The UNHCR is also diplomatically active on behalf of detainees. It has issued general guidelines to officials that reflect the best humanitarian practices when detaining migrants and asylum-seekers. These guidelines include:[33]

- the right to asylum must be respected;
- the rights of liberty and security of person and to freedom of movement apply to all asylum-seekers;
- detention must be in accordance with and authorized by law;
- detention must not be arbitrary;
- detention must not be discriminatory;
- indefinite detention is arbitrary and maximum limits should be established in law;
- decisions to detain or extend detentions must be subject to minimal safeguards;
- conditions of detention should be humane and dignified;
- special circumstances and the needs of particular asylum-seekers (victims of trauma, torture, women, children, LGBTQ) must be taken into account;
- detention should be subject to independent monitoring and inspection.

The monitoring and inspection of detention facilities can be conducted by UNHCR officials themselves, as well as a range of international, regional, and national bodies (national human rights commissions and ombudsman offices). The UNHCR also recommends allowing civil society actors to perform these functions as well.[34] Part of the diplomatic struggle regarding migrants and asylum-seekers is whether state officials will allow access to those detained at the frontier. This frontier space is a grey area that is technically not the territory of a state, and therefore, domestic laws do not apply. States have become quite effective in border enforcement by detaining migrants on islands and creating bureaucratic mazes that leave migrants in legal limbo.[35] States deliberately make it difficult for migrants to reach their territory, create grey spaces, and detain migrants away from lawyers and NGOs that might inform them of their rights or assess their well-being. In Sidebar 7.1, Ivan Gayton, of MSF, describes the difficulties he and his colleagues have encountered in negotiating access to migrants detained in Europe. These vulnerable people are kept in "migration controls" which are often beyond the reach of human rights and humanitarian groups.

Sidebar 7.1 Ivan Gayton (MSF) – negotiating access

I work for Medecins Sans Frontieres, an emergency medical humanitarian agency. I've spent most of the last decade in war and disaster areas.

Our mandate is to save life, alleviate suffering, and restore dignity. Saving life is accomplished via direct action; we provide medical care, water and sanitation, vaccination, and teach people how to avoid disease. To alleviate suffering, and in particular to restore dignity, is often beyond the reach of direct medical action, rather we must use our voice to provoke action.

It is easy to speak out. What is more difficult is to do so in such a way that provokes real change for the people we are speaking on behalf of rather than simply generating publicity for its own sake.

MSF has worked with vulnerable migrant populations for decades, but has always struggled to gain access to the places where they suffer most. Immigration detention centres are notoriously prone to becoming sites of ill-treatment for people with little or no recourse, even in high-income democratic societies. The situation in poorer and less politically stable countries, where immigration controls are often funded by and implemented on behalf of high-income countries, can be and often is unspeakable.

I, along with many of my colleagues, have participated in negotiations to access immigration detention centres. Along Europe's southern and eastern borders, MSF has been able to access holding centres, though often under restrictive circumstances; for example I have been patted down to check for hidden cameras when entering European migrant detention centres, where the administrators openly admit that they do not wish for the conditions to be publicly known. The conditions I have seen within have varied from reasonable to horrific; in one of the worst cases I have seen hundreds of people confined in tiny areas with a single overflowing toilet, so cramped that the migrants could not all lie down and had to take shifts sleeping. However, conditions in the worst of these centres do not even compare to the horrors of "externalized" migration controls, to which MSF and other humanitarian agencies have little or no access at all.

Since 2010, Libya has implemented migration controls at the behest of Italy, providing capture, detention, and deterrence of irregular migrants in exchange for cash payments and diplomatic support. During the Arab Spring uprising, I personally met many of the survivors of this system who had fled to Tunisia after the detention centres collapsed; the stories of the torture and exploitation they experienced would have been unbelievable had they not been so consistent from one person to the next.

While funded and mandated by Europe, the detention centres in Libya are nevertheless beyond the reach of humanitarian oversight and assistance; Libya has never signed the Geneva Conventions or Refugee Convention. Neither the fallen Gaddafi regime nor the current government is inclined to allow foreign scrutiny of their prison system, and the European funders of the detention centres have not exhibited much interest in demanding access for humanitarian services and oversight. The detention centres in Malaysia, Indonesia, and Turkey, to name but a few, are similarly opaque.

MSF continues to take an interest in the condition of vulnerable migrants, but we have thus far failed to make sufficient use of our voice to gain meaningful access. The ultimate arbiters of access to migrant detention centres are not the countries being paid to run them; he who pays the piper calls the tune. The piper is paid, by and large, by democratic governments, ultimately under the control of their citizens. It is to these citizens that we must take our case, and demand that whenever migration controls are delegated to third countries, humanitarian agencies must be guaranteed meaningful access.

It is not easy to make a case for our right to assist those who do not have the sympathy of the Western public; by and large irregular migrants are the target of political fear-mongering and parochial hatred. However, MSF and the humanitarian community in general has always stood for universal medical ethics and human rights; we should not let the difficulty of the discussion dissuade us. Our ultimate weapon is humanization, bearing witness to the humanity and suffering of those we treat, and we have tremendous experience using it to build empathy for our patients, even those in areas tremendously far-removed from the experience of the average citizen of high-income countries. We need not wait to see the conditions in these detention centres to make the public case for the essential humanity of their inmates, and to demand access to them in the name of universal medical ethics and human rights.

Still, IGOs and NGOs are quite resourceful in gaining access to detained migrants and strive to adhere to the highest professional standards. In 2014, the Association for the Prevention of Torture, the International Detention Coalition, and the UNHCR teamed up to write *Monitoring Immigration Detention: Practical Manual*.[36] This step-by-step manual details how to prepare for a detention visit, decide which officials need to be contacted, what to look for during the inspection, and how to write the follow-up report.

The aim is to establish a consistent monitoring methodology that can be used by professionals from IGOs and NGOs to insure the human dignity of incarcerated migrants.

Another category of detainee are those convicted of crimes. Jails and prisons are also monitored by human rights professionals. While not always using the language of international human rights, national and international NGOs have become important tools in protecting the basic rights of the convicted. While most have committed and been convicted of horrific crimes, they are still entitled to human dignity while incarcerated. Also, many states have (intentionally or not) incarcerated large numbers of mentally ill persons with the convicted population. Prison facilities around the world are characterized by deplorable conditions where basic human rights are routinely violated. Moreover, the suffering of convicts (or adult male migrants of color) do not generate the same kinds of international compassion as suffering women, children, or POWs. In 1990, the UN General Assembly adopted Resolution 45/111 which outlined eleven principles for the treatment of prisoners:

1. All prisoners shall be treated with the respect due to their inherent dignity and value as human beings.
2. There shall be no discrimination on the grounds of race, colour, sex, language, religion, political or other opinion, national or social origin, property, birth or other status.
3. It is, however, desirable to respect the religious beliefs and cultural precepts of the group to which prisoners belong, whenever local conditions so require.
4. The responsibility of prisons for the custody of prisoners and for the protection of society against crime shall be discharged in keeping with a State's other social objectives and its fundamental responsibilities for promoting the well-being and development of all members of society.
5. Except for those limitations that are demonstrably necessitated by the fact of incarceration, all prisoners shall retain the human rights and fundamental freedoms set out in the Universal Declaration of Human Rights, and, where the State concerned is a party, the International Covenant on Economic, Social and Cultural Rights, and the International Covenant on Civil and Political Rights and the Optional Protocol thereto, as well as such other rights as are set out in other United Nations covenants.
6. All prisoners shall have the right to take part in cultural activities and education aimed at the full development of the human personality.
7. Efforts addressed to the abolition of solitary confinement as a punishment, or to the restriction of its use, should be undertaken and encouraged.
8. Conditions shall be created enabling prisoners to undertake meaningful remunerated employment which will facilitate their reintegration into the country's labour market and permit them to contribute to their own financial support and to that of their families.
9. Prisoners shall have access to the health services available in the country without discrimination on the grounds of their legal situation.
10. With the participation and help of the community and social institutions, and with due regard to the interests of victims, favourable conditions shall be created for the reintegration of the ex-prisoner into society under the best possible conditions.
11. The above Principles shall be applied impartially.

By establishing international standards, the General Assembly enables the OHCHR to spearhead training and educational programs. The OHCHR produces manuals for prison officials and educates national human rights commissions, ombudsman offices, and local NGOs on how to monitor prisons. Successful oversight of detention facilities requires that human rights and humanitarian professionals conform to the highest professional and ethical standards to be effective. Otherwise, their poor behavior will be used against them by officials, access will be denied, and the plight of those largely hidden from public view will decline. They must also be sensitive to the local politics and the worldview of local officials toward international human and humanitarian principles if they are to be successful in negotiating access.

The diplomatic role of other professionals

Human rights and humanitarian principles are also pursued by other kinds of professionals such as artists, journalists, and academics and their work has an indirect impact on diplomacy at all levels. Acting independently or as member of an NGO (e.g. Artists for Human Rights, Journalists for Human Rights, Lawyers for Human Rights, Scholars at Risk) other professionals can shape the diplomatic discourse by presenting, dramatizing, depicting, and advancing human rights issues or humanitarian situations within their professions. In Sidebar 7.2 award-winning photojournalist Greg Constantine discusses his work in documenting the rights of stateless persons. This kind of work raises awareness and creates public pressure on state and IGO officials to "do something." It also educates local communities about international efforts to promote and protect human rights and principles.

Sidebar 7.2 Greg Constantine (photojournalist)

The majority of the stories I have dedicated myself to during my career as a photographer have focused on human rights and social injustices. Stories that explore the intersection between the universal acknowledgement that all people are born with what we prescribe as human rights and the deliberate denial of these rights by others. While *rights* can be defined by some as being black and white, the majority of the people I have met as a photographer would say their *rights* have been lost (or have sunk) into a vast sea of gray.

For the past nine years, I've worked on stories about stateless people around the world. People who have been denied or stripped of the *right to have rights*. People who exist and survive in this gray sea where the moral, political and legal discussion and debate about human rights collide like no other. Most of these people describe how they live without human rights. They explain how they feel as if they don't exist in this world. Still, almost all, in their own way, say they want the world to know about their story.

As a photographer, I spend my time doing everything I can to explore and expose this ugly, complicated and more often than not, tragic sea of gray. What can I do to visually articulate the consequences the denial of human rights have on people and communities in their day to day lives in a way that is nuanced, truthful, intelligent and respectful? How can I share these stories with others not just for the broader purpose of exposing them but more importantly, how can I share these stories in a way that people better *understand* them? I am always trying to discover the ways in which these stories represent or reflect on the larger themes that construct the times in which we live. But always, the fundamental motivation of my work is to tell stories of people.

Because I work on stories about human rights, people ask if I am an activist. How can you not be when you work on these kinds of stories? Yet at the same time, I am fully aware of my professional boundaries. So then, what role do photography projects about human rights play? Photography for me is not just about visual documentation. I believe it goes beyond photography and visual storytelling. It is about engagement.

What can these photographs achieve? How can they encourage discussion? How can they inform? How far can I get these photographs and stories into the eyes of a variety of audiences? How can they make a contribution to a wider discussion that will hopefully spark some kind of change for the people in the photographs, however large or small that change might be? With each new story, I always ask myself these questions, and with each story I hold a huge sense of responsibility and obligation to make sure people learn about the stories of the people I photograph.

We now live in a time when newspapers, magazines and a handful of television and radio broadcasters do not serve as the only gatekeepers to our lifeline of what is happening out in the world as well as in our own backyard. Is getting the work published enough? Absolutely not! We live in a time when the mechanisms in which we receive information and can become engaged in stories about human rights are vast and expanding each year. I place equal importance on how I get the work and these stories out to people as I do on actually creating the work. I believe it is my responsibility to harness and exploit this expanding landscape of engagement. Why? Because the stories and the people in the stories demand and deserve more.

I have always viewed my work as producing ammunition for others to then utilize, to build on, to take into discussions with others that I am not able to reach myself. This requires strategy and it requires collaboration. Strategy in the sense of identifying the audiences who need to be exposed most to the work and collaboration in executing the most effective way of delivering this work to those audiences. I regularly collaborate with international and local human rights organizations, NGOs, civil society groups and universities. Together we plot out ways to engage people and this comes as a result of having shared goals and objectives; to do something that will inevitably contribute toward improving the lives of the people I photograph (and the people they advocate on behalf of).

> Exhibitions, panel discussions, lectures, installations, projections, books, online multimedia features, documentary films, social media, educational platforms: each can be used to reach specific audiences that individually have their own unique interests and influence yet collectively can move a conversation forward that will hopefully crystalize into some action. Actions that will nudge or change the status quo for situations where human rights abuse occur. For many of the stateless people I have met, this absence, denial or postponement of rights has suffocated individuals and communities for years, decades and for some, generations.
>
> These stories are far too easily lost to the always-changing headlines of the moment. They are far too easily lost to a variety of agendas that unfortunately brush the lives of real people suffering human rights abuse underneath the rug of realpolitik.
>
> I believe in documentary photography and in what it can accomplish. I believe that it can give a voice and serve as an incredibly powerful and effective bridge between people and their understanding of complex global issues and the lives of others, however distant they may be. It provides visual evidence that in so many ways is a prerequisite to engagement, to understanding, to change. It provides evidence that holds those who perpetrate human rights abuses – often times with impunity – to account and opens up a space for people to question, re-think and challenge those authorities who hold and abuse power or are in a position to enforce the protection of rights but for any number of reasons choose not to.

Academics are useful for providing careful, although often unwelcome, analyses of current diplomatic approaches to advancing international human rights and humanitarian principles. They provide the necessary intellectual history and review the mechanics of creating law and norms. However, sometimes the good intentions of state, IGO, and NGO diplomatic efforts are usually not enough to push other actors to positions where they are not ready to go. The moral and ethical high ground many states, IGOs, and NGOs believe they occupy may prompt them to pursue ill-advised strategies that may backfire and set back diplomatic efforts. Academics are usually among the first to point to the shortcomings of existing approaches.

Art, academia, law, and journalism are the types of professions that tend to be active in promoting and protecting human rights because rights such as the freedom of expression and thought, equality under the law, the right to counsel, access to competent legal tribunals, and a fair and impartial hearing foundational to the professions. Members are often targeted for persecution and even killed in the course of their work. This means diplomacy is necessary not only for their physical protection but also for them to practice their professions.

Conclusion

Human rights and humanitarian professionals include those who see themselves, and are seen by others, as the rank and file promoters and protectors of human rights and humanitarian principles in the field. Concerted efforts to define the professional involve establishing professional guidelines and ethical codes of conduct. It involves training the professional in negotiating techniques and effective decision-making in difficult and opaque situations. The human rights and humanitarian officer, lawyer, and detention monitor are examples of the kind individual operating in the field or in offices every day. They work to secure access and gather reliable data for assessing human rights and humanitarian situations. Professionals from other fields also are on the front lines of human rights and humanitarian diplomacy, raising awareness and informing public opinion. These individuals, and the professional associations they belong to, must also work to protect their members and their work as they are essential to realizing human rights and humanitarian principles in the field.

Key terms

Field diplomacy, professionalization, freedom of movement, leverage, quiet advocacy, loud advocacy, material assistance, professional expertise, allies, human rights officers, International Law Commission (ILC), cause lawyers.

Discussion questions

1. What is field diplomacy and who is involved in its conduct?
2. What steps have been taken to define "the professional" in terms of operational guidelines and ethical codes of conduct?
3. Compare and contrast the roles of the field officer and lawyer in protecting and promoting international human rights and humanitarian principles.
4. Describe different kinds of detainees and the challenges detentions monitor face in protecting the human rights of detainees.

Notes

1 Larry Minear, "The Craft of Humanitarian Diplomacy", in *Humanitarian Diplomacy: Practitioners and their Craft*, ed. Larry Minear and Hazel Smith (New York: United Nations University Press, 2007), 8.
2 The International Committee of the Red Cross, *Professional Standards for Protection Work Carried Out by Humanitarian and Human Rights Actors in Armed Conflict and*

Other Situations of Violence (ICRC: Geneva, 2013), accessed October 4, 2015. www.icrc.org/eng/assets/files/other/icrc-002-0999.pdf.
3 UN High Commissioner for Refugees (UNHCR), *Handbook and Guidelines on Procedures and Criteria for Determining Refugee Status under the 1951 Convention and the 1967 Protocol Relating to the Status of Refugees*, December 2011, HCR/1P/4/ENG/REV. 3, accessed September 20, 2014. www.refworld.org/docid/4f33c8d92.html.
4 Human Rights Law Centre, University of Nottingham, *Guiding Principles for Human Rights Field Officers Working in Conflict and Post-Conflict Environments*, 2008, accessed October 4, 2015. http://reliefweb.int/report/world/guiding-principles-human-rights-field-officers-working-conflict-and-post-conflict.
5 Human Rights Law Centre, University of Nottingham, *Statement of Ethical Commitments of Human Rights Professionals* (2008), 22–23, accessed October 4, 2015. http://reliefweb.int/report/world/guiding-principles-human-rights-field-officers-working-conflict-and-post-conflict.
6 UN High Commissioner for Refugees (UNHCR), *UNHCR Manual on Refugee Protection and the European Convention on Human Rights (April 2003, Updated August 2006)*, August 2006, accessed September 20, 2014. www.refworld.org/docid/3f4cd5c74.html.
7 United Nations Human Rights Office of the High Commissioner, *Manual on Human Rights Monitoring* (Geneva, 2001), accessed October 4, 2015. www.ohchr.org/Documents/Publications/OHCHRIntro-12pp.pdf.
8 High Commissioner for Human Rights Centre for Human Rights, *Human Rights Training: A Manual on Human Rights Training Methodology*. Professional Training Series No.6 (Geneva and New York: United Nations, 2000), accessed October 4, 2015. www.ohchr.org/Documents/Publications/training6en.pdf.
9 The Code of Conduct for the International Red Cross and Red Cresent Movement and Non-Governmental Organizations (NGOs) in Disaster Relief (Geneva, 1994), accessed October 4, 2015. www.icrc.org/eng/resources/documents/publication/p1067.htm.
10 Michael O'Flaherty and George Ulrich, "The Professional Identity and Development of Human Rights Field Officer," in *The Professional Identity of the Human Rights Field Officer*, ed. Michael O'Flaherty and George Ulrich (Burlington: Ashgate, 2010), 7–32.
11 Human Rights Law Centre, University of Nottingham, "Guiding Principles for Human Rights Field Officers Working in Conflict and Post-Conflict Environments," 2008, accessed October 4, 2015. http://reliefweb.int/report/world/guiding-principles-human-rights-field-officers-working-conflict-and-post-conflict.
12 Anji E. Wall, *Ethics for International Medicine: A Practical Guide for Aid Workers in Developing Countries* (Hanover: Dartmouth University Press, 2012).
13 Human Rights Law Centre, University of Nottingham, "Statement of Ethical Commitments of Human Rights Professionals." Also see commentary: George Ulrich, "The Statement of Ethical Commitments of Human Rights Professionals: A Commentary," in *The Professional Identity of the Human Rights Field Officer*, ed. Michael O'Flaherty and George Ulrich (Burlington: Ashgate, 2010), 49–82.
14 Deborah Mancini-Griffoli and Andre Picot, *Humanitarian Negotiation: A Handbook for Securing Access, Assistance and Protection for Civilians of Armed Conflict* (Geneva: Centre for Humanitarian Dialogue, 2004), 20.
15 Mancini-Griffoli and Picot, *Humanitarian Negotiation*.

16 Mancini-Griffoli and Picot, *Humanitarian Negotiation*, 15.
17 Mancini-Griffoli and Picot, *Humanitarian Negotiation*, 69–89.
18 Claire Magone, Michael Neuman, and Fabrice Weissman (eds.), *Humanitarian Negotiations Revealed: The MSF Experience* (London: Hurst and Company, 2011).
19 Gerard McHugh and Manuel Bessler, *Humanitarian Negotiations with Armed Groups: A Manual for Practitioners*, United Nations Office for the Coordination of Humanitarian Affairs (2006), accessed October 4, 2015. https://docs.unocha.org/sites/dms/Documents/HumanitarianNegotiationswArmedGroupsManual.pdf.
20 Clive Baldwin, "Implementation through Cooperation? Human Rights Officers and the Military in Kosovo," *International Peacekeeping*, 13:4 (December 2005), 199–2002, 489–501.
21 Josh Kron, "South Sudan Expels a UN Rights Officer," *New York Times*, November 6, 2013, A7.
22 Nell Moley, "Confronting the Ethical Challenges of Ethical Accountability in International Human Rights Lawyering," *Stanford Journal of International Law*, 59:2 (2014), 359–392.
23 Linda Reif, *The Ombudsman, Good Governance, and the International Human Rights System* (Leiden: Maritinus Nijhoff Publishers, 2004), 2.
24 *International Law Commission*, "Membership," accessed September 25, 2014, www.un.org/law/ilc/index.htm.
25 Stephen Meili, "U.K. Refugee Lawyers: Pushing the Boundaries of Domestic Court Acceptance of International Human Rights Law," *Boston College of International And Comparative Law Review*, 36:2 (Spring 2013), 1123–1148.
26 Lis Hajjar, "Cause Lawyering in Transnational Perspective: National Conflict and Human Rights in Israel/Palestine," *Law and Society Review*, 31:3 (1997), 473–504.
27 Frank Munger, "The Cause Lawyer's Cause," *Law in Context*, 28:2 (2010), 95–106, 95.
28 Jonathan Todres, "Lawyers and the Universal Declaration of Human Rights," *International Law News*, 38:1 (Winter 2009), 12–13.
29 Paul Bouvier, "Humanitarian Care in Small Things is Dehumanised Places," *International Review of the Red Cross*, 94:888 (Winter 2012), 1537–1550, 1538.
30 The International Committee of the Red Cross, "Working for the ICRC," accessed September 16, 2014. www.icrc.org/eng/who-we-are/jobs/.
31 The International Committee of the Red Cross, "Respect for the Life and Dignity of Detainees," 2010, accessed September 29, 2014. www.icrc.org/eng/what-we-do/visiting-detainees/overview-visiting-detainees.htm.
32 *The New Republic*, "Seeing Red," December 29, 2004, accessed September 29, 2014. www.newrepublic.com/article/red-cross-geneva-conventions-guantanamo%3Dbay-al-qaeda.
33 The United Nations High Commissioner for Refugees, *Detention Guidelines: Guidelines on the Applicable Criteria and Standards relating to the Detention of Asylum-Seekers and Alternative to Detention*, 2012, accessed September 30, 2014. www.unhcr.org/505b10ee9.html.
34 The United Nations High Commissioner for Refugees, *Detention Guidelines*, 69.
35 Alison Mountz, *Seeking Asylum: Human Smuggling and Bureaucracy at the Border* (Minneapolis: Minnesota University Press, 2010).
36 The Association for the Prevention of Torture, the International Detention Coalition, and the United Nations High Commission for Refugees, *Monitoring Immigration Detention: Practical Manual*, June 2014, accessed September 30, 2014. www.apt.ch/content/files_res/monitoring-immigration-detention_practical-manual.pdf.

8
Conclusion

Human rights and humanitarian diplomacy today

International human rights and humanitarian principles, as currently defined and applied, are the product of diplomacy conducted at multiple levels by states, IGOs, NGOs and individuals. After the initial post-World War II flurry of diplomatic activity that gave rise to the UDHR, the Geneva Conventions, the Genocide Convention, and the Convention Relating to the Status of Refugees, the Cold War lull saw only occasional advancements in human rights and humanitarian protections. Differences in worldview regarding the role, priority, and importance of human rights and humanitarianism in world affairs stymied diplomatic efforts. The thaw in the 1970s led to renewed efforts to advance rights and principles. The binding covenants on Civil and Political Rights and Economic, Social, and Cultural Rights entered into force, the Helsinki Accords were embraced, the United States (under the Carter Administration) made human rights a foreign policy priority, and two Protocols of the Geneva Conventions were adopted to protect victims during armed conflict. The return of the Cold War in the 1980s slowed progress, but the Gorbachev–Reagan summits marked an important diplomatic turning point when the taboo against discussing human rights during summitry was broken.

The end of the Cold War in 1989 led to renewed optimism for multilateral human rights and humanitarian diplomacy. The UN Security Council took decisive action explicitly on behalf of human rights and humanitarian principles. While not necessarily fully embracing new directions, China and Russia and states from the Global South were willing to expand multilateral operations, including peacekeeping, peacemaking, and peacebuilding. The diplomatic framework of IGOs was strengthened, with secretaries-general publicly engaging in human rights and humanitarian diplomacy. They were supported by the IGO diplomacy of high commissioners and other officials. Civil society actors proliferated as governments became more permissive and responsive to internal and external influence and pressure. The human rights of women, LGBTQ persons, indigenous peoples, and disabled people have been advanced by NGO diplomacy.

Still, post-Cold War challenges were unprecedented. The violent dismembering of multinational/ethnic states, and weak, ineffective governments, led to gross violations of human rights and humanitarian principles on an alarming scale. Moreover, the rules of world order, especially traditional notions of sovereignty and the corresponding principle of nonintervention, worked against effective multilateral responses to genocide, war crimes, gross violations of human rights, and crimes against humanity. The general legal prohibition against the use of force, unless in self-defense or authorized by the UN Security Council, made confronting complex humanitarian emergencies exceptionally difficult. Still, multilevel diplomacy resulted in international and hybrid courts, R2P, and a renewed commitment to peacekeeping.

The outcomes of these initiatives have not always been desirable. While groundbreaking, international and hybrid criminal courts are expensive, cumbersome, and require political support. They are easily politicized in that governments willing to extensively fund or support them are doing so for multiple reasons. Governments have self-referred situations to the ICC not to help end the impunity of those committing crimes but to criminalize the domestic political opposition. Often legal approaches and invoking legal language can backfire in diplomacy. The application and outcome of R2P in Libya has, at best, made states cautious. At worst, in the case of Russia and China, R2P is an unacceptable and undesirable outcome for multilateral human rights and humanitarian diplomacy. The advancement of certain categories of human rights have not been widely embraced because of religious and cultural reasons, as well as concerns about sovereignty.

Events and political choices have also conspired against a deepening of commitment to human rights and human principles. Terrorist attacks against the United States in 2001, and subsequent attacks around the world, have led states that are generally supportive of human rights and humanitarian principles to adopt policies that run counter to the letter and spirit of the law. Use of drones, targeted assassinations, extraordinary renditions, extensive surveillance, detention, secret detention and interrogation centers, and enhanced interrogation techniques call into question how international human rights and humanitarian principles figure in the twenty-first century. While it was the United States that has taken these steps, other liberal states have followed and many agree with at least some of them. The exponential advancements in technology, the Internet, and social media create problems as well as opportunities. Newly created or reformed regional human rights arrangements are inconsistent with global norms suggesting fractures in the fragile international consensus under construction since the end of World War II.

The lofty aspirations represented by international human rights and humanitarian principles belie the hard, grinding, and often distasteful diplomacy necessary to build enough consensus among enough actors to create principles and move them forward. The advancement of human rights and humanitarian principles is not necessarily neat, progressive, or linear. There are many false starts and serious setbacks. In short, there is nothing inexorable about the evolution of international human rights and principles. This makes analyzing human rights and humanitarian diplomacy somewhat discouraging. Important and thoughtful works by experts suggest that the world is witnessing the end of human rights.[1] These justifiably pessimistic analyses show that while the classical human rights movement has made great strides, the current framework is now encountering stiff resistance in principle and practice.[2] This resistance is coming from authoritarian, non-Western democracies, and deeply religious societies. However, resistance does not mean the Herculean efforts to promote and protect human rights have been for naught. Rather, it makes human rights and humanitarian diplomacy even *more* necessary and vital for human dignity. It also means that human rights and humanitarian principles at the end of the twenty-first century may look different because they will need to be adapted to account for different preferences and worldviews. How they are adapted will depend on multilevel diplomacy.

One way to think about human rights and humanitarian diplomacy in this context is to think about the process of building a figurative house. This house must be constructed in such a way that it can be inhabited by almost everyone, not just those who possess Western values and aspire to the secular, Western ideal. There is a blueprint for that house but in the process of building the house, mistakes were made, fires were accidentally set, walls needed to be moved around, and additions constructed. The house is still structurally sound and while some people are thinking of moving out and others do not like some of the people living there, very few want to burn it down. But some renovations need to be made. This chapter examines three interrelated challenges to the existing human rights and humanitarian regime: illiberal states and ideologies; failed states; and globalization and business. It highlights that there are more vehicles for individuals to participate in human rights and humanitarian diplomacy and that diplomacy should be judged, not by how close it meets a particular ideal, but whether at a particular place and time, human dignity was preserved. As long as the status of human dignity is better than it was before, then diplomacy was successful.

Illiberal states and ideologies

For the most part, international human rights and humanitarian principles are largely liberal constructs and a lot of diplomacy has centered on advancing those constructs. The very idea that human rights are universal is a liberal value and aspiration. Pushback by illiberal states is nothing new. Even though the UDHR is a laundry list of rights and values and the drafters sought to accommodate the wishes of the fifty-eight UN members, the Soviet Union, Saudi Arabia, and South Africa abstained. As the number of states grew, more expressed concern that their values and preferences were not considered or that some were incompatible. They were also concerned that human rights would be used to justify imperialism, intervention, or interference. States that fought so hard to gain their sovereignty from colonial rule were worried about weakening the principle of state sovereignty that has undergirded much international relations for centuries. Most have no problem with other states and IGOs pursuing human rights and humanitarian principles through dialogue and standard-setting, as long as they can define and implement them without undue external interference. The current 193 states are quite diverse and that means more diversity regarding the definition and implementation of human rights. While most states are party to most international human rights treaties, that diversity is reflected in formal reservations and uneven application. Recognizing diversity is the first step in valuing and accommodating others. At the same time, national, local practices, and religious practices that are harmful to human dignity must continually be confronted and eventually abandoned.

The liberal world order, which was fostered, financed, and militarily protected by the United States, created the political space for the current international human rights and humanitarian frameworks to be built. In spite of its problems, the liberal order has been conducive to the spread of values, including the rule of law and the importance of individual freedom. However, in spite of its inclusiveness, this order has had difficulty in protecting the security of persons, in providing for the basic human needs of the world's poor, and reconciling its colonial past.

The challenge of illiberalism is complex. Increasingly, China's model of authoritarian development is being emulated by states in Asia and Africa. China has made great strides in improving the quality of life of its citizens. It has done much to eradicate extreme poverty, achieve universal primary education, reduce child mortality, and improve maternal health. Its record on civil and political rights, however, is not so good. In addition to the usual authoritarian techniques of forced disappearances, arbitrary arrest, detention, torture, and summary executions, China also violates human rights in other ways. According to Freedom House, an NGO that monitors and measures freedom around the world, modern authoritarians capture the institutions that undergird political pluralism.[3] China's pattern of authoritarianism relies on dominating the institutions of civil society. The government controls universities and the media. It polices and censors the Internet, creating the "great firewall" to keep out unwanted influences and information. National courts and the domestic legal systems are politicized.

China is also willing to do business with states that have poor human rights records, which makes China's approach more palatable to "unfree" states around the world. China's example is compelling, especially in areas not steeped in the Western liberal tradition. It should also be noted that China's willingness to do business with states based on "mutual respect" regardless of human rights violations is matched by the willingness of Western liberal states to do business with China. There is little evidence to suggest that as societies become more advanced, modern, and developed, they will become more liberal and embrace liberal notions of human rights. The slide in civil and political rights in recent years indicates that quality democracy may be at bay.

Even when civil and political rights are protected and democracy is possible, there is no guarantee that people will choose liberalism, with its emphasis on pluralism, tolerance, minority rights, equality under law, rule of law, or an independent judiciary. Illiberal democracies threaten the existing character of the international human rights regime because their societies are only partly free or they embrace ideologies or religious doctrines that are incompatible with contemporary human rights norms.[4] Ranging from modern authoritarian to mostly free, illiberal democracies reflect national or regional identities. Freedom House classifies many illiberal democracies (for example Russia, Venezuela, Ukraine) as "modern authoritarian" because they cripple the opposition without annihilating it and maintaining a veneer of order, legitimacy, and prosperity.[5] Other illiberal democracies (such a Hungary, Ecuador, and Pakistan) are similar in that they make it difficult for civil society to function outside of the cultural norm. Human beings exercising their human rights may freely choose to embrace the values of virulent nationalism, xenophobia, fascism, or religious extremism. The recent elections that brought Hamas and the Muslim Brotherhood to power in Gaza and Egypt, respectively, show that democracy does not translate into liberal values.

The growing multi-polarity of international affairs and the decline of the liberal world order means diplomats, especially at the state, multilateral, and IGO levels, may have to adjust their negotiating strategies to account for a weakening bargaining position. They may also need to be more accepting of a multicultural international human rights regime. This regime, for all intents and purposes, will not be significantly different, except that it would dispense with the conceit that all the human rights outlined in the corpus of international human rights law are universal, indivisible, and equal. The post-World War II history of human rights diplomacy shows that this is an impossible ideal. Women's rights have never been fully embraced in large swaths of the world and in some places are practically non-existent. Tolerance of religion and religious minorities is weakening. States continue to use multilateral fora to shield gross violators of human rights. The proliferation of regional human rights regimes by the states that comprise ASEAN, the Arab League, the OIC, and the AU does not represent a renewed commitment to universal human rights but serious dissatisfaction with the existing order, so much so states are willing to create alternatives.

The status of international humanitarian principles and law, especially among state parties (whether liberal, authoritarian, or otherwise), generally works well because states have a self-interest in adhering to IHL. It protects their armed forces, wounded, and POWs during armed conflict. Reciprocity also encourages compliance, especially as it relates to individuals who are no longer bearing arms. More progress needs to be made protecting civilians in conflict zones especially since they are often the targets of growing number of militias and irregular military forces who reject the existing law.

Failed states

Failed states pose a Gordian knot for the protection of international human rights and humanitarian principles. States fail for a variety of reasons that are not mutually exclusive: poor governance, dismemberment because of secessionism, civil or sectarian war to control the government, and foreign occupation or interference. As states bear the main duty of protecting human rights and humanitarian principles domestically, their failure creates chaos in the existing order and poses a grave threat to the basic human rights of the population. The current interstate system is simply not equipped to handle failed states in part because other states have vested interests in the outcome of conflicts and IGOs do not have significant independent capacity. As such, the collapse of states (or governments) often lead to the gravest of human rights violations: genocide and crimes against humanity. Peacekeeping and peacebuilding can only do so much and the lack of viable civil society actors mean political and civil vacuums exist. In the context of a civil war, shifting internal and external alliances, coupled with extremist and nihilist elements, puts human rights and humanitarianism at risk. This is a problem that the international community has yet to manage successfully. One the one hand, humanitarian aid and intervention creates a moral hazard that can cause or prolong the conflict. On the other hand, belligerents in the conflicts know that if you create an ugly and unsafe environment for foreign state, IGO, and NGO aid personnel, they will go home. It is not surprising that areas where respect for human rights and humanitarian principles is low are areas of prolonged crises in failed or failing states such as Congo, Somalia, Ethiopia, Yemen, Sudan, Afghanistan, Iraq, and Syria. R2P is one attempt to manage the situation; however, some kind of formal "receivership" maybe necessary in order to stabilize the situation and do the hard work of rebuilding the society. This may mean reviving the "trustee system" and even recognizing that some states ought not to be retained in their current form.[6]

Globalization and business

Globalization is also complicating the protection of human rights because it challenges the primacy of the state. Globalization means many different things, but at its essence it involves economic, political, and social forces that affect everyone, regardless of geography. The globalization of transportation, telecommunications, the Internet, markets, and production means societies linked together to an unprecedented degree. While globalization brings many benefits, those benefits are not evenly distributed within and between states. Globalization also has a malevolent side. Terrorists, diseases, and criminal syndicates trafficking in people, weapons, and drugs move almost as freely as global corporations. Weapons of mass destruction in the wrong hands mean that once thriving societies can be left in ruins in an instant. Economic instability and crisis in one country or region can easily be transmitted around the world. States can no longer can guarantee security, economic well-being, and good paying jobs. Powerful global corporations, seeking to maximize profits for shareholders around the world, resist state efforts to restrict or regulate their activities. They certainly do not like the use of sanctions to punish violators of human rights and humanitarian principles because the cost-burden falls on them. Also, corporate profits come from reduced labor costs, and without proper oversight, corporations can engage in exploitation and human rights violations, especially as it relates to fair remuneration for labor.[7] Unsafe and inhumane working conditions, wage theft, unequal pay, child labor, and slave labor are pernicious human rights problems in the global economy that require concerted state, IGO, and NGO efforts to address. NGOs have been part of a social movement to "name and shame" corporations; however, not all companies are well known nor are they "shameable."[8]

Part of the problem is that corporations are treated as separate from "civil society." Recall from Chapter 6 that most analysts distinguish between private, nonprofit organizations (such as NGOs) and private, for-profit organizations (such as national and multinational corporations), with the former being principled organizations, and therefore part of civil society; and the latter being self-interested, and therefore, not a civil society actor.[9] This conception of civil society is unnecessarily narrow for several reasons. First, private for-profit actors have significant influence over states, important civic interests, and are important sources of funding for many NGOs. Second, the original Hegelian conception of civil society was grounded in market relationships separate from the state. Third, IGOs, such as the UN, have embraced multinational corporations in a variety of partnerships including development and the promotion of human rights. Finally, human rights and humanitarian NGOs effectively function as businesses that are concerned with revenue, marketing, expenditures, and compete with other NGOs for donor money.[10] This makes the artificial distinction between principle and profit less clear.

Kofi Annan's "Global Compact" initiative is an effort to bring businesses and corporations into the human rights and humanitarian dialogue, not just as targets of diplomacy but as advocates. Businesses have the potential to be important protectors of human rights and humanitarian principles, as well as principal source of violations. Mainstreaming international human rights into corporate practices will help corporate decision-makers to consider the human rights consequences of their activities. This is especially important when states subcontract government activities such as detention, security, and logistics to private companies.

While much attention is paid to state sovereignty, very little is paid to the consequences of "market sovereignty." Liberal economic thought is based on the idea that markets are the preferred way to distribute goods, services, and resources because the workings of the market force their efficient production at a price consumers are willing to pay. Liberals may disagree on the extent to which government should be involved in the market either as consumer or regulator, but at its essence, liberalism prefers markets. This often translates into privatizing the provision of goods and services necessary for the realization of rights (food, water, health care) or state-owned industries that earn the state income to help pay for the realization of certain human rights.[11] Liberals would argue that as long as individuals are maximally free to chart their own course in life and participate in public life, that markets and privatization are the more efficient way to ensure everyone has access to food, water, and medical care. Economic globalization and transnational corporations are potential "disruptors" to traditional state methods of promoting and protecting human rights. States attempting to regulate their behavior often find corporations relocating to other countries.

Markets and free enterprise have generated enormous wealth, life-saving and -enhancing innovations, and unprecedented levels of prosperity. They have also created a tremendous amounts of poverty and economic inequality. How the international community addresses poverty and inequality will have a profound effect on the quality of human rights and humanitarian principles in the future. Some observers worry that the evolution of human rights and humanitarian principles means permanent zones of freedom and repression in the future.[12]

Conclusion

Absent a world government, multilevel human rights and humanitarian diplomacy defines what human rights and humanitarian principles mean in theory and practice. That meaning is not static. The post-World War II diplomacy is quite impressive in that it constructed an elaborate, flexible framework that allowed states a great deal of leeway to customize human rights to national preferences. It is also impressive because it is easier to maintain the status quo than to affect change. But affect change it did. Human rights and humanitarian diplomacy is difficult and often unsuccessful, but cannot be abandoned. While liberalism is at bay, it is still an exceptionally powerful and potent force in world politics that illiberal states and actors must contend with. Like-minded actors must build alliances by finding common ground and discovering the leverage to move forward. Human rights and humanitarian diplomats must also rethink some of their strategies and initiatives. Good intentions alone are not enough to advance human rights. Hard-nosed decisions have to be made and diplomats cannot fall prey to the "justification of effort" whereby they value institutions and laws simply because they have invested a lot of effort in them.

At the end of the day, individuals comprise states, IGOs, NGOs, and global corporations, and the more individuals know about existing international human rights and humanitarian principles, the easier it will be to build upon and modify them. However, individuals also need to know and at least understand (if not respect) differences as they related to worldview and prioritizing rights and principles. Human rights and humanitarian diplomacy is not about reaching some Western European socialist ideal about the relationship of the state to its citizens, but rather constructing a house where everyone can comfortably live while preserving human dignity and respecting cultural differences.

Discussion questions

1. If the UDHR were put to a vote in the General Assembly today, would it pass?
2. How does the decline of the liberal world order affect the implementation of international human rights and humanitarian principles?
3. Discuss the challenges of illiberal and failed states to the international human rights and humanitarian framework.
4. How does globalization complicate the protection of human rights? Why are corporations and businesses necessary participants in the diplomatic process?

Notes

1 See Costas Douzinas, *The End of Human Rights: Critical Legal Thought at Turn of the Century* (London: Hart Publisher, 2000); Stephen Hopgood, *The Endtimes of Human Rights* (Ithaca: Cornell University Press, 2013).
2 Stephen Hopgood, "The End of Human Rights," *Washington Post*, January 3, 2014.
3 Freedom House, "Freedom in the World 2014," accessed October 11, 2014. http://freedomhouse.org/report/freedom-world/freedom-world-2014?gclid=CJqhmPubpcECFQMT7Aod1CoA8Q#.VDl1Yo10yYN.
4 Fareed Zakaria, "The Rise of Illiberal Democracy," *Foreign Affairs*, 76:1 (1997), 22–43.
5 Freedom House, "Freedom in the World 2014."
6 Rosa Ehrenreich Brooks, "Failed States or State as Failure," *University of Chicago Law Review*, **72**:4 (2005), 1159–1196.
7 Delphine Rabet, "Human Rights and Globalization: The Myth of Corporate Social Responsibility," *Journal of Alternative Perspectives in the Social Sciences*, 1:2 (May 2009), 463–475.
8 Tim Bartly and Curtis Child, "Shaming the Corporation: The Social Production of Targets and the Anti-Sweatshop Movement," *American Sociological Review*, 79:2 (August 2014), 653–679.
9 See for example Kathryn Hochstetler, "Civil Society," in *The Oxford Handbook of Modern Diplomacy*, ed. Andrew F. Cooper, Jorge Heine, and Ramesh Thakur (Oxford: Oxford University Press, 2013), 176–191.
10 Thomas G. Weiss, *Humanitarian Business* (Cambridge: Polity, 2013), 2–5.
11 Kristin L. Retherford, "Regulating the Corporate Tap: Applying Administrative Law Principles to Achieve the Human Right to Water," *Indiana Law and Journal*, 88:2 (Spring 2013), 811–835, 811.
12 Hopgood, "The End of Human Rights."

Glossary

1951 Convention Relating to the Status of Refugees a United Nations multilateral treaty that legal defines a refugee as someone "owing to a well-founded fear of being persecuted for reasons of race, religion, nationality, membership of a particular social group or political opinion, is outside the country of his nationality, and is unable to, or owing to such fear, is unwilling to avail himself of the protection of that country; or who, not having a nationality and being outside the country of his habitual resident as a result of such events, is unable or, owing to such fear, in unwilling to return to it." It provides the legal framework for the protection of refugees.

1954 Convention Relating to the Status of Stateless Persons a UN multilateral treaty that defines a stateless person as someone who is not considered a national by any state. It provides the legal framework for the protection of stateless persons.

1961 Convention on the Reduction of Statelessness a United Nations multilateral treaty in which states agree to reduce the incidence of statelessness.

1961 Vienna Convention on Diplomatic Relations a keystone treaty that recognized and reaffirmed the principles of the independence and sovereignty of states and codified centuries of custom related to how states are to treat each other and their emissaries.

The 1967 Protocol a key provision of refugee law that removed the temporal and geographic limitations of the 1951 Convention Relating to the Status of Refugees.

2005 World Summit a meeting of all United Nations member states on the 60th anniversary of the UN. The meeting was called to reform the UN to make it more effective in the areas of development, security, and human rights.

Ad hoc international criminal tribunals judicial bodies that are created to try individuals accused of war crimes, crimes against humanity, and gross violations of human rights. These tribunals are created for a limited time and for a specific conflict. Examples include the ICTY and ICTR.

African Charter on Human and Peoples' Rights (Banjul Charter) the central human rights treaty of the AU that includes collective rights such as self-determination and the right to natural resources.

African Court on Human and Peoples' Rights a human rights court created by the Organization of African Unity (now the African Union) in 1998 and became operational in 2004 after being ratified by fifteen member states.

African Union (AU) a regional IGO established May 26, 2001 consisting of fifty-four African states. Its predecessor was the Organization of African Unity.

Allies a kind of leverage used by human rights and humanitarian professionals involving the mobilization of important people who can exert influence.

American Declaration on the Rights and Duties of Man (1948) the original human rights statement of the OAS.

Amicus curiae a "friend of the court" brief that serves to educate national and international lawyers and judges by providing them with the legal reasoning for potentially deciding a case.

Amnesty International an NGO founded in 1966 to raise international awareness regarding human rights abuses. It seeks to promote and protect human rights through research, action, and advocacy.

Anarchy the absence of a higher authority in international relations.

António Guterres the 10th United Nations High Commissioner for Refugees (2005–present).

Arab Charter on Human Rights the organizing regional human rights law of the Arab League first adopted in 1994.

Arab Human Rights Committee independent experts who advise Arab League member states on human rights and humanitarian issues.

Arbitration a form of conflict-resolution similar to mediation in that the "legal right or wrong" of the parties are not as important in reaching a settlement, but in which the parties agree ahead of time to be bound by the decision of the arbiter.

ASEAN Declaration of Human Rights the organizing regional human rights law for the Association of Southeast Asian Nations.

ASEAN Intergovernmental Commission on Human Rights a forum for multilateral human rights diplomacy for the Association of Southeast Asian States.

Assimilation the most likely solution to the plight of refugees wherein the refugee remains in the country of first asylum.

Ban Ki-moon the eighth Secretary-General of the United Nations. He served from 2007 to 2015.

Bertrand Ramacharan acting UN High Commissioner for Human Rights, 2003–04.

Boutros Boutros-Ghali the sixth Secretary-General of the United Nations. He served from 1992 to 1996.

Cairo Declaration on Human Rights in Islam the central organizing human rights document adopted by the Organization of Islamic Conference (now Cooperation) in 1990. This declaration interprets human rights in the context of Islam and Sharia Law.

Capitalism an economic system and mode of production that is based on markets, private property, wage labor, and private ownership of the means of production.

Cause lawyers politically motivated lawyers who formulate and advance social and political causes, including human rights.

Celebrity diplomacy the promotion and protection of human rights and humanitarian principles by famous personalities.

Charter-based bodies human rights bodies provided for by the UN Charter and supported by the OHCHR.

Citizen diplomacy a concept that came into vogue during the Cold War meaning that citizens have a responsibility to be unofficial ambassadors for their countries. After the Cold War, the definition of citizen diplomacy evolved to mean the process by which ordinary people can shape human rights and humanitarian values of a society, whether their own or global civil society's.

Civil society consists of hundreds of thousands of private civic actors including NGOs and individuals.

Clapper v. *Amnesty International USA* **(2013)** a US Supreme Court case involving US surveillance policies.

Cluster Coordination a strategy for delivering humanitarian aid during complex emergencies. Developed by the UN OCHA, the strategy centers around organizing humanitarian aid groups into sectors of humanitarian aid, such as food or shelter, which then are responsible for providing the humanitarian assistance.

Commission diplomacy usually refers to the "high level panels" and commissions that issue reports on human rights and humanitarian issues which then shape official policies. Another variation of commission diplomacy centers on the work of human rights commissions within IGOs. For the most part, this variation of commission diplomacy is a form of multilateral diplomacy consisting of the representatives of member states who have responsibility of promoting human rights and sometimes even protecting human rights by hearing individual petitions. Examples include the now defunct UN Commission on Human Rights (since replaced by the HRC) and the European Commission on Human Rights (1954–98), similarly defunct, which allowed private petitions and investigated complaints. The League of Arab States, the African Union, Organization of American States, and the Association of South East Asian Nations have respective human rights commissions that are engaged more on promotional activities such as standard setting, rather than direct protection.

Commission on Human Rights (1946–2006) a fifty-three member body that was elected by the United Nation Economic and Social Council (ECOSOC) to promote and protect human rights. It was replaced by the HRC in 2006.

Commissions of inquiry panels appointed on an ad hoc basis by the HRC to investigate gross violations of human rights.

Committee diplomacy centers on the bodies created to monitor the implementation of specific human rights treaties. The committees are comprised of independent human rights experts.

Common Article 3 a legal provision that extended the protection of civilians under the Geneva Conventions to include internal, as well as international, conflicts.

Conference diplomacy is a form of multilateral diplomacy that is often conducted under the auspices of an IGO, usually the UN or a regional organization.

Constructivism an approach used by academics and analysts to explain how the central theories, concepts, norms and values in international relations are socially constructed and change over time.

Convention on the Prevention and the Punishment of Genocide (1948) a treaty that defined genocide in legal terms as acts committed with the intent to destroy, whole or in part, a national, ethnic, racial, or religious group. The treaty advised all participating countries to prevent and punish acts of genocide.

Convention on the Prohibition of the Use, Stockpiling, Production and Transfer of Anti-Personnel Mines and on their Destruction a treaty that aims to eliminate anti-personnel landmines (also known as the Ottawa Treaty or the Mine Ban Treaty).

Corporate Social Responsibility (CSR) an initiative to educate businesses and corporations about internationally recognized human rights and to recruit them as partners in the protection of human rights.

Council of Europe a forty-seven-member-state IGO for cooperation in Europe in the areas of human rights, rule of law, and democracy.

Counter-summits protest meetings by NGOs and other civil society actors who use the occurrence of state summits to raise human rights issues.

Démarches official diplomatic positions of protests delivered by one government to another through the ministry of foreign affairs.

Diplomacy 2.0 diplomacy that uses social media such as Twitter, Tumblr, Snapchat and Facebook to communicate with people all around the world.

Diplomatic immunity affords diplomats special protection while conducting relations abroad.

Diplomatic recognition when states formally acknowledge each other by establishing embassies and consulates in each other's territory and accepting the credentials of their representatives.

Emergency Relief Coordinator (ERC) an under-secretary general that heads the OCHA.

European Union a twenty-eight-member-state regional organization devoted to political and economic integration.

EU Annual Report on Human Rights and Democracy an analysis of the status of international human rights issued annually by the European Union.

The European Convention on Human Rights and Fundamental Freedoms (1950) a regional treaty that forms the legal basis for human rights protection in Europe.

European Court on Human Rights a regional human rights court based in Strasbourg, France that hear cases involving human rights violations. Individuals and groups may bring cases, as well as states.

Field diplomacy the negotiating, bargaining, and advocating activities of human rights and humanitarian professionals during routine and complex missions.

First generation human rights civil and political rights.

First generation peacekeeping missions that include lightly armed personnel and observers who are deployed with the consent of the host government and other belligerents after a ceasefire had been negotiated.

First UN a way of conceptualizing the United Nations as an organization comprised of sovereign states who bring their different capabilities, values, interests, and rivalries to the table.

Foreign minister or secretary an individual at the top of the MFA who reports to the head of state and is the public face of a state's day-to-day diplomacy.

Freedom of movement an important principle during human rights and humanitarian field operations that allows IGO and NGO officials access to at-risk populations or allows at-risk populations to move to safety.

Geneva Conventions a series of treaties regulating the treatment of civilians, prisoners of war (POWs) and soldiers during armed conflict.

Genocidaires the name given to the perpetrators of the Rwandan genocide.

Global Compact a UN initiative to recruit businesses as partners and encourage businesses to embrace the principles of the UN including the promotion and protection of human rights.

Good offices a term for using the prestige of diplomatic officials to resolve conflict.

Goodwill Ambassadors celebrities who use their fame to raise the profile of human rights and humanitarian organizations, such the United Nations High Commissioner for Refugees. They are a key component of celebrity diplomacy.

Hegemonic power where a state possesses a preponderance of military and economic capabilities, enough so that they are able to create and control the central institutions of the international system.

Helsinki Accords a series of high level agreements signed in 1975 that led to a thaw in the Cold War and put human rights on the international agenda.

Helsinki Summit a summit meeting held during July 31 to August 1, 1975 that was the capstone to the signing of the Helsinki Accords.

Helsinki Watch an NGO created as a result of the Helsinki Accords to monitor the human rights progress of the signatories, particularly the Soviet Union. This NGO later became Human Rights Watch.

Human rights and humanitarian diplomacy is the bargaining, negotiating, and advocating process involved with promoting and protecting international human rights and humanitarian principles.

Human-rights based approach a strategy of placing respect for international human rights at the center of an organization's operation. It requires officials to consider the human rights implications of their actions and policies.

Human rights officers professionals whose job it is to monitor and report on human rights situations for an NGO or IGO.

Human rights reports written analyses of human rights situations produced by states, IGOs, and NGOs. These analyses are usually country-based or thematic reports.

Human Rights Watch a prominent human rights NGO known for its thorough human rights reports. It was formerly known as Helsinki Watch.

Human security the idea that the individuals (rather than states) should be safe, healthy, and free from harm.

Humanitarian diplomacy a term used by the International Federation of the Red Cross and other humanitarian aid organizations to refer to the process whereby NGOs are involved with persuading decision-makers and opinion leaders to act at all times in the interests of vulnerable people and with full respect for fundamental humanitarian principles.

Humanitarian space a geographical and theoretical area where the priorities of actors and organizations are reducing harm and meeting the basic human needs of people during armed conflict and complex emergencies. Diplomatic efforts are often centered on creating this space on the ground and in the minds of belligerents.

Humanitarianism action taken by states and other actors, not because individuals have a legal right, but because it is the humane thing to do.

Hybrid courts criminal tribunals staffed by local judges and lawyers, as well as international jurists and legal experts.

IGO diplomacy when independent officials representing IGOs engage in diplomatic activities to galvanize international attention, carry out their mandates, and liaise with states, NGOs, and other IGOs.

Imperialism (colonialism) when states, controlled by capitalists, scrambled for captive territories to serve as outlets for excess goods and services that cannot be consumed at home.

The Independent International Commission on Kosovo a body of autonomous experts, established and funded by Sweden, to investigate the Kosovo conflict and the military intervention by NATO. Its main finding was that the intervention was "illegal but legitimate."

Independent Permanent Human Rights Commission a body of experts in Islamic human rights. It was created by the Organization of Islamic Cooperation in 2008 to complement the Cairo Declaration on Human Rights in Islam.

The InterAmerican Commission on Human Rights a body of experts charged with investigating human rights situations for the OAS.

The InterAmerican Convention of Human Rights (1968) the cornerstone human rights treaty for the OAS.

InterAmerican Court for Human Rights a regional human rights court that complements the InterAmerican Convention of Human Rights. It is authorized to hear cases brought by states but individuals do not have the right to petition the court.

Intergovernmental organizations (IGOs) organizations created by states to help them take collective action.

Internally displaced persons (IDPs) a special category of person who flee armed conflict or natural disaster but are unable to cross an international border.

International Bill of Rights contains the human rights articulated in the UDHR, the ICCPR, and the ICESCR.

International Campaign to Ban Landmines (ICBL) a coalition of civil society actors that mobilized to pressure states to create the Convention on the Prohibition of the Use, Stockpiling, Production and Transfer of Anti-Personnel Mines and on their Destruction (also known as the Ottawa Treaty or the Mine Ban Treaty).

International civil service is the bureaucracy of global and regional IGOs. It is often referred to as the secretariat.

The International Commission on Intervention and State Sovereignty an independent panel of legal and human rights experts created by Canada to explore the issue of humanitarian intervention. It sought to redefine sovereignty to include the R2P.

The International Committee of the Red Cross a Swiss NGO created in 1863 to assist the victims of armed conflict. It eventually took on a formal monitoring role that is codified in the Geneva Conventions.

International Covenant on Civil and Political Rights (ICCPR) (1966) treaty that includes many first generation human rights such as the right to: the freedom from torture or slavery; recognition and equality under the law; the freedom of thought and religion; the freedom of expression and opinion; and the freedom of assembly and association, among others.

International Covenant on Economic, Social and Cultural Rights (ICESCR) (1966) treaty that includes many second generation human rights such as: labor rights, the right to health, the right to education, and the right to an adequate standard of living.

The International Criminal Tribunal for the former Yugoslavia (ICTY) the first ad hoc international criminal tribunal since the post-World War II Nuremberg and Tokyo tribunals. Established by the UN Security Council in 1993, the court is responsible trying those accused of war crimes and crimes against humanity during the break-up of the former Yugoslavia.

The International Criminal Tribunal for Rwanda (ICTR) established by the UN Security Council in 1994 to try those accused of genocide, war crimes and crimes against humanity during the Rwandan genocide. It is the first international court in history to indict persons for genocide and define rape as a war crime.

International humanitarian law (IHL) focused on promoting human dignity and governs the conduct of armed conflict.

International law the formal rules and principles that govern the relations and the behavior of states.

International Law Commission (ILC) comprised of thirty-four legal experts nominated by member states of the UN who produce treaty drafts and conduct legal research on substantive questions related to the progressive development of international law.

International legal personality means that states have the capacity to create international law and have rights and duties under that law.

The International Red Cross and Red Crescent Movement a network of international humanitarian organizations affiliated with the ICRC.

International relations theory a set of assumptions or propositions that describe, explain, analyze, and predict world affairs.

Jan Egeland was the UN Under-Secretary General of Humanitarian Affairs and ERC from 2003 to 2006.

Jose Ayala-Lasso the first UN High Commissioner for Human Rights (1994–97).

Keynesian liberalism a school of liberal thought that sees the state as an important force for leveling the economic and political playing field and for correcting for market excesses and imperfections.

Kofi Annan the seventh Secretary-General of the United Nations. He served from 1997 to 2006.

Landmine Ban Treaty a treaty that aims to eliminate anti-personnel landmines around the world (also known as the Ottawa Treaty or the Convention on the Prohibition and the Use, Stockpiling, Production, and Transfer of Anti-Personnel Mines and on their Destruction).

The League of Arab States a regional IGO consisting of twenty-two member states.

Letter-writing campaigns a grassroots technique designed to bring pressure on those committing human rights violations.

Leverage a form of influence or power utilized to achieve a desired outcome.

Liberalism fundamentally an economic theory that is very suspicious of government, often seeing government as a necessary evil (in contrast to realism). Liberalism is premised on equality under the law, rule of law, democratic government, and maximally free markets.

Loud advocacy a kind of leverage used by human rights and humanitarian professionals involving denunciation.

Louis Arbour the fifth UN High Commissioner for Human Rights (2004–08).

Marxian a worldview that sees the market as a way for the dominant capitalist class to accumulate vast wealth by maximizing profits which comes at the expense of wages.

Mary Robinson the second UN High Commissioner for Human Rights (1997–2002).

Material assistance a kind of leverage used by human rights and humanitarian professionals to gain access to at-risk populations.

Médecins Sans Frontières (MSF) a humanitarian NGO that delivers emergency aid to people affected by armed conflicts, natural disasters, and complex emergencies and operates under the principles of neutrality, impartiality, and medical ethics.

Mediation a form of conflict-resolution that is often nonbinding and usually involves finding a solution to a dispute that works for the parties rather than trying to assess who is legally right and wrong.

Megaphone diplomacy a form of diplomacy that uses media to advance human rights and humanitarian principles by building public awareness and informing the public debate.

Ministry of Foreign Affairs (MFA) government bureaucracies generally responsible for maintaining diplomatic relations with other states and IGOs (including staffing and supporting missions abroad), dealing with foreign diplomats at home, and conducting a state's public diplomacy.

Most Favored Nation (MFN) a special trade status that makes a state eligible for a preferential trade concessions.

Multilateral diplomacy when states use IGOs to help them take collective action relating to a specific issue.

Naming and shaming a strategy of publicly calling out gross violators of human rights in order to push them to change their policies and behaviors.

National human rights commissions independent bodies created to oversee the implementation of human rights domestically. Sometimes these bodies also investigate past human rights abuses.

Navanethem (Navi) Pillay the sixth UN High Commissioner for Human Rights who served from 2008 to 2014.

Neoclassical liberals a school of liberal thought that sees the role of the state to promote free market values, but with very limited government regulation of the market, unless it is to help the supply (business) side of the economic equation.

Network diplomacy when IGO officials engage with other non-state actors in human rights and humanitarian diplomacy.

NGO diplomacy when NGO officials independently advocate or negotiate on behalf of human rights and humanitarian principles.

Nongovernmental organizations (NGOs) private, not-for-profit, voluntary organizations that have policy goals.

Nonintervention a companion legal principle to sovereignty that means that states have the duty not to intervene in the internal affairs of other states.

Nonrefoulement a principle articulated by the 1951 Convention Relating to the Status of Refugees in which signatories are legally obligated not to return individuals with refugee status, or those seeking such status, back to a situation of persecution.

Ombudsman an independent official or office that investigates complaints of human rights violations.

Operation Turquoise the name of the 1994 UN intervention force in Rwanda. Led by France, this military operation sought to create safe haven for Rwandan refugees.

The Organization for Security and Cooperation in Europe (OSCE) a fifty-seven-member-state regional IGO. It provides a forum for security and human rights issues.

Organization of American States (OAS) a thirty-five-member regional IGO that promotes cooperation among American states.

The Organization of Islamic Cooperation (formerly Conference) (OIC) an IGO comprised of fifty-seven member states that embrace Islam.

Ottawa Treaty a treaty that aims to eliminate anti-personnel landmines around the world (also known as the Convention on the Prohibition and the Use, Stockpiling, Production, and Transfer of Anti-Personnel Mines and on their Destruction or the Mine Ban Treaty).

The P-5 the five permanent members of the UN Security Council (Russia, China, the United Kingdom, the United States, and France) who have veto power over council decisions.

Parallel conferences civil society conferences held by NGOs in tandem with IGO conferences.

Peace enforcement (also known as second generation peacekeeping) involves preventative diplomacy and enforcing Security Council decisions. Peace enforcement often means creating safe areas and using more "robust" measures to deliver humanitarian aid.

Peace of Westphalia a series of peace treaties that ended the Thirty Years War and the Eighty Years War.

Peacebuilding centers on the reconstruction of post-conflict societies (also known as third generation peacekeeping).

Peacebuilding Commission a United Nations agency created in 2005 to help with the reconstruction of war-torn societies.

Peacekeeping a UN innovation which helps societies create the conditions for peace. Peacekeeping often consists of stationing lightly armed forces and civilian observers in conflict zones with the consent of the involved parties.

persona non grata a declaration made by a state that requires an individual to leave the country for any reason.

Pledging conferences meetings organized by the UN and other organizations to raise money for the victims of armed conflict or natural disasters.

Preventative diplomacy a form of diplomacy that involves taking steps to stop a conflict from escalating.

Private diplomacy (also known as "quiet" diplomacy) involves the behind-the-scenes, quiet approach to protecting and promoting human rights and humanitarian principles.

Professional expertise a kind of leverage used by human rights and humanitarian professionals whereby they bring their skills and knowledge to bear in resolving a crisis situation.

Professionalization (of human rights and humanitarian work) the process by which the activities of human rights and humanitarian aid workers become standardized or even accredited. Evidence of this process includes the proliferation of handbooks, codes, and guidelines issued by states, IGO, and NGOs on human rights and humanitarian work.

Public diplomacy a tactic whereby an issue is placed squarely on a foreign policy agenda, or in the media, and is subject to public scrutiny and comment.

Quiet advocacy a kind of leverage used by human rights and humanitarian professionals involving behind-the-scenes bargaining and persuasion.

Reagan–Gorbachev summits a series of meetings between President Reagan and Soviet General-Secretary Gorbachev held between 1985 and 1988 where human rights and humanitarian concerns became part of superpower summitry.

Realism one of the oldest theories in international relations that centers on the exercise of power by states against other states in the international system.

Resettlement a solution to the plight of refugees whereby UNHCR officials engage in ongoing diplomacy to encourage other states to permanently accept refugees.

Resolution 688 the first unambiguous recognition of a human rights and humanitarian situation within a state as a threat to international peace and security.

Responsibility to Protect (R2P) an evolving international norm that redefines sovereignty to mean that the state has the duty to protect its population from genocide, crimes against humanity, and gross violations of human rights. If the state is unable or unwilling to do so, the duty shifts to the international community.

Second generation human rights economic, social and cultural rights.

Second generation peacekeeping (often referred to as peace enforcement) involves preventative diplomacy and enforcing Security Council decisions. It often involves creating safe areas and using more "robust" measures to deliver humanitarian aid.

Second UN the system of decision- and policy-making by UN officials (the UN bureaucracy) who are independent and not instructed by states.

Secretariat the professional bureaucracy of an organization.

Securitization of aid a problem that arises in the humanitarian partnership between states and NGOs whereby the security interests of donor states often determine NGO relief activities. The securitization of aid also compromises the neutrality of NGOs.

Sergio Vieira de Mello the third UN High Commissioner for Human Rights (2002–03). He was killed in a terrorist attack on UN headquarters in Iraq in 2003.

Sovereignty a centuries' old legal principle that holds that the state, or representatives of the state (the government), has the final say within its territorial jurisdiction.

Special rapporteurs independent experts that investigate country-specific and thematic issues relating to human rights or humanitarian situations.

Standing a requirement that means in order to bring a case in court, petitioners must have sufficient legal capacity. This often means that petitioners must have a stake in the outcome or show actual harm requiring adjudication.

State a geographic and political entity that has a defined territory, population, and a government. States possess sovereignty.

Structuralism a term often used to describe attributes of the international system that influences actor behavior. In Marxian theory, capitalism is a systemic attribute.

Subjects actors that are regulated by international law. States are the principal subjects of international law but non-state actors may be subjects as well as long as they are legally recognized as such.

Summit diplomacy a channel of diplomacy that involves the heads of state or leaders of governments.

Third generation human rights collective human rights such as the rights of peoples to self-determination, or development, or the rights of specific groups (minorities, children, women, refugees, stateless persons, and indigenous peoples).

Third generation peacekeeping a type of peacekeeping that focuses on the reconstruction of post-conflict societies (also known as peacebuilding).

Third UN the network of NGOs, independent experts, and other civil society actors that attempt influence states and IGOs to adopt certain values and develop certain policies.

Track 1 diplomacy the official diplomacy practiced by state and IGO officials using traditional channels and tools.

Track 2 diplomacy expands diplomatic activity to include the more unofficial interactions that involve civil society actors such as NGOs and prominent individuals.

Treaty-based bodies the committees and monitoring bodies that oversee the implementation of international human rights law.

Truth commissions special human rights commissions at the national level established on an ad hoc basis to investigate human rights violations that occurred under previous regimes.

United Nations High Commissioner for Human Rights a position created in 1993 and the official head of the OHCHR.

Universal Declaration of Human Rights (UDHR) (1948) a nonbinding UN General Assembly resolution that represents the existing international consensus regarding the definition and importance of human rights in the post-World War II order.

Universal Periodic Review (UPR) a staggered peer review process where all 193 UN members report on the status of their domestic human rights and explain how they are meeting their obligations under international human rights law.

Valerie Amos the Under-Secretary General and ERC (2010–present).

Voluntary repatriation a solution to the plight of refugees whereby UNHCR officials mediate the safe return of individuals to their home country.

Worldviews sets of widely held beliefs that provide a mental map as to how the world works.

Zeid al-Hussein the seventh United Nations High Commissioner for Refugees (2014–present).

Appendix

Statement of ethical commitments of human rights professionals[1]

As human rights professionals, we share an unwavering dedication to human rights as enshrined in the Universal Declaration of Human Rights and other international instruments and hold to values of human dignity, equality and non-discrimination, justice, rule of law, international solidarity, mutual understanding and tolerance, and respect for the capabilities and values of others.

Our vision is a world in which every man, woman and child may live in dignity and freedom. We contribute to the attainment of this vision through strong personal commitment and the highest degree of professional integrity. We must undertake our work with truthfulness, humility and compassion. We shall at all times uphold the highest ethical standards.

As human rights professionals, we work in a variety of institutional settings. Irrespective of our affiliation and location, we affirm this statement of the main ethical principles and standards that guide us in our work:

1. The primary commitment of human rights professionals is to the human rights of the individuals, communities and peoples they serve; in cases of professional dilemma or uncertainty, this commitment shall be the fundamental consideration.
2. In all of their actions, human rights professionals shall promote and protect human rights on the basis of the international standards.
3. Human rights professionals are obliged to recognise and respect the dignity of every human being and to honour the principles of equality and non-discrimination on the grounds of race, colour, gender, sexual orientation, language, religion, opinion, national or social origin, disability, age, property, birth or other status.
4. Human rights professionals recognise their special responsibility towards the most vulnerable members of society, in particular regarding the protection, as a matter of the highest priority, of individuals who face immediate risk of grave human rights violations.
5. Human rights professionals in all their acts and expressions shall demonstrate and ensure respect for the dignity of victims and others affected by human rights violations. They shall act with a sense of propriety and cultural sensitivity.

6. Human rights professionals shall seek to anticipate any risks of harm to others that may arise in connection with their work and shall take every possible measure to avoid exposing individuals, communities or peoples to undue risks of harm.
7. Human rights professionals in all their activities shall respect the principle of participation that empowers individuals, communities and peoples. Human rights professionals shall strive to ensure the participation of the most marginalised and vulnerable members of society in activities and decisions that affect them.
8. Human rights professionals, both in their personal and official capacities, shall demonstrate respect for all individuals, irrespective of their cultural, religious and other values. This does not preclude the legitimacy of candid dispute, disagreement or action regarding practices that may affect human rights.
9. Human rights professionals are committed to be impartial in the promotion and protection of human rights irrespective of the identity or status of perpetrators and victims. They shall endeavour to ensure that their impartiality is evident to all relevant actors.
10. Human rights professionals have a duty to react to actual and impending human rights violations that they confront and to alert their own organisations and, where appropriate, government authorities and other relevant actors.
11. Human rights professionals shall recognize the primary and fundamental importance of effective local human rights protection structures, governmental and otherwise, and shall seek to strengthen them.
12. Human rights professionals shall engage with colleagues and other counterparts, regardless of position and contractual status, in a just, respectful and constructive manner.
13. Human rights professionals shall be aware of any power or privilege that their position commands and refrain from abusing their status, especially in relations with members of the local community.
14. Human rights professionals shall work loyally and in conformity with the aims and regulations of their organisation. They bear a responsibility to bring to the attention of the organisation any of its policies or practices that they consider to be incompatible with human rights.
15. Human rights professionals have a duty to react appropriately to any serious ethical misconduct or human rights abuse, including sexual exploitation, that comes to their knowledge. This duty extends to acts committed by persons contracted by their own and partner organisations. The reaction may include reporting the misconduct to the competent authorities.
16. Human rights professionals shall be guided under all circumstances by the need to accomplish the objectives of their mission. This includes the avoidance of unnecessary and/or disproportionate risks to themselves and people working with them in the conduct of their professional activities.
17. Human rights professionals are obliged to stay informed about developments in international human rights standards and mechanisms, and to practice their profession accordingly.
18. Human rights professionals, in particular those in managerial positions, shall expend every effort to foster a work environment in which these ethical principles can be upheld.

This *Statement* should not be interpreted as restricting or limiting any ethical commitments made in the context of specific institutional employment.

Note

1 In *Guiding Principles For Human Rights Field Officers Working in Conflict and Post Conflict Environment. 2008*, 22–23, accessed October 4, 2015. http://resourcecentre.savethechildren.se/sites/default/files/documents/6030.pdf.

Bibliography

"About MSF." Médecins Sans Frontières. Accessed November 27, 2013. www.msf.org/about-msf.

"About Us." Human Rights Watch. www.hrw.org/about.

Addo, Michael K. "The Practice of United Nations Treaty Bodies in the Reconciliation of Cultural Diversity with Universal Respect for Human Rights." *Human Rights Quarterly* 32:2 (2010): 601–664.

"African Commission on Human and Peoples' Rights." African Commission on Human and Peoples' Rights. Accessed September 4, 2014. www.achpr.org/instruments/achpr/.

"The African Court on Human and Peoples' Rights." African Union. Accessed September 4, 2014. www.au.int/en/organs/cj.

Alleyne, Mark D. "The United Nations' Celebrity Diplomacy." *SAIS Review of International Affairs* 25:1 (2005) 175–185.

Alston, Philip, and Ryan Goodman. *International Human Rights: The Successor to International Human Rights in Context: Law, Politics and Morals: Text and Materials.* Oxford: Oxford University Press, 2013.

Alston, Philip, Jason Morgan-Foster, and William Abresch. "The Competence of the UN Human Rights Council and Its Special Procedures in Armed Conflicts: Extrajudicial Executions and the War on Terror." *European Journal of International Law* 19 (2008): 183–209.

Amao, Olufemi. *Corporate Social Responsibility, Human Rights, and the Law: Multinational Corporations in Developing Countries.* Abingdon: Routledge, 2011.

The Association for the Prevention of Torture, the International Detention Coalition, and the United Nations High Commission for Refugees *Monitoring Immigration Detention: Practical Manual* (June 2014). Accessed September 30, 2014. www.apt.ch/content/files_res/monitoring-immigration-detention_practical-manual.pdf.

Aston, Philip. "Neither Fish nor Fowl: The Quest to Define the Role of the UN High Commissioner for Human Rights." *European Journal of International Law* 8:2 (1997): 321–335.

Baldwin, Clive. "Implementation through Cooperation? Human Rights Officers and the Military in Kosovo." *International Peacekeeping* 13:4 (December 2005): 489–501.

Bartly, Tim, and Curtis Child. "Shaming the Corporation: The Social Production of Targets and the Anti-Sweatshop Movement." *American Sociological Review* 79:2 (August 2014): 653–679.

Bassiounit, M. Cheriff. "The Institutionalization of Torture Under the Bush Administration." *Case Western Reserve Journal of International Law* 37:2/3 (2006): 389–425.

Berridge, G.R. *Diplomacy: Theory and Practice.* New York: Palgrave, 2002.

Bhatt, Kean. "The Hypocrisy of Human Rights Watch." *NACLA Report on the Americas* 46:4 (Winter 2013): 44–48.

Binet, Laurence. "Ethiopia: A Fool's Game in Ogaden." In *Humanitarian Negotiations Revealed: The MSF Experience*, ed. Claire Magone, Michael Neuman, and Fabrice Weissman. New York: Columbia University Press, 2011, 35–46.

Blakely, Ruth. "Dirty Hands, Clean Conscience? The CIA Inspector General's Investigation of 'Enhanced Interrogation Techniques' in the War on Terror and the Torture Debate." *Journal of Human Rights* 10:4 (October 2011): 544–561.
Bohmekt, Tobias. "Civil Society Lobbying and Countries' Climate Change Policies: A Matching Approach." *Climate Policy* 13:6 (2013): 698–717.
Boutros-Ghali, Boutros. *Unvanquished: A U.S.-U.N. Saga.* New York: Random House, 1999.
Bouvier, Paul. "Humanitarian Care in Small Things is Dehumanised Places." *International Review of the Red Cross* 94:888 (Winter 2012): 1537–1550.
Brooks, Rosa Ehrenreich. "Failed States or State as Failure." *University of Chicago Law Review* 72:4 (2005): 1159–1196.
Brown, Charles J. "The Limits of Institutional Diplomacy." *Freedom Review* 25:4 (April 1994): 31–33.
Brown, Widney. "Human Rights Watch: An Overview." In *NGOs and Human Rights: Promise and Performance*, ed. Claude Emerson Welch. Philadelphia: University of Pennsylvania Press, 2001, 72–84.
Burke, Jason. "India Cracks Down on US Embassy Club in Diplomatic Row." *Guardian*. Last modified January 8, 2014. Accessed April 12, 2014. www.theguardian.com/world/2014/jan/08/india-us-american-embassy-club-row.
Callaway, Rhonda L., and Julie Harrelson-Stephens. *Exploring International Human Rights: Essential Readings.* Boulder: Lynne Rienner Publishers, 2007.
Cardenas, Sonia. "Transgovernmental Activism: Canada's Role in Promoting National Human Rights Commissions." *Human Rights Quarterly* 25:3 (2003): 775–790.
Carr, E.H., and Michael Cox. *The Twenty Years' Crisis, 1919–1939: An Introduction to the Study of International Relations.* New York: Palgrave, 2001.
Cerf, Vinton G. "Internet Access is Not a Human Right." *New York Times*. Last modified January 5, 2012. Accessed October 4, 2015. www.nytimes.com/2012/01/05/opinion/internet-access-is-not-a-human-right.html?_r=0.
Chandler, David G. "The Road to Military Humanitarianism: How Human Rights NGOs Shaped a New Humanitarian Agenda." *Human Rights Quarterly* 23:3 (2001): 678–700.
Clark, Ann Marie. *Diplomacy of Conscience: Amnesty International and Changing Human Rights Norms.* Princeton: Princeton University Press, 2001.
Clark, Ben. "Contemporary Legal Doctrine on Proportionality in Armed Conflicts: A Select Review." *Journal of International Humanitarian Legal Studies* 3:2 (2012): 391–414.
"Cluster Coordination." United Nations Office for the Coordination of Humanitarian Affairs. Accessed September 1, 2014. www.unocha.org/what-we-do/coordination-tools/cluster-coordination.
Clymer, K. "Jimmy Carter, Human Rights and Cambodia." *Diplomatic History* 27:2 (April 2003): 561–593.
The Code of Conduct for the International Red Cross and Red Cresent Movement and Non-Governmental Organizations (NGOs) in Disaster Relief. Last modified 1994. Accessed October 4, 2015. www.icrc.org/eng/resources/documents/publication/p1067.htm.
"Commissioner for Human Rights." The Council of Europe. Accessed September 4, 2014. www.coe.int/en/web/commissioner/mandate.
"Confidentiality: Key to the ICRC's Work but Not Unconditional." The International Committee of the Red Cross. Accessed March 2014. www.icrc.org/eng/resources/documents/interview/confidentiality-interview-010608.htm.

Conklin, Alice L. "Colonialism and Human Rights, A Contradiction in Terms? The Case of France in West Africa, 1895–1914." *The American Historical Review* 103:2 (April 1998): 419–442.
Cooper, Andrew F. *Celebrity Diplomacy*. Boulder: Paradigm Publishers, 2008.
Cooper, Andrew F., Jorge Heine, and Ramesh Thakur. "Introduction: the Challenges of 21st Century Diplomacy." In *The Oxford Handbook of Modern Diplomacy*, ed. Andrew F. Cooper, Jorge Heine, and Ramesh Thakur. Oxford: Oxford University Press, 2013, 1–31.
Daalder, Ivo. "Leadership, Lisbon and Libya: Remarks to the Aspen Group." NATO. Last modified June 10, 2011. Accessed August 21, 2014. http://nato.usmission.gov/ambassador-speeches/aspenstrategy20110610.html.
"Description of OCHCR Field Operations and Staff." UN Office for the Coordination of Humanitarian Affairs. Accessed October 4, 2015. www.ohchr.org/EN/Countries/Pages/WorkInField.aspx.
"Detention Guidelines: Guidelines on the Applicable Criteria and Standards relating to the Detention of Asylum-Seekers and Alternative to Detention." The United Nations High Commissioner for Refugees. Accessed September 30, 2014. www.unhcr.org/505b10ee9.html.
Devroy, Ann. "Clinton Grants China MFN, Reversing Campaign Pledge." Last modified May 27, 1994. Accessed October 4, 2015. http://tech.mit.edu/V114/N27/china.27w.html.
"Devyani Khobragade Row: India Targets US Nationals." BBC. Last modified December 28, 2013. Accessed April 11, 2014. www.bbc.com/news/world-asia-india-25534144.
Diehl, Paul F. *The Politics of Global Governance: International Organizations in the Post Cold War Era*. Boulder: Lynne Rienner Publishers, 1998.
Dinsmore, Greg. "Debate: When Less is Really Less- What's Wrong with Minimalist Approaches to Human Rights." *Journal of Political Philosophy* 15:4 (2007): 473–483.
Donnelly, Jack. *International Human Rights*. Boulder: Westview Press, 1993.
Donnelly, Jack. "International Human Rights Law: Six Decades after the UDHR and Beyond." In *International Human Rights Law: Six Decades after the UDHR and Beyond*, ed. Mashood A. Baderin and Manisuli Ssenyonjo. Surrey: Ashgate, 2013, 39–48.
Douzinas, Costas. *The End of Human Rights: Critical Legal Thought at Turn of the Century*. London: Hart, 2000.
Durham, Helen. "The Role of Civil Society in Creating the International Criminal Court Statute: Ten Years On and Looking Back." *International Humanitarian Legal Studies* 3 (2012): 3–42.
Egeland, Jan. "Humanitarian Diplomacy." In *The Oxford Handbook of Modern Diplomacy*, ed. Andrew F. Cooper, Jorge Heine, and Ramesh Thakur. Oxford: Oxford University Press, 2013, 352–368.
Ejaz, Imam, Shaikh Babar, and Rizvi Narjis. "NGOs and Government Partnership for Health Systems Strengthening: A Qualitative Study Presenting Viewpoints of Government, NGOs and Donors in Pakistan." *BMC Health Services Research* 11:1 (2011): 122–128.
Engle, Eric. "Human Rights According to Marxism." *Guild Practitioner* 65:4 (2008): 249–256.
English, John. "The Ottowa Convention on Anti-Personnel Landmines." In *The Oxford Handbook of Modern Diplomacy*, ed. Andrew F. Cooper, Jorge Heine, and Ramesh Thakur. Oxford: Oxford University Press, 2013, 797–808.
Esse de Lang, Niki. "The Establishment and Development of the Myanmar National Human Rights Commission and its Conformity with International Standards." *Asia Pacific Journal on Human Rights and Law* 13:1 (2012): 1–41.

Evans, Gareth. "Commission Diplomacy." In *The Oxford Handbook of Modern Diplomacy*, ed. Andrew F. Cooper, Jorge Heine, and Ramesh Thakur. Oxford: Oxford University Press, 2013, 278–302.

"Fact Sheet No.2 (Rev. 1.) The International Bill of Rights." Office of the High Commissioner for Human Rights. Last modified 1996. Accessed June 25, 2013. www.ohchr.org/ Documents/Publications/FactSheet2Rev.1en.pdf.

Farre, Sabastien. "The ICRC and the Detainees in Nazi Concentration Camps (1942–1945)." *International Review of the Red Cross* 94:888 (2012): 1381–1408.

"First UN High Commissioner for Human Rights Named." *Africa Report* 39:1 (March/April 1994): 10–12.

Forsythe, David P. "Human Rights." In *The Oxford Handbook of Modern Diplomacy*, ed. Andrew F. Cooper, Jorge Heine, and Ramesh Thakur. Oxford: Oxford University Press, 2013, 658–674.

Forsythe, David P. *Human Rights and Peace: International and National Dimensions.* Lincoln: University of Nebraska Press, 1993.

Forsythe, David P. "The UN Secretary-General and Human Rights." In *The Challenging Role of the UN Secretary-General: Making "The Most Impossible Job in the World" Possible*, ed. Benjamin Rivlin and Leon Gordenker. Westport: Praeger, 1993, 211–232.

Freedman, Rosa. *United Nations Human Rights Council: A Critique and Early Assessment.* New York: Routledge, 2013.

"Freedom in the World 2014." Freedom House. Last modified October 11, 2014. Accessed October 4, 2015. http://freedomhouse.org/report/freedom-world/freedom-world-2014 ?gclid=CJqhmPubpcECFQMT7Aod1CoA8Q#.VDl1Yo10yYN.

Gordenker, Leon. *Refugees in International Politics.* London: Croom Helm, 1987.

"Governance and Organization: How the UNHCR is Structured." United Nations High Commission for Refugees. Accessed October 4, 2015. www.unhcr.org/pages/49c3646c80. html.

Gowan, Richard. "Diplomatic Fallout: Vieira de Mello and the Dark Side of U.N. Diplomacy." *World Politics Review.* Last modified August 12, 2013, accessed September 21, 2014. www.worldpoliticsreview.com/articles/13156/diplomatic-fallout-vieira-de-mello-and-the-dark-side-of-u-n-diplomacy.

Green, Christian M. "Religion." In *The Oxford Handbook of International Human Rights Law*, ed. Dinah Shelton. Oxford: Oxford University Press, 2013, 9–13.

Greenhouse, Stephen. "Report Outlines the Abuse of Foreign Domestic Workers." *New York Times.* Last modified June 14, 2001.

"Guiding Principles for Human Rights Field Officers Working in Conflict and Post-Conflict Environments." Human Rights Law Centre, University of Nottingham. Last modified 2008. Accessed October 4, 2015. http://reliefweb.int/report/world/ guiding-principles-human-rights-field-officers-working-conflict-and-post-conflict.

Hafner-Burton, Emilie. *Making Human Rights a Reality.* Princeton: Princeton University Press, 2013.

Hajjar, Lis. "Cause Lawyering in Transnational Perspective: National Conflict and Human Rights in Israel/Palestine." *Law and Society Review* 31:3 (1997): 473–504.

Hammarberg, Thomas, and Isil Gachet. "Commissioner for Human Rights." In *Human Rights Diplomacy: Contemporary Perspectives*, ed. Michael O'Flaherty, Zdzisław Kędzia, Amrei Müller and George Ulrich. Leiden: Martinus Nijhoff, 2011, 101–128.

"Handbook and Guidelines on Procedures and Criteria for Determining Refugee Status under the 1951 Convention and the 1967 Protocol Relating to the Status of Refugees."

UN High Commissioner for Refugees (UNHCR). Last modified December 2011. Accessed September 20, 2014. www.refworld.org/docid/4f33c8d92.html.

Hellinger, Daniel, and Dennis R. Judd. *The Democratic Facade*, 2nd edition. New York: Wadsworth, 1994.

Hicks, Peggy. "Human Rights Diplomacy: The NGO Role." In *Human Rights Diplomacy: Contemporary Perspectives*, ed. Michael O'Flaherty, Zdzisław Kędzia, Amrei Müller and George Ulrich. Leiden: Martinus Nijhoff, 2011, 117–222.

Hill, Jr., Daniel W., Will H. Moore, and Bumba Mukherjee. "Information Politics Versus Organization Incentives: When are Amnesty International's 'Naming and Shaming' Reports Biased?" *International Studies Quarterly* 57:2 (June 2013): 219–232.

Hochstetler, Kathryn. "Civil Society." In *The Oxford Handbook of Modern Diplomacy*, ed. Andrew F. Cooper, Jorge Heine, and Ramesh Thakur. Oxford: Oxford University Press, 2013, 171–191.

Hopgood, Stephen. "The End of Human Rights." *Washington Post*, October 11, 2014.

Hopgood, Stephen. *The Endtimes of Human Rights*. Ithaca: Cornell University Press, 2013.

Hossain, Kamal, Leonard F.M. Besselink, Haile Selassie, Gebre Selassie, and Edmond Volker. *Human Rights Commissions and Ombudsman Offices: National Experiences throughout the World*. The Hague: Kluwer Law International, 2000.

Human Rights Law Centre, University of Nottingham, "Guiding Principles for Human Rights Field Officers Working in Conflict and Post-Conflict Environments," 2008. Accessed October 4, 2015. http://reliefweb.int/report/world/guiding-principles-human-rights-field-officers-working-conflict-and-post-conflict.

Human Rights Law Centre, University of Nottingham, *Statement of Ethical Commitments of Human Rights Professionals*, 2008, 22–23. Accessed October 4, 2015. http://reliefweb.int/report/world/guiding-principles-human-rights-field-officers-working-conflict-and-post-conflict.

"Human Rights Training: A Manual on Human Rights Training Methodology. Professional Training Series No.6." High Commissioner for Human Rights Centre for Human Rights. Last modified 2000. www.ohchr.org/Documents/Publications/training6en.pdf.

Human Rights Watch. "Civil Society Denounces Adoption of Flawed ASEAN Human Rights Declaration." Accessed October 1, 2014. www.hrw.org/news/2012/11/19/civil-society-denounces-adoption-flawed-asean-human-rights-declaration.

"Humanitarian Diplomacy." International Federation of the Red Cross and Red Crescent Societies. Accessed December 26, 2013. www.ifrc.org/en/what-we-do/humanitarian-diplomacy/humanitarian-diplomacy-policy/.

"Humanitarian Operations." U.S. State Department. Accessed April 25, 2014. www.state.gov/t/pm/iso/c21542.htm.

Ibhawoh, Bonny. *Imperialism and Human Rights: Colonial Discourses of Rights and Liberties in African History*. Albany: State University of New York Press, 2007.

Ignatieff, Michael, and Amy Gutmann. *Human Rights as Politics and Idolatry*. Princeton: Princeton University Press, 2001.

International Committee of the Red Cross. "Professional Standards for Protection Work Carried Out by Humanitarian and Human Rights Actors in Armed Conflict and Other Situations of Violence." The International Committee of the Red Cross. Last modified 2013. Accessed October 4, 2015. www.icrc.org/eng/assets/files/other/icrc-002-0999.pdf.

International Committee of the Red Cross. 2010. "Respect for the Life and Dignity of Detainees." Accessed September 29, 2014. www.icrc.org/eng/what-we-do/visiting-detainees/ overview-visiting-detainees.htm.

"The ICTR in Brief." Accessed October 4, 2015. www.unictr.org/en/tribunal.

"The ICTR Remembers: 20th Anniversary of the Rwandan Genocide." Accessed October 4, 2015. www.unmict.org/ictr-remembers.

Joseph, Sarah. *Blame It on the WTO? A Human Rights Critique*. Oxford: Oxford University Press, 2011.

Kapp, Clare. "Brazilian Diplomat Moves Into the Hot Seat." *The Lancet* 360:9337 (September 21, 2002).

Karns, Margaret P., and Karen A. Mingst. "International Organizations and Diplomacy." In *The Oxford Handbook of Modern Diplomacy*, ed. Andrew F. Cooper, Jorge Heine, and Ramesh Thakur. Oxford: Oxford University Press, 2013, 142–159.

Keck, Michelle. "State Funded NGO in Civil Wars: the US Case." *BMC Health Services Research* 17:4 (December 2011): 411–427.

Keck, M., and C. Sikkink. *Activists beyond Borders*. Ithaca: Cornell University Press, 1998.

Korey, William. "The Helskinki Accords: Good Intentions." *New Republic*, August 2, 1975, 6–7.

Krain, Matthew. "J'accuse! Does Naming and Shaming Reduce the Severity of Genocides or Politicides?" *International Studies Quarterly* 56:3 (September 2012): 574–589.

Kron, Josh. "South Sudan Expels a UN Rights Officer." *New York Times*, November 6, 2013, A7.

Lewis, Anthony. "Abroad at Home; Human Rights Delimma." *New York Times*. Last modified February 13, 1986.

Li, Yitan, and A. Cooper Drury. "Threatening Sanctions When Engagement Would Be More Effective: Attaining Better Human Rights in China." *International Studies Perspectives* 5:4 (November 2004): 378–394.

Loescher, Gilburt D. *Beyond Charity: International Cooperation and the Global Refugee Crisis*. Oxford: Oxford University Press, 1996.

Londono, Ernesto. "Bahrain Orders Senior U.S. Diplomat to Leave." *Washington Post*. Last modified July 7, 2014. Accessed July 8, 2014. www.washingtonpost.com/world/national-security/bahrain-orders-senior-us-diplomat-to-leave/2014/07/07/982655 4c-0609-11e4-8a6a-19355c7e870a_story.html.

MacFarquhar, Neil. "Open Search Urged for U.N. Rights Job." *New York Times*. Last modified June 10, 2008, A9. Accessed October 4, 2015. www.nytimes.com/2008/06/10/world/10nations.html?_r=0.

Magone, Claire, Michael Neuman, and Fabrice Weissman. *Humanitarian Negotiations Revealed: The MSF Experience*. London: Hurst and Company, 2011.

Mancini-Griffoli, Deborah, and Andre Picot. "Humanitarian Negotiation: A Handbook for Securing Access, Assistance and Protection for Civilians of Armed Conflict." Centre for Humanitarian Dialogue. Accessed October 4, 2015. www.hdcentre.org/uploads/tx_news/188HumanitarianNegotiation.pdf.

"Manual on Human Rights Monitoring." United Nations Human Rights Office of the High Commissioner. Last modified 2001. www.ohchr.org/Documents/Publications/OHCHRIntro-12pp.pdf.

McHugh, Gerard, and Manuel Bessler. "Humanitarian Negotiations with Armed Groups: A Manual for Practitioners." United Nations Office for the Coordination of Humanitarian Affairs. Last modified 2006. Accessed October 4, 2015. https://docs.unocha.org/sites/dms/Documents/HumanitarianNegotiationswArmedGroupsManual.pdf.

Meili, Stephen. "U.K. Refugee Lawyers: Pushing the Boundaries of Domestic Court Acceptance of International Human Rights Law." *Boston College of International and Comparative Law Review* 36:2 (Spring 2013): 1123–1148.

"Membership." UN International Law Commission. Accessed September 25, 2014. www.un.org/law/ilc/index.htm.

Minear, Larry. "The Craft of Humanitarian Diplomacy." In *Humanitarian Diplomacy: Practitioners and Their Craft*, ed. Larry Minear and Hazel Smith. Tokyo: United Nations University Press, 2006, 7–35.

The Ministry of Foreign Affairs of the Federation of Russia. Last modified December 6, 2012. Accessed August 1, 2014. www.mid.ru/brp_4.nsf/0/F6501F42C40A25EE44257ACC004971FC.

Moley, Nell. "Confronting the Ethical Challenges of Ethical Accountability in International Human Rights Lawyering." *Stanford Journal of International Law* 59:2 (2014): 359–392.

"Monitoring Immigration Detention: Practical Manual." The Association for the Prevention of Torture, the International Detention Coalition, and the United Nations High Commission for Refugees. Last modified June 2014. Accessed September 30, 2014. www.apt.ch/content/files_res/monitoring-immigration-detention_practical-manual.pdf.

Morgenthau, Hans. *Politics Among Nature: The Struggle for Power and Peace*, 5th edition. New York: Alfred Knopf, 1978.

Mountz, Alison. *Seeking Asylum: Human Smuggling and Bureaucracy at the Border*. Minneapolis: University of Minnesota Press, 2010.

Mueller, Sherry. "The Nexus of U.S. Public Diplomacy and Citizen Diplomacy." In *Routledge Handbook of Public Diplomacy*, ed. Nancy Snow and Philip M. Taylor. New York: Routledge, 2007, 100–110.

Munger, Frank. "The Cause Lawyer's Cause." *Law in Context* 28:2 (2010): 95–106.

Murphy, Ray, and Mohamed M. El Zeidy. "Prisoners of War: A Comparative Study of the Principles of International Humanitarian Law and the Islamic Law of War." *International Criminal Law Review* 9:4 (2009): 623–649.

Naples-Mitchell, Joanna. "Perspectives of UN Special Rapporteurs on their Role: Inherent Tensions and Unique Contributions to Human Rights." *International Journal of Human Rights* 15:2 (February 2011): 232–248.

Nye, Joseph S. *Soft Power: The Means to Success in World Politics*. New York: Public Affairs, 2004.

"OCHA on Message: Humanitarian Principles." UN Office for the Coordination of Humanitarian Affairs. Accessed June 2012. https://ochanet.unocha.org/p/Documents/OOM-humanitarianprinciples_eng_June12.pdf.

O'Flaherty, Michael. "The United Nations Human Rights Treat Bodies." In *Human Rights Diplomacy: Contemporary Perspectives*, ed. Michael O'Flaherty, Zdzisław Kędzia, Amrei Müller and George Ulrich. Leiden: Martinus Nijhoff Publishers, 2011, 155–171.

O'Flaherty, Michael, and George Ulrich. "The Professional Identity and Development of Human Rights Field Officer." In *The Professional Identity of the Human Rights Field Officer*. Online edition. Burlington: Ashgate, 2010, 7–32.

Olivares, Alanis, and Efren C. Goettingen. "Indigenous Peoples' Rights and the Extractive Industry: Jurisprudence from the Inter-American System of Human Rights." *Journal of International Law* 5:1 (2013): 187–214.

"Our Mission." Amnesty International. Accessed October 22, 2013. www.amnestyusa.org/about-us/our-mission.

Pease, Kelly-Kate S. *International Organizations*. New York: Pearson, 2012.

Petrasek, David. "New Powers, New Approaches? Human Rights Diplomacy in the 21st Century." *International Journal on Human Rights* 10:19 (2013): 6–15.

Pflantz, Mike. "African Union Leaders Give Themselves Immunity from War Crimes Prosecution." *Telegragh*. Last modified July 2, 2014. Accessed September 13, 2014.

www.telegraph.co.uk/news/worldnews/africaandindianocean/10940047/African-leaders-vote-to-give-themselves-immunity-from-war-crimes-prosecutions.html.

Pinheiro, Paulo Sergio. "Being a Special Rapporteur: A Delicate Balancing Act." *International Journal of Human Rights* 15 (2011): 162–171.

Pinheiro, Paulo Sergio. "Musings of a UN Special Rapporteur on Human Rights." *Global Governance* 9 (2003): 7–13.

Poe, Steven C. "Human Rights and Economic Allocation Under Ronald Reagan and Jimmy Carter." *American Journal of Political Science* 36:1 (February 1992): 147–167.

Poe, Steven C., and C. Neal Tate. "Repression of Human Rights to Personal Integrity in the 1980s: A Global Analysis." *American Political Science Review* 88:4 (1994): 853–872.

Pogge, Thomas. "Recognized and Violated by International Law." *Leiden Journal of International Law* 18:4 (2005): 717–745.

Power, Samantha. *Chasing the Flame: One Man's Fight to Save the World*. New York: Penguin Books, 2008.

Power, Samantha. "The Envoy." *The New Yorker*, January 7, 2008, 42–55.

Preston, Julia. "New U.N. Chief Invites Controversy by Declining to Oppose Hussein Execution." *New York Times*. Last modified January 3, 2014. Accessed October 4, 2015. www.nytimes.com/2007/01/03/world/middleeast/03nations.html?fta=y&_r=0.

Public Library of US Diplomacy. Accessed April 28, 2014. www.wikileaks.org/plusd/cables/02ROME3647_a.html.

Rabet, Delphine. "Human Rights and Globalization: The Myth of Corporate Social Responsibility." *Journal of Alternative Perspectives in the Social Sciences* 1:2 (May 2009): 463–475.

Rana, Kishan S. *21st Century Diplomacy: A Practitioner's Guide*. New York: Bloomsbury, 2011.

Reif, Linda C. *The Ombudsman, Good Governace and the Internal Human Rights System*. Leiden: Nijhoff, 2004.

"Respect for the Life and Dignity of Detainees." The International Committee of the Red Cross. Accessed September 29, 2014. www.icrc.org/eng/what-we-do/visiting-detainees/overview-visiting-detainees.htm.

Retherford, Kristin L. "Regulating the Corporate Tap: Applying Administrative Law Principles to Achieve the Human Right to Water." *Indiana Law and Journal* 88:2 (Spring 2013): 811–835.

Rinehart, Liz Clark. "Clapper v. Amnesty International USA: Allowing the FISA Amendment Act of 2008 to Turn Incidentally in Certainly." *Maryland Law Review* 73:3 (2014): 1018–1048.

Roach, Steven C. *Governance, Order, and the International Criminal Court: Between Realpolitik and a Cosmopolitan Court*. Oxford: Oxford University Press, 2009.

Roberg, Jeffrey L. "The Importance of International Treaties: Is Ratification Necessary." *World Affairs* 169:4 (Spring 2007): 181–186.

Roberts, Steven V. "The Moscow Summit: The Serious Side; Reagan and Gorbachev Begin Summit Parley in the Kremlin; Strike Sparks Rights Issue." *New York Times*. Last modified May 30, 1988.

Robinson, Piers. *The CNN Effect: The Myth of News, Foreign Policy, and Intervention*. New York: Routledge, 2002.

Russell, James M. "The Ambivalence about the Globalization of Telecommunications: The Story of Amnesty International, Shell Oil Company, and Nigeria." *Journal of Human Rights* 1:2 (September 2002): 405–416.

Russett, Bruce M. *Grasping the Democratic Peace: Principles for a Post-Cold War World.* Princeton: Princeton University Press, 1994.
"Russia Attacks EU Human Rights Record after Criticism." BBC. Last modified December 7, 2012. Accessed August 2, 2014. www.bbc.com/news/world-europe-20644214.
Sappideen, Razeen. "Property Rights, Human Rights, and the New International Trade Regime." *International Journal of Human Rights* 15:7 (October 2011): 1013–1030.
Schabas, William. *The UN International Tribunals: The Former Yugoslavia, Rwanda and Sierra Leone.* Cambridge: Cambridge University Press, 2006.
Schmitz, David F., and Vanessa Walker. "Jimmy Carter and the Foreign Policy of Human Rights: The Development of a Post- Cold War Foreign Policy." *Diplomatic History* 28:1 (January 2004): 113–143.
"Second International Pledging Conference for Syria." UN Office for the Coordination of Humanitarian Affairs. Last modified January 15, 2014. Accessed April 18, 2014. https://docs.unocha.org/sites/dms/Documents/SyriaPledging_MediaInfo_EN.pdf.
"Seeing Red." *New Republic.* Last modified December 29, 2004. Accessed September 29, 2014. www.newrepublic.com/article/red-cross-geneva-conventions-guantanamo%3Dbay-al-qaeda.
Shannon, Roisin. "Playing with Principles in the Era of Securitized Aid: Negotiating Humanitarian Space in Post 9–11 Afghanistan." *Progress in Development Studies* 9:1 (January 2009): 15–36.
Shultz, George Pratt. *Turmoil and Triumph: My Years as Secretary of State.* New York: Scribner's, 1993.
Sirleaf, Matiangai V.S., "The Truth about Truth Commissions: Why they Do Not Function Optimally in Post-Conflict Societies." *Cardozo Law Review* 35:6 (2014): 2263–2347.
Spanheimer, Ryan. "Justification for Creating an Ombudsman Privilege in Today's Society." *Marquette Law Review* 96:2 (2012): 161–168.
"Special Procedures of the Human Rights Council." United Nations Office of the High Commissioner for Human Rights. Accessed June 25, 2014. www.ohchr.org/en/HRBodies/SP/Pages/Welcomepage.aspx.
"Special Rapporteur on Torture and Other Cruel, Inhuman or Degrading Treatment or punishment." United Nations Office of the High Commissioner for Human Rights. Accessed January 15, 2014. www.ohchr.org/EN/Issues/Torture/SRTorture/Pages/SRTortureIndex.aspx.
Spieler, Paula. "The Maria da Pheha Case and the Inter-American Commission on Human Rights: Contributions to the Debate of Domestic Violence Against Women in Brazil." *Indiana Journal of Global Legal Studies* 18:1 (2011): 121–143.
Ssenyonjo, Manisuli. "Economic, Social and Cultural Rights." In *International Human Rights Laws: Six Decades after the UDHR and Beyond*, ed. Mashood A. Baderin and Manisuli Ssenyonjo. Surrey: Ashgate, 2009, 49–88.
"Statement of Ethical Commitments of Human Rights Professionals." Human Rights Law Centre, University of Nottingham. Last modified 2008. Accessed October 4, 2015. http://reliefweb.int/report/world/guiding-principles-human-rights-field-officers-working-conflict-and-post-conflict.
Steinberg, Gerald M. "Human Rights Watch Protects Arab Tyrants." *Middle East Quarterly* 20:3 (Summer 2013): 49–58.
Stephens, Beth, Judith Chomsky, Jennifer Green, Paul Hoffman, and Michael Ratner. *International Human Rights Litigation in U.S. Courts*, 2nd edition. Leiden: Martinus Nijhoff Publishers, 2008.

Taylor, Paul. "The United Nations and International Organizations." In *The Globalization of World Politics: An Introduction to International Relations*, ed. John Baylis, Steve Smith, and Patricia Owens. Oxford: Oxford University Press, 1998, 264–283.
Terry, Fiona. *Condemned to Repeat? The Paradox of Humanitarian Action*. Ithaca: Cornell University Press, 2002.
Tharoor, Ishaan. "At Last, A Western Country Stands Up to Saudi Arabia on Human Rights." *Washington Post*, March 12, 2014, accessed March 15, 2015. www.washingtonpost.com/blogs/worldviews/wp/2015/03/12/at-last-a-western-country-stands-up-to-saudi-arabia-on-human-rights/?tid=HP_more?tid=HP_more.
Thomas, Daniel C. "Boomerangs and Superpowers: International Norms, Transnational Networks, and US Foreign Policy." *Cambridge Review of International Affairs* 15:1 (2001): 25–44.
Thomas, Daniel C. *The Helsinki Effect: International Norms, Human Rights, and the Demise of Communism*. Princeton: Princeton University Press, 2001.
Todres, Jonathan. "Lawyers and the Universal Declaration of Human Rights." *International Law News* 38:1 (Winter 2009): 12–13.
"Treaties States Parties to Such Treaties." The International Committee for the Red Cross. Accessed September 14, 2014. www.icrc.org/applic/ihl/ihl.nsf/Treaty.xsp?documentId=AA0C5BCBAB5C4A85C12563CD002D6D09&action=openDocumenthttps://www.icrc.org/applic/ihl/ihl.nsf/Treaty.xsp?documentId=AA0C5BCBAB5C4A85C12563CD002D6D09&action=openDocument.
"Twitter Diplomacy: State Department 2.0." *NPR All Things Considered*. Podcast audio. February 21, 2012. Accessed October 4, 2015. www.npr.org/blogs/alltechconsidered/2012/02/21/147207004/twitter-diplomacy-state-department-2-0.
Ulrich, George. "Framework for the Analysis of Human Rights Diplomacy." In *Human Rights Diplomacy: Contemporary Perspectives*, ed. Michael O'Flaherty, Zdzisław Kędzia, Amrei Müller, and George Ulrich. Leiden: Martinus Nijhoff, 2011, 19–42.
"UNHCR Manual on Refugee Protection and the European Convention on Human Rights." UN High Commissioner for Refugees (UNHCR). Last modified 2006. Accessed September 20, 2014. www.refworld.org/docid/3f4cd5c74.html.
"United Nations General Assembly Resolution, A/RES/20/2131, 'Declaration on the Inadmissibility of Intervention in the Domestic Affairs of States and the Protection of their Independence and Sovereignty,' (21 December 1965)." Accessed September 1, 2013. www.un-documents.net/a20r2131.htm.
"United Nations General Assembly Resolution 428 (v), December 14, 1950." United Nations. Accessed October 4, 2015. www.un.org/documents/ga/res/5/ares5.htm.
UN High Commissioner for Refugees (UNHCR), *Handbook and Guidelines on Procedures and Criteria for Determining Refugee Status under the 1951 Convention and the 1967 Protocol Relating to the Status of Refugees*, December 2011, HCR/1P/4/ENG/REV. 3, Accessed September 20, 2014. www.refworld.org/docid/4f33c8d92.html.
US State Department. Accessed October 4, 2015. www.state.gov/s/h/tst/2013/index.htm.
"Vienna Convention on Diplomatic Relations." United Nations Audio Visual Library of International Law. Accessed January 23, 2014. http://legal.un.org/avl/ha/vcdr/vcdr.html.
Vincent, R.J. *Human Rights and International Relations*. Cambridge: Cambridge University Press, 1988.
von Clausewitz, Carl. *On War*. Ed. Michael Howard and Peter Paret. Princeton: Princeton University Press, 1976.

Wall, Anji E. *Ethics for International Medicine: A Practical Guide for Aid Workers in Developing Countries*. Hanover: Dartmouth College Press, 2012.
Weintraub, Bernard. "Reagan to Resist One Issue Summit." *New York Times*. August 22, 1986. Accessed October 4, 2015. www.nytimes.com/1986/08/22/world/reagan-to-resist-one-issue-summit.html.
Weiss, Thomas George. *Humanitarian Business*. Cambridge: Polity, 2013.
Weiss, Thomas George. *The United Nations and Changing World Politics*, 7th edition. Boulder: Westview Press, 2014.
Weiss, Thomas George, Tatiana Carayannis, and Richard Jolly. "The Third United Nations." *Global Governance* 15:1 (2009): 123–142.
Weiss, Thomas George, David P. Foysythe, Roger A. Coate, and Kelly-Kate Pease. *The United Nations and Changing World Politics*, 7th edition. Boulder: Westview Press, 2014.
Weissman, Fabrice. "Silence Heals … From the Cold War to the War on Terror, MSF Speaks Out: A Brief History." In *Humanitarian Negotiations Revealed: The MSF Experience*, ed. Claire Magone, Michael Neuman, and Fabrice Weissman. New York: Columbia University Press, 2011, 177–197.
Weissman, Fabrice. "Sri Lanka: Amid All-Out War." In *Humanitarian Negotiations Revealed: The MSF Experience*, ed. Claire Magone, Michael Neuman, and Fabrice Weissman. New York: Columbia University Press, 2011, 14–33.
Welch, Claude E., Jr. *NGOs and Human Rights: Promise and Performance*. Philadelphia: University of Pennsylvania Press, 2001.
Welch, Claude E., Jr. and Ashley F. Watkins. "Extending Enforcement: The Coalition for the International Criminal Court." *Human Rights Quarterly* 33:4 (November 2011): 927–1032.
Wendt, Alexander. "Anarchy is what States Make of It: The Social Construction of Power Politics." *International Organizations* 46 (Spring 1992): 291–324.
Wheeler, Mark. "Celebrity Diplomacy: United Nations' Goodwill Ambassadors and Messengers of Peace." *Celebrity Studies* 2:1 (2011): 6–18.
"Who We Are." Amnesty International. Accessed September 1, 2014. www.amnesty.org/en/who-we-are/about-amnesty-international.
"Who We Are." United Nations Office for the Coordination of Humanitarian Affairs. Accessed September 1, 2014. www.unocha.org/about-us/who-we-are.
Williams, Jody, and Stephen D. Goose. "Citizen Diplomacy and the Ottawa Process." In *Banning Landmines: Disarmament, Citizen Diplomacy, and Human Security*, ed. Jody Williams, Stephen D. Goose, and Mary Wareham. Lanham: Rowman & Littlefield, 2008, 181–198.
Winston, Morton E. "Assessing the Effectiveness of International Human Rights NGOs: Amnesty International." In *NGOs and Human Rights: Promise and Performance*, by Claude Emerson Welch. Philadelphia: University of Pennsylvania Press, 2001, 25–54.
Witt, John Fabian. *Lincoln's Code: The Laws of War in American History*. New York: Free Press, 2012.
"Working for the ICRC." The International Committee of the Red Cross. Accessed September 16, 2014. www.icrc.org/eng/who-we-are/jobs/.
Zakaria, Fareed. "The Rise of Illiberal Democracy." *Foreign Affairs* 76:1 (1997): 22–43.

Index

Note: Page numbers with 't' are tables.

1951 Convention Relating to the Status of Refugees (and the 1967 Protocol) 37, 124, 125
1954 Convention Relating to the Status of Stateless Persons 37
1961 Convention on the Reduction of Statelessness 37
1961 Vienna Convention on Diplomatic Relations 43–44, 46
1967 Protocol 37, 125, 156
1969 American Convention on Human Rights 94, 128
2005 World Summit 68, 81, 91, 101, 108

academics 167, 169
actors 7–9, 13, 14, 15, 173
   civil society 179
ad hoc international criminal tribunals 86
advocacy 134–136
Africa 94–95
African Charter on Human and Peoples' Rights (Banjul Charter) 94, 128
African Commission on Human and Peoples' Rights 128
African Court on Human and Peoples' Rights 94, 129
African Union (AU) 12, 83, 94, 128, 177
   regional courts 129
Albright, Madeleine 48, 79
allies 158
American Convention of Human Rights (1969) 94, 128
American Declaration on the Rights and Duties of Man (1948) 94
the Americas 93–94, 127–128, 129
amicus curiae 142–143, 161
Amnesty International 2, 138–139, 142
   Clapper v. *Amnesty International USA* 142

   letter to UN 143–145
Amos, Valerie 126
anarchy 20
Annan, Kofi 104
   Global Compact initiative 9, 102, 179
   In Larger Freedom 102
   More Secure World: Our Shared Responsibility, A 101–102
Arab Charter on Human Rights 95, 128
Arab Human Rights Committee 95, 128
Arab League 95, 177
arbitration 14
Arbour, Louise 104–105
artists 169
ASEAN *see* Association of South East Asian Nations
Asia, IGOs 95
Assad, Bashar al- 36, 85
Assange, Julian 61
assimilation 124
assistance, humanitarian 15
Association of South East Asian Nations (ASEAN) 12, 95, 129, 177
   Intergovernmental Commission on Human Rights 128
AU *see* African Union
authoritarianism 56, 175, 176–177, 178
Axworthy, Lloyd 47–48
Ayala-Lasso, Jose 103

Bahrain 44
Balkans 68, 76–77, 79, 159
Banjul Charter 94, 128
Ban Ki-moon 102, 126, 143
Bashir, Omar el- 86
Beneson, Peter 138
Bessler, Manuel 158
bilateral diplomacy 47

Boutros-Ghali, Boutros 103
  Agenda for Peace, An 101
Burke, Jason 45
Bush, George W. 91, 140
business 178–179

Cairo Declaration on Human Rights in Islam 95
Canada 47–48, 62
capitalism 25–26
Carter, Jimmy 31–34
cause lawyers 161
celebrity diplomacy 137
charter-based bodies 113
China 173, 174, 176
  Balkans 79
  Internet 176
  as Most Favored Nation 30–31
  Resolution 688 76
citizen diplomacy 137–138
civil service
  OCHA 125–126
  regional 126–129
  UN High Commissioner for Human Rights 102–113, 121
  UN Secretaries-General 100–102
civil society actors 1, 9, 11, 56, 67, 134, 163, 173
civil society space 55, 56
Clapper v. *Amnesty International USA* 142
Clausewitz, Carl von 21
Clinton, Bill 30–31
Clinton, Hillary 61
Cluster Coordination approach 126
Coalition for the International Criminal Court 136
colonialism *see* imperialism
commission diplomacy 12, 80
Commission on Human Rights 89–91
commissions, national human rights 61–62, 63
commissions of inquiry 121
committee diplomacy 12–13, 123
Common Article 3 (Geneva Conventions) 37
conference diplomacy 11–12
Constantine, Greg 167–169
constructivism 27

controversy of human rights 4–6
Convention on the Prevention and the Punishment of Genocide 37
Convention on the Prohibition of the Use, Stockpiling, Production and Transfer of Anti-Personnel Mines and on their Destruction (Ottawa Treaty) 48, 137
Corporate Social Responsibility (CSR) 9, 102
Costello, Joe 53–58
Council of Europe 93, 127
counter-summits 11
"Country Reports on Human Rights Practices" (US State Dept) 34
courts/tribunals 86, 94, 174
  ICC 15, 83, 94–95, 136
  regional 128–129
CSR *see* Corporate Social Responsibility
cultural relativism 5

Daalder, Ivo 48
Dayton Peace Accords 77
démarches 58, 60
democracy 26, 177
Democratic People's Republic of Korea (DPRK) 53–54
d'Escoto Brockman, Miguel 88
detention monitors 162–167
Diana, Princess of Wales 138
dignity *see* human dignity
diplomacy 2.0 10, 53
diplomacy
  channels 10–13
  heads of state 27–36
  tools and strategies 13–15
  types 9–10, 14, 82–83, 121, 123, 137–138
  see also international diplomatic law
diplomatic immunity 44
diplomatic recognition 44
Dunant, Henry 146

ECOSOC (Economic and Social Council) 89, 91
Egeland, Jan 126
Emergency Relief Coordinator (ERC) 126
Ethiopia 150
European Convention on Human Rights and Fundamental Freedoms (1950) 93

European Court on Human
    Rights 93, 128
European Court of Justice 128
European Union (EU) 93
    Annual Report on Human Rights and
        Democracy 52
    Balkans 80
    regional civil service 126–127

failed states 177–178
field diplomacy 13, 155
    negotiation 157–158
first/second/third generation human
    rights 3, 6
first/second/third generation
    peacekeeping 68, 69–74t, 75, 173
first/second/third UN 67, 78, 81, 102
Follow the Money 148–149
foreign ministers/secretaries 47–48
foreign policy 1, 19, 21, 22, 23
    United States 30–34
    see also Ministries of Foreign Affairs
        (MFA)
Fox, Hosanna 147–150
Freedom House 176–177
freedom of movement 157
Frelick, Bill 139–142

Gaddafi, Muammar 83–84
Gayton, Ivan 164–165
Gebauer, Thomas 137
gender equality 57, 107, 162
generations (first/second/third) of human
    rights 3, 6
Geneva Conventions 7, 37, 39
    ICRC 146, 162–163
genocidaires 78
Global Compact initiative 9, 102, 179
globalization 178–179
Global South 47, 87, 173
Goldstone, Richard 80
good offices 101
Goodwill Ambassadors 125
Gorbachev, Mikhail 29–30
Guterres, António 125

handbooks for human rights/humanitarian
    workers 156, 157–158

heads of state 20, 27–36, 31–32
hegemonic power 21–22, 23
Helsinki Summit/Accords 28–29, 39,
    139, 173
Helsinki Watch 29
Hicks, Peggy 135
HRC *see* Human Rights Council
human dignity 2–4, 7, 16, 175–176
    cultural/religious practices 5, 6, 180
    detention 162, 166
    Helsinki Accords 29
    IHL 7
    Marxism 26
humanitarian diplomacy 13, 15, 135
humanitarianism (defined) 7
humanitarian space 136
human-rights based approach 101
Human Rights Council (HRC) (UN)
    89–92, 106, 109
    special procedures 114, 115–118t
human rights (defined) 2–4
human rights officers 158–159
human rights reports 52
Human Rights Watch 29, 44, 45–46, 135,
    139–142
    From a Flood to a Trickle 141
    letter to UN 143–145
    Silent Treatment, The 140
human security 12, 48, 75, 101, 137
human security network 137
hybrid courts 86, 174

ICBL *see* International Campaign to Ban
    Landmines
ICC *see* International Criminal Court
ICCPR *see* International Covenant on Civil
    and Political Rights
ICISS *see* International Commission
    on Intervention and State
    Sovereignty
ICRC *see* International Committee of the
    Red Cross
ICTR *see* International Criminal Tribunal
    for Rwanda
ICTY *see* International Criminal Tribunal
    for the former Yugoslavia
IDPs *see* internally displaced
    persons

IGO diplomacy (network diplomacy) 11, 92–95, 100, 125, 129
　and OHCHR 113
　regional 127
　see also United Nations (UN)
IGOs see intergovernmental organizations
IHL see international humanitarian law
ILC see International Law Commission
imperialism (colonialism) 26, 178
Independent International Commission on Kosovo (Kosovo Commission) 80
Independent Permanent Human Rights Commission 95, 128
India
　Khobragade incident 44–46, 58
　Ministry of External Affairs 47
　Resolution 688 76
InterAmerican Commission on Human Rights (1959) 94, 127–128
InterAmerican Court of Human Rights 94, 129
intergovernmental organizations (IGOs) 8, 9, 15, 20, 92–95, 173
　see also European Union; IGO diplomacy; United Nations
internally displaced persons (IDPs) 125
International Bill of Rights 2, 127
International Campaign to Ban Landmines (ICBL) 137
international civil service 100
International Commission on Intervention and State Sovereignty (ICISS) 12, 81, 82
International Committee of the Red Cross (ICRC) 2, 37, 145–147, 151, 160
　detention monitoring 162–3
International Convention on the Elimination of All Forms of Racial Discrimination 3
International Covenant on Civil and Political Rights (ICCPR) 2, 7, 89
International Covenant on Economic, Social and Cultural Rights (ICESCR) 2, 89
International Criminal Court (ICC) 15, 83, 94–95, 136, 174
International Criminal Tribunal for the former Yugoslavia (ICTY) 77, 80, 86

International Criminal Tribunal for Rwanda (ICTR) 79
international diplomatic law 43–47
international humanitarian law (IHL) 7, 13, 22, 36–39, 177
　detention monitoring 162–163
　landmines 137
　negotiations 158
International Law Commission (ILC) 160
international legal personality 19
International Red Cross and Red Crescent Movement 146, 156
international relations theory 19, 20
Internet 145, 174, 176
intervention/nonintervention 4, 23, 35, 47, 81, 173
Iran, and the US 46
Iraq
　and Kuwait 75–76
　refugees 140–141
　United States 76, 82, 91
Ireland, MFA 53–58
Israel 89

jails/prisons 166
Jefferson, Thomas 24
journalists 169

Kenya 82–83
Kenyatta, Uhuru 83, 86
Keynesian liberalism 24, 25
Khan, Irene 145
Khobragade, Devyani 44–46, 58
Kosovo Commission see Independent Commission on Kosovo
Kuwait, and Iraq 75–76

landmines 137–138
language 46
lawyers 159–162, 169
League of Arab States 94
Leahy, Patrick 137
Lesbian, Gay, Bisexual, Transgender and Queer/Intersex (LGBTQ/I) 11, 57, 113, 135, 161, 162, 163, 173
letter-writing campaigns 138
leverage 158

liberalism 23–25, 29, 179, 180
  see also states, illiberal
Libya 83–85, 165
lobbying 142
loud/quiet advocacy 158
low politics 22

McHugh, Gerard 158
McMillion, Margaret 58–61
Malinowski, Tom 44
Mancini-Griffoli, Deborah,
  Humanitarian Negotiation 157–158
market sovereignty 179
Marxian worldview 25–26, 29
Marx, Karl 26
material assistance 158
Médecins Sans Frontières (MSF) 2, 145,
    147–151
  detention monitoring 164–165
  Humanitarian Negotiations Revealed
    (McHugh and Bessler) 158
media 121
  see also social media
mediation 14
megaphone diplomacy 121
MFN *see* Most Favored Nation
Middle East, IGOs 94–95
Milosevic, Slobodan 79, 80, 105
Mine Ban Treaty *see* Convention on the
    Prohibition of the Use, Stockpiling,
    Production and Transfer of Anti-
    Personnel Mines and on their
    Destruction (Ottawa Treaty)
Ministries of Foreign Affairs (MFA) 47,
    48–61, 62–63
  US Department of State 48–52, 52t
Most Favored Nation (MFN) status,
    China 30–31
MSF *see* Médecins Sans Frontières
Muller, Bobby 137
multilateral diplomacy 8, 129, 173
  see also IGO diplomacy; United Nations
Myanmar 83

naming and shaming 145, 178
national human rights commissions 61–62
NATO (North Atlantic Treaty
    Organization)
  Balkans 48, 77, 79, 80
  Libya 84
negotiation 157–158
neoclassical liberals 24–25
network diplomacy *see* IGO diplomacy
NGO diplomacy 8, 134–143, 173
nongovernmental organizations (NGOs)
    8–9, 15
  experts 135–136
  Freedom House 176–177
  Helsinki Watch 29
  humanitarian 145–151
  humanitarian diplomacy 13, 15
  human rights 138–142
  Human Rights Watch 29
  Rwanda 78
  third UN 67
  see also NGO diplomacy
nonintervention/intervention 4, 23, 35, 47,
    81, 173
nonrefoulement 124

OAS (Organization of American States) 12,
    93–94, 128, 129
OCHA (Office for the Coordination of
    Humanitarian Affairs) 125–126
  *Humanitarian Negotiations with Armed
    Groups* (McHugh and Bessler) 158
O'Flaherty, Michael 156
OHCHR (Office of the High
    Commissioner for Human
    Rights) 8, 101, 102–113, 167
ombudsman offices 61–62, 63
Operation Turquoise 78
Organization of Islamic Cooperation
    (OIC) 94, 129, 177
Organization for Security and Cooperation
    in Europe (OSCE) 80, 93
Ottawa Convention 15
Ottawa Treaty 48, 137

the P-5 67–68, 81
  and Secretaries-General 100–101
parallel conferences 11
peacebuilding 68, 75, 173, 178
Peacebuilding Commission 68,
    101–102
peace enforcement 68, 75

peacekeeping 68, 69–74t, 75, 77, 173, 178
Peace of Westphalia 7–8
persona non grata (PNG) 44
Picot, Andre, *Humanitarian Negotiation* 157–158
Pillay, Navanethem (Navi) 105–112
Pinheiro, Paulo Sergio 89–91, 119–121
pledging conferences 11
power 21–22
preventative diplomacy 82–83
prisons/jails 166
private diplomacy 10
professional expertise 158
professionalization of human rights/humanitarianism 155–157, 167–169, 170
　detention monitors 162–167
　human rights officers 158–159
　lawyers 159–162
　negotiation 157–158
Pronk, Jan 126
propaganda 10
protests 11
public diplomacy 10, 114
　heads of state 31–32
　Putin 35–36, 85
　Robinson 104
Putin, Vladimir 35–36, 85

quiet diplomacy 10, 105, 114
quiet/loud advocacy 158

R2P *see* Responsibility to Protect (R2P)
Ramcharan, Bertrand 104, 119
rapporteurs, special 114, 115–118t, 119, 121
　Pinheiro 89–91, 119–120
Reagan, Ronald 29–30
realism 20–23, 26, 29
Red Cross/Crescent *see* International Red Cross and Red Crescent Movement
refugees
　1951 Convention Relating to the Status of Refugees (and the 1967 Protocol) 37, 124, 125
　Iraqi 140
　UNHCR 123–125, 140–141
regional approaches to human rights 92–95
regional civil service 126–129

repatriation, voluntary 124
reprisals 56
resettlement 124
Resolution 45/111 166
Resolution 688 75–76
Resolution 1973 72t, 83–84, 85
Responsibility to Protect (R2P) 81–87, 88, 89, 108, 174, 178
responsibility while protecting (RWP) 84
Robinson, Mary 9, 35, 103–104
Roth, Kenneth 145
Russia 173, 174
　Balkans 79–80
　human rights reports 52–53
Rwanda 68, 76, 78–79, 80, 105
　United States on 58–61

Saudi Arabia, Wallstrom incident 48
Sauerbrey, Ellen R. 141
Schultz, George 29–30
secretariats 100
secretaries *see* foreign ministers/secretaries
securitization of aid 136
security, human 12, 48, 75, 101, 137
social media 10, 53, 145, 174
Somalia 76, 77–78, 80
South Africa 87
sovereignty 4–5, 22, 35, 47, 81, 173
　and the Helsinki Summit/Accords 28
　ICC 86
　imperialism 26
　market 179
　regional human rights 94
special rapporteurs *see* rapporteurs, special
Sri Lanka 151
standing 142
stateless people 167–168
Statement of Ethical Principles for Human Rights Professionals 157
states 7–8, 9, 14, 19–27, 177
　authoritarian 56, 175, 176–177, 178
　development of international law 36–39
　failed 177–178
　heads of 20, 27–36
　illiberal 175–177
　international diplomatic law 43–47
　and NGOs 136, 142
structuralism, *see* Marxian worldview

subjects of international law 19
Sudan 86, 102
summit diplomacy 10–11, 27–28
Sweden, MFA 48
Syria 54, 85–86
   Putin on 35–36, 85

terrorism 174, 178
theory 20, 27
track 1/2 diplomacy 1, 14–15, 134
treaties, human rights 3, 37, 38t
   monitoring bodies 121–123, 122t
treaty-based bodies 113
treaty monitoring 2, 12, 113, 121, 122t, 123, 126–128, 160
trustee systems 178
truth commissions 62

UDHR *see* Universal Declaration of Human Rights
Ukraine 54
Ulrich, George 156
UNHCR (United Nations High Commissioner for Refugees) 123–125, 140–141, 160
   detention monitoring 163–164
   Monitoring Immigration Detention 165
United Kingdom (UK)
   and Assange 61
   Foreign and Commonwealth Office 47
   Iraq 76, 82
   Libya 84
   Rwanda 60
United Nations (UN) 4, 8
   Charter 4–5, 66–67
   General Assembly 87–89
   High Commissioner for Human Rights 102–113, 121, 143–145
   HRC 89–92
   OCHA 125–126, 158
   OHCHR 8, 101, 102–113
   Secretaries-General 100–102, 173
   Security Council 62–68, 69–74t, 75–82, 173
      courts 86–87
      R2P 81–86
   Special Committee on Apartheid 87
   treaty monitoring bodies 121–123, 122t
   UNHCR 123–125

United States
   and Boutros-Ghali 101
   Department of Defense 51
   Department of State 47, 48–52, 52t, 141
   detention monitoring by ICRC 163
   foreign policy 30–31
   as hegemon 21, 23
   Helsinki Accords 29–30
   and Human Rights Watch 140–141
   international diplomatic law 43
      Bahrain incident 44
      and Iran 46
      Khobragade incident 44–46
   Iraq 76, 82, 91, 140–141
   liberal worldview 176
   Libya 84
   realist worldview 23
   regional human rights 94
   Rwanda 58–61
   Somalia 77–78
   Syria 85
Universal Declaration of Human Rights (UDHR) 2, 2–4, 37, 39, 89, 106, 175
universalism 5
Universal Periodic Review (UPR) 92, 106, 109, 110

victims of war 7
Vieira de Mello, Sergio 104
Vienna Convention *see* 1961 Vienna Convention on Diplomatic Relations
voluntary repatriation 124

Wallstrom, Margot 48
war 22, 46
World Trade Organization (WTO) 31
worldviews 13, 26–27, 39, 45, 80, 173
   and the Helsinki Summit/Accords 29
   liberalism 23–25
   Marxian 25–26
   realism 20–23

Yugoslavia *see* Balkans

Zeid al-Hussein, Prince 112–113